D1058718

Beyond *Bend It Like Beckham*

BEYOND
Bend It Like
BECKHAM

THE GLOBAL PHENOMENON
OF WOMEN'S SOCCER

Timothy F. Grainey • *Foreword by Brittany Timko*

UNIVERSITY OF NEBRASKA PRESS • LINCOLN AND LONDON

Library of Congress
Cataloging-in-Publication Data

Grainey, Timothy F.
Beyond "Bend it like Beckham": the
global phenomenon of women's soccer
/ Timothy F. Grainey; foreword by
Brittany Timko.
p. cm.
Includes bibliographical references.
ISBN 978-0-8032-3470-3 (pbk.: alk.
paper)
1. Soccer for women—Cross-cultural
studies. 2. Soccer—Social aspects—
Cross-cultural studies. I. Title.
GV944.5.G73   2012
796.334082—dc23   2011047387

Set in Sabon by Kim Essman.
Designed by Annie Shahan.

#759915533

To my wife, April,
and daughter, Arianna:
two precious gems
who make my life better
in infinite ways

Contents

List of Illustrations   ix

Foreword   xi

Acknowledgments   xv

Introduction   xvii

PART ONE   Rapid Growth in the United States

1   Title IX, Soccer Moms, and
     Pioneering Players   3

2   U.S. National Team, 1996–1999:
     "Welcome to Our Party"   17

3   Professional Women's Soccer and the WUSA:
     "The Best Three Years of My Life"   35

4   Women's Professional Soccer (WPS)   65

PART TWO   Challenges in the Middle East, Africa,
               and Latin America

5   The State of the Game in the
     Middle East   105

6   Challenges and Successes in Africa   123

7 Latin America: Fighting Machismo
Attitudes   139

8 Women Athletes: Objects versus
Wholesome Role Models   163

PART THREE   Building Leagues and National Team Programs

9 Ancestral Roots: Leveraging the Diaspora
to Build the Game Abroad   181

10 National Leagues around the World   201

11 Overcoming a Fifty-Year Ban
in England   215

12 Canada's Youthful Road to Success   231

Conclusion: "The Future of Football
Is Feminine"   241

Afterword: 2011 Women's World Cup   247

Appendix of Tables   255

Selected Bibliography   267

Illustrations

1 Brittany Timko   xii

2 Macke Mutz's flip throw   9

3 Cindy Parlow coaching at a clinic in Bahrain   122

4 Goalkeeper Anna Picarelli versus
Abby Wambach in an international match   183

5 Queensland (now Brisbane) Roar
celebrate their 2008–9 title win   212

6 Queensland (now Brisbane) Roar coach and
captain address the media   213

7 Canadian Women's National Team
coaching staff   233

Foreword

When I was five years old I dreamed of playing in a World Cup, at the Olympics, and professionally. I told my parents, who have always been supportive. They told me to work hard at my dreams, and the opportunities would be endless. At the time, what I didn't know was that some of my dreams weren't very realistic. In 1990 there was no official women's World Cup, women's soccer wasn't a part of the Olympics, and playing professionally would almost be laughable, as most countries barely recognized women as being able to play soccer. For me, my role models were male. I watched a documentary on Pele, and he immediately became my favorite player. I believed that if I had faith, when it was time for me to play, the opportunities would be there. So every day I went down to the park and juggled, dribbled, and kicked the ball against a wall. I would miss birthday parties for games because the games were just that much more fun for me. At school I waited for the bell to ring so I could play at recess and lunch. That was the highlight of my school day.

Close to twenty years later, soccer has helped me to live my dreams and continue to make new ones. I've played in two world youth championships; in 2002 at the finals, we played in front of fifty thousand Canadians and had over a million watching on TV. I've been able to represent my country in two World Cups and recently the 2008 Olympics. It paid for my education, allowing me to

1. Brittany Timko with the Canadian National Team. (CanadaSoccer.Com/ Tony Quinn.)

attend the University of Nebraska–Lincoln on an athletic scholarship. Soccer has allowed me to travel the world, competing against other countries, and has also allowed me to live and experience different cultures. And although it seemed unrealistic at the time, soccer has allowed me to play professionally. After graduating, I participated in the first year of the Australian W-League and saw firsthand the potential that the league has to grow over the coming years. From Australia I went to Sweden, where the league is already one of the best in the world and will undoubtedly continue to flourish. Then my travels took me to Germany's top competitive league, as the country builds toward the 2011 World Cup as host.

Looking forward, I think that Sepp Blatter was correct when he stated that "the future of football is feminine." The passion and excitement that girls have to play soccer is continuing to grow. It is now realistic to dream of playing professionally. And finally, we are given the opportunities to show the world that we can play the beautiful game too.

Beyond Bend It Like Beckham brings to life examples of women who have gone through highs and lows to achieve their dreams. It also shows us how far women's soccer has come through the years and more importantly, that the sky is the limit in terms of how far it can go.

Acknowledgments

This book celebrates the amazing journey of girls' and women's soccer, focusing on why the sport has become the number 1 sport for females globally and a vehicle for societal change.

I'd like to thank Robert Taylor and his publishing team at the University of Nebraska Press, especially editorial assistant Courtney Ochsner, for their excellent guidance, effort, and belief in the project; my wife, April, for her poignant suggestions on the manuscripts; my daughter, Arianna, for her photographic ideas; and Dan Lauletta, a freelance writer and womensprosoccer.com columnist, for his review of the WUSA and WPS chapters.

I am indebted to Chris Vaughn Griffiths of *World Football Pages of Canada*, who brought me into the soccer journalism realm; John Turnbull of TheGlobalGame.com, and David Fleenor of Soccer365 .com, for their continued support of my articles on women's soccer.

Special mention for their assistance in numerous ways over the years must go to Rob Penner, the director of communications of Women's Professional Soccer; Richard Scott, media officer of Canada Soccer; David Applegate in communications at U.S. Soccer; Dan Courtemanche at Major League Soccer (ex-WUSA); the Equalizer soccer website founder, Jeff Kassouf; and the superb soccer correspondent Scott French.

This book is a testament to the passion and commitment of women soccer players, coaches, and administrators around the world. There's not enough space to thank all those who so freely gave of their time. Their stories were always enjoyable and edifying, but I would like to single out some who were instrumental in shaping this book (in alphabetic order): Tonya Antonucci, Melissa Barbieri, Eleni Benson, Shek Borkowski, Ian Bridge, Josee Busilacchi, Ann Chiejine, Marilyn Childress, Dr. Bob Contigulia, Leo Cuellar, Tonny Dijkhuizen, Dr. Sahar El-Hawary, Mary Harvey, Emma Hayes, Jeff Hopkins, Monica Jorge, Tanya Kalivas, Dalton Kaufmann, Noel King, Daniel Lato, Melissa Lesage, Jill Loyden, Aivi Luik, Anton Maksimov, Laura Pappano, Even Pellerud, Anna Picarelli, Ben Popoola, Katie Ratican, Jennifer Rottenberg, Monika Staab, Brittany Timko, Tim Ward, Tiffany Weimer, Kacey White, and Joao Maria Xavier.

College head coaches Kevin Boyd at Arizona State and Brad Evans at the University of Toledo always shared ideas and contacts with players all over the world. FC Indiana head coach Shek Borkowski and general manager Anton Maksimov, now with the LTA Agency, allowed me to closely follow FC Indiana for years and tap into the team's unbelievable source of international players. Arizona Rush (Tucson) WPSL team coaches and directors Dalton Kaufman and Chris Sydney have openly and perceptively shared their approach to building a top-level women's franchise. Kinsley Nyce has been a constant soccer traveler with me for years. Thanks to Brittany Timko for agreeing to share her story of "living the dream."

Introduction

This book examines why soccer has become the most popular team sport for women and girls, not just in North America but globally as well. This process has taken only a few decades, which is shocking since some countries like Brazil and Germany even banned the sport in the 1960s and 1970s. Federation Internationale de Football Association (FIFA), the sport's governing body, determined through its Big Count global survey of participants that 26 million women played the sport in 2006; this is 10 percent of the estimated 265 million total players. Four million women and girls registered with a FIFA member for an organized team, an increase of 54 percent since the previous survey in 2000. Millions around the world watch the Women's World Cup every four years. Nowhere do so many girls and women play the game as in the United States, whose 1.6 million registered players are more than the sum total of the fourteen nations who rank behind it. Women's soccer has brought new energy, ideas, opportunities, and fans to the sport. In the United States it is the biggest women's college sport. In Canada, fully a third of all players are female, the highest percentage of any country or territory in the world, contributing to soccer eclipsing hockey as the most popular game among Canadian youth. How did women's soccer grow so quickly? What obstacles did it overcome, what problems does it still face, and what does the future hold?

Part 1 examines the history of the sport in the United States. The

United States was a late adopter of soccer, a solid decade behind the major Western European markets. However, the combination of federal legislation aimed at equal spending in colleges by gender (Title IX), along with the discovery by parents that soccer was an inexpensive, safe, healthy, and socially beneficial activity for children of both sexes, led to an explosion in the sport's numbers. Women's soccer electrified the country in the United States during the 1999 Women's World Cup, bringing unheard of publicity and attention. The result was unfathomable even months before; a national poll conducted in 2007 found that 48 percent of Americans knew who three-time FIFA World Player of the year Mia Hamm was, but only 9 percent could identify Landon Donovan — the top American-born male player—and Hamm had been retired *for three years.*

The two attempts to professionalize the sport in the United States, via the Women's United Soccer Association (WUSA) from 2001 to 2003 and Women's Professional Soccer (WPS) starting in 2009, have ramifications for players' career choices, marketing, other women's professional sports enterprises, and the growth of national team programs. This book explores why players postpone their careers, additional education, marriage, and children to "live the dream," even when salaries are far below what they would make in other professions.

Part 2 looks at the sport internationally, particularly how it struggles to gain a foothold in some countries since it defies perceptions of traditional roles for women. We will focus on the Middle East, Africa, and Latin America. Then we look specifically at perceptions of women athletes, including sexual portrayals, which frequently are excused under the guise of "marketing the game." We look at lingering definitions of how women should play the game, which are discriminatory and different from those for men.

Part 3 covers different ways in which the national teams and leagues have expanded around the world. We will look at why North American athletes are going abroad to play for clubs and the national teams of their parents and grandparents. Some countries have done a better job than others in leveraging their diaspora for long-term growth at home. We then turn attention to the pressing need of a number of countries to establish national leagues for their top athletes (whether completely amateur, semiprofessional, or professional setups.) We will look at how a number of countries have approached the issue, including Australia, England, the Netherlands, Russia, and Sweden. We then explore how Canada leveraged a rich vein of youth players to turn around a national team program that was floundering from a lack of support and direction.

The conclusion discusses the biggest problems facing the expansion of the sport globally and presents some future hopes for the sport.

The book's title refers to Gurinder Chadha's independent film *Bend It Like Beckham*, which featured two soccer-mad teenage girls in England (one with traditional Sikh parents) who defy family and social pressures to play the game at a high level. The movie was a surprise success in the United States when released in spring 2003, grossing $43 million by the end of the year. *Bend It Like Beckham* treated soccer, and particularly women's soccer, with respect, arguably a first for the sport in North America, where previous movies showed the sport in an unrealistic or condescending fashion.

Beyond *Bend It Like Beckham*

ONE

Rapid Growth in the United States

1

Title IX, Soccer Moms, and Pioneering Players

Today, all over the United States, soccer is seen as a "normal" sport for girls to play. You see them playing in television advertisements, in movies, and on television shows; there's no shame or shock in the activity. You see them in their uniforms in restaurants and shopping malls. For a high school girl, it is one of the most popular sports to play and has the additional carrot of there being a significant number of college scholarships available. In short, it is a very common activity for American girls.

Things were very different four decades ago. The year 1972 is seen as a watershed for all women's sports, because Title IX was passed into law that year. Title IX of the Education Amendments Act was a federal ruling mandating gender equity in athletic opportunities for colleges that received federal funds. Sporting equality was hardly the focal point of the legislation, but its effects proved far reaching. Since both private and public universities and colleges received government funding, they had to adjust their athletic budgets in proportion to the ratio of male and female athletes and, as one writer penned, "The edict developed into perhaps the most contentious issue in the history of college sports." Further guidelines in 1993 required that the male–female ratio of participants reflect the university's total enrollment, and not just a school's athletes. Though this was not the intent, detractors have long blamed Title IX for any reductions in funding for male teams.

Starting the Sport

In the early seventies when Title IX came into effect, women simply didn't play the sport of soccer in any significant numbers. Some girls played it on rare occasion, perhaps as a PE activity at school, but that ended before high school. Formalized training or coaching was nonexistent. Team sports for women were limited to field hockey, softball, volleyball, and some basketball. You didn't see boys playing soccer very often either outside of heavily ethnic centers. Many people didn't know what soccer was and those that did heaped scorn on it. A neighbor of mine summed up the general mindset when he declared it was "a sport played by f#*&ing foreigners." A major event like a World Cup was available for viewing in the 1970s only via Closed Circuit in theaters or arenas, and then just in large cities. PBS had some German soccer on TV, but you had a better chance of seeing a UFO than a full soccer game on television forty years ago.

Women's college soccer was played at only a handful of colleges during the seventies, beginning as club soccer at a few schools in the northeastern states. Matches were generally a glorified version of kickball. In 1977 Phil Pincince started the first varsity women's college team at Brown University. He had a few experienced players, some good athletes from other sports such as tennis, and some who were new to sports. In addition to building a team, he had to build a schedule with other colleges that were starting programs in his area, including Ontario's Lake Champlain College, which had had a team for a few years and gave Brown their only loss that first year. By the following season, the Ivy League had enough teams to hold a championship at Brown that included Dartmouth, Harvard, Princeton, and Yale. In 1979 Brown hosted the first Eastern Regional Championships.

The Northeast had always been where the majority of schools with women's programs were centered. That changed in 1980 when Anson Dorrance, already coaching the men's college team at the University of North Carolina, started a women's program at the bequest of his athletic director. After his first season, Dorrance wanted a national championship for the sport. With fewer than fifty college teams in the United States, the National Collegiate Athletic Association (NCAA) wasn't yet an option, as it required at least eighty participating teams for a championship, so the Association for Intercollegiate Athletics for Women sanctioned the first intercollegiate championship in 1981, which North Carolina won. The NCAA got on board in 1982 with a championship tournament, and Dorrance's team won the first three NCAA championships and seven of the first eight to close the first full decade of women's intercollegiate soccer.

Title IX dovetailed with Baby Boomer parents discovering that soccer was a fun, relatively safe sport that their children could start as young as age four. It was a game that *anyone* could play—football required greater bulk, basketball skewed towards taller players, and track and tennis needed exceptional speed—soccer was accessible to any average athlete; and *anyone* meant girls as well as boys. The result: now you can even find soccer leagues for people in wheelchairs and little people (under four-foot-ten). Soccer became the favorite sport of young families, plus it had low entry costs — all you needed to start was a ball, shin guards, and some soccer shoes—it was the ultimate egalitarian sport. Women who carted their kids to games for years in minivans even became a targeted demographic by political parties and marketers during the nineties—*Soccer Moms*. The combination of the federal legislation and the discovery of a new recreational activity for children resulted in an explosion of youth clubs, high school programs, and fully funded college teams that actively sought women players. Pele's arrival in 1975 to play for the New York Cosmos of the North American Soccer League (NASL) helped to popularize the sport, along with the United States hosting the Men's World Cup in 1994 and the launch of another pro league in 1996 (Major League Soccer, which replaced the NASL, which had folded in 1984 after eighteen seasons). These events all helped to diffuse the sport of its "ethnic" baggage, but it was largely the tremendous growth of youth soccer that helped to end that stigma. It became *the* sport of suburbia; *Washington Post* columnist Steve Twomey labeled it "the game that ate suburbia."

Throughout the 1980s and 1990s, youth leagues blossomed. Young girls would begin by playing with boys, but by age seven or eight parents would start looking for leagues for girls only, sometimes having to start them with a few other parents. Experienced coaches from overseas started to run clinics for girls, include them in camps, and launch elite girls' teams. Parents even hired experienced pros by the hour to work with their children a couple of times a week—all tax free with no records kept, of course. Studies have shown that girls who participate in sports have higher self esteem, are more likely to graduate from high school, and are less likely to become pregnant, which is an answer to parents' prayers. Sports encourage girls to work as a team and develop skills, and reinforces their enthusiasm for healthy activities.

There were an estimated 18 million soccer players in the United States in 2007, half of whom were females, with an average age of fifteen. Participation in girls' youth soccer has doubled over the past decade, while youth participation in all other sports has dropped. It's the same story at the high school level, where participation in women's sports like basketball and volleyball has leveled off, while the percentage of girls who play soccer has increased significantly. In 1972, twenty-eight high schools in the entire country had girls' teams, but as of this writing, it's eight thousand. The number of elite female players rose from 700 in 1972 to 290,000 today. There are now three times more female soccer players in the United States than there are Girl Scouts. The numbers of girls pouring into youth programs tipped the scales in terms of money and influence for the sport. The growth of boys' soccer was significant, but when you added the girls, it overwhelmed everything: the availability of coaches, leagues, and existing fields. The first two could be overcome with volunteer parents, at least during a child's early years, while later on Boomer parents became a force, lobbying civic authorities for more dedicated soccer parks. Soccer-only fields were unheard of before 1990 except for a few privately held fields that ethnic clubs owned. These social networks of parents were good at organizing, learned quickly that their numbers provided political clout, and were doing it for the best reason of all—their children. There are currently over 100 dedicated soccer complexes in the country with 150 more planned in the next few years, which has further helped to establish soccer as an "American sport."

In the meantime, colleges, trying to keep out of the Title IX legislative dragnet, crunched numbers and found that soccer's low equipment costs combined with squads of twenty would appreciably help their gender balance numbers. The number of NCAA schools that added women's programs was staggering, rising from 80 in 1981–82 to 951 in 2007–8. The most rapid growth came during the 1990s; in ten years the number of women's Division I programs tripled while men's growth was relatively flat. Just in 1995–96 alone, over 115 new women's teams were fielded over the previous academic year. In 1997 women's programs outnumbered men's programs in Division I for the first time. In 2007 there were 307 Division I women's soccer programs and a total of 951 in all divisions. Today, there are more women playing soccer in college than any other sport (see table 1 in the appendix).

The few top-shelf women's programs of the late 1980s and early 1990s, notably Anson Dorrance's University of North Carolina teams but also the University of Portland, the University of Virginia, Santa Clara University, and Colorado College, began to face competition in the later nineties. What was most astounding was the number of schools that were adding women's programs that didn't even field a men's side, including the University of Nebraska, Purdue University, Louisiana State University, Arizona State University, and Florida State University. The explosion of youth soccer meant that there were so many quality players emerging that new programs could compete almost immediately. This was unrealistic in other sports, where it took years to build a dominant program. Of course, to qualify for the playoffs within the first few years, an administration had to provide sufficient support and uncover a clever coach who could leverage the university's other benefits in recruiting, while constructing a strong unit. The best example was the University of Florida, which, led by future U.S. National Team stars Danielle Fotopoulos, Heather Mitts, and Abby Wambach, captured the 1998 NCAA Division I title in only the team's fourth year of existence. Even more enlightening, their coach was a woman. Their success spurred other schools to invest in women's soccer, through providing the maximum number of scholarships (currently fourteen) but also by supplying dedicated stadiums and training fields. This contrasts sharply with the men's teams, who work with a maximum limit of nine-and-nine-tenths full rides, and some schools only provide a few partial scholarships or have even disbanded their men's programs (such as Illinois State and Central Michigan Universities) while still supporting the distaff side. Certainly some of this was due to Title IX compliance, but some men's coaches have blamed women for all of their woes. The coach of BYU's men's club team complained, "It's fair to say gender equity has hurt the development of men's soccer in the U.S."

The easy counterargument is this: how can something be hurt that for the most part has been in a stupor for nigh on thirty years? Freeing a heavy-duty truck from quicksand is easier than turning men's college soccer around. Men's programs struggle to figure out what their mission is to players, the school, and fans; that hasn't changed for decades. Men's college soccer has been damaged significantly by the NCAA steadfastly operating outside FIFA, tampering with rules such as multiple substitutions, and focusing more on recreational than elite player development. Top quality players now skip college for the pros, but for women, you get to national teams and the pros through college soccer. College soccer became a target for the top women athletes to continue their sport after high school; the image of coaches dangling the golden ticket of a college scholarship at youth tourneys played well with parents, who were all too happy to munch. Many didn't stop to crunch the numbers; out of six hundred thousand high school players, there are only about ten thousand full-tuition scholarships in soccer for both genders, with

2. Macke Mutz of the University of Arizona performing the acrobatic flip-throw in. (Luke Adams, University of Arizona Athletics.)

women accounting for 60 percent of those. Parents responded to the stories like "Cathy's friend's daughter across town got a full ride to Stanford," which encouraged them to spend more on elite clubs, coaches, tournament travel, and equipment. The colleges capitalized on the growing number of youth players, which in turn helped to attract more new players to soccer. Women injected new energy into the sport at all levels. Many colleges correctly read their tea leaves; women's soccer was hot. The 1999 Women's World Cup (wwc) success in America simply validated their strategy and made them look like clairvoyant geniuses.

A side benefit of the growth of women's soccer is that it has provided women another avenue to stay associated with the game through coaching. As colleges added teams, they turned to experienced women players to coach, some of whom were the first beneficiaries of the government's mandate. Some were ex–national team players, while others combined coaching with a professional career. Some still in their mid-twenties were appointed to head coaching slots, even at major universities. UNC graduate Lori Walker was appointed as head coach of the new University of Kansas program in 1995 at age twenty-four, and her schoolmate Angela Kelly started at the University of Tennessee at twenty-five. U.S. National Team forward Lindsay Tarpley, a former UNC player and now in Women's Professional Soccer (WPS), when asked in college what she wanted to do after her soccer career, said, "I'm majoring in communications and mentoring in exercise science. But I'd really like to coach and be able to train [for the National Team]. I'd love to coach at the college level."

As colleges added programs and scholarships, they started to attract top international athletes. Women from Germany, France, Italy, and Scandinavia came to America to further their education both in the classroom and on the soccer field. Another important difference is that women didn't have to fight against an established dominant sport for players like the men did with football. All women's sports expanded thanks to Title IX.

Launch of the United States Women's National Team

In 1985 U.S. women were invited to play their first match as a women's national team in Italy as part of an international tournament. They lost three games and tied one after only three days of practices and were forced to wear hand-me-down men's uniforms. Italy, Sweden, and Norway had formed women's national teams a decade or more before the Americans. U.S. Soccer realized they had to arrest the gap in ability if they were serious about competing. The first women's coach, part-timer Mike Ryan, made way for Anson Dorrance; but even the dominant women's college soccer coach was still forced to lobby the U.S. Soccer Federation for the job in 1986. Many viewed Dorrance as arrogant, but no one could deny his record (by this time, he had won four national team titles at UNC; his team was virtually unstoppable). Longtime U.S. Soccer Women's National Team Media Chief Aaron Heifetz called

Dorrance "the Christopher Columbus of his sport," and continued, "Anson had vision and he was always ahead of the game. He figured out this women's soccer thing way before anyone else. He got a head start on everybody." Dorrance made the switch to the women's game years before his colleagues because he was able to look at the big picture. The men's game on the national level was "an old boy's network," and at that point seemed light years away from qualifying for a Men's World Cup spot. There was little room to grow. The women's game was less established but with unlimited potential, and once he accepted the women's national team coaching job, there was never any question which way Dorrance had plotted his future. Three years later, in 1989, he resigned from the North Carolina men's team and took over the women's team full time. Dorrance said, "I saw women's soccer in America as a sleeping giant, and my goal was to wake it up. I don't think UNC alone started the boom, but I do think we were a beacon for it, because we didn't want to just win, we wanted to win attractively."

Dorrance's U.S. team won their first tournament title in 1986 in Blaine, Minnesota, in a triangular event with Canada and Norway. He brought the same unique approach to the national team that he had with the Tar Heels. He escalated the level of competitiveness in practice sessions and in games, which had not previously been a prevalent theme with women's teams. He would keep track of who won individual drills in practices, sprint races, and the like, and he stressed conditioning. Dorrance created what he liked to call "a competitive cauldron" to build soccer excellence. He demanded the same commitment he had from his men's team. However, he felt that men's and women's teams had to be coached differently, stressing that "different doesn't mean unequal. It just means different." Tim Crothers, who wrote a biography of the coach and knew him for many years, quoted Dorrance on the differences of coaching men versus women:

To coach men, you've got to dominate them, drive them with the intensity of your personality and walking up and down the sidelines, burying them always seems to get them going. I always wanted to rail at my women the same way, but while it made me feel good, I learned they weren't going to hear a thing. I could vent my spleen and have a heart attack, but it's not going to make them better players. You don't drive women, you lead them, and you don't lead them effectively with intimidation. You relate to them personally. You lead them by caring about them. Women have to understand that your relationship with them is never in jeopardy.

Dorrance found that he enjoyed coaching women more than men: "Women are easier to coach than men because they listen to criticism, but they're difficult to manage because most are sensitive to slights, and their bond is stronger than on a men's team. Therefore, when you bench a female player, her teammates feel empathy. They experience a debilitating catharsis towards that player and it affects them, whether the benched girl gives a damn or not." Dorrance's successor as national team coach, Tony DiCicco, echoed his predecessor's thinking when he said,

It takes subtlety to coach girls, and humanity. To girls, the coach is a member of the team, or not. They will choose their own hierarchy, their own leaders, and sometimes it's not the players a coach might expect based on his or her objective assessment. That's the first thing you have to figure out. Who have they chosen? You have to coach the team through the team, through their leaders. It's very humbling for a coach and, I think, it's been good for the game. We're now seeing that leadership style take hold everywhere—and not just in soccer. . . . I think that's what women's soccer has brought to the world of sports. Emotional honesty, the sense that we're all in this together, and that the coach doesn't have all the answers. He or she is still the boss, there should never be any doubt about that, but the team bears the first responsibility for its fate, and the coach is part of the team.

Dorrance's approach was the antithesis of a recreational sports culture that held back competition for women because achieving success might come at the expense of being liked, so winning wasn't all that important. To Anson Dorrance, soccer was serious business, and if you weren't on board, then you could find another sport or college.

Dorrance also had an uncanny eye for talent, spotting Julie Foudy, Kristine Lilly, and Mia Hamm when they were fifteen- to-sixteen-years-of-age and teamed them with Brandi Chastain, Joy Bielfeld-Fawcett, and former UNC players Carla Werden-Overbeck and April Heinrichs (who would later coach the team to the 2004 Olympic Gold Medal). Within five years he had built a team that could compete with the world's elite at the first Women's World Championship in China in late 1991.

For the players, competing at the top level after college was extremely difficult. There were no salaries to speak of; they only received per-diem expenses when they were at a team camp or game. They worked part-time jobs, because regular jobs wouldn't hold a position for them while they were away. They lived at home or shared rooms with friends, sometimes even sharing a bed. Social lives were secondary to pursuing their sport; some even put off marriage and starting families. They had to practice on their own for long periods of time. Lauren Gregg, the team's assistant and a former player said, "It was hard. It reinforced for us that we weren't playing just because people were watching or because we were being paid a lot of money." Finally, in 1991, U.S. Soccer paid for a three-week training camp, common for men but new for women, before the regional qualifying tournament. The regional championships were held in Haiti, where the U.S. women won their way through to the World Championships from a weak group, scoring at least ten goals each against Mexico, Martinique, Trinidad and Tobago, and Haiti before cinching their spot with a 5–0 win over Canada in the final.

Dorrance was still concerned that the team was not quite at the level of the Scandinavians and Italians, so they traveled extensively before the World Championships in 1991, playing games in Bulgaria, China, Denmark, France, Germany, and Holland, as well as four games at home along the eastern seaboard. As it turned out, the U.S. team was rampant in China, going undefeated in six games. In the first round, they struggled in the opener against Sweden before coming out on top 3–2, then beat Brazil 5–0 and Japan 3–0. They blasted Taiwan 7–0 in the quarterfinals, topped Germany 5–2 in the semifinals, and then became World Champions on a late Michelle Akers goal against Norway, their most dangerous competitor in the tournament. Akers led the tournament with ten goals, followed by Carin Jennings (six) and Heinrichs (four)—the aptly named "triple edged sword." Akers won top scorer (Golden Shoe award), and Jennings was deemed the tournament's best player (Golden Ball award). Mia Hamm scored two goals as a seventeen-year-old, the same number she would score in each of the subsequent three World Cups during her illustrious career. The women loved their time in China; they played in front of enthusiastic crowds, including 65,000 for the final in Guangzhou. The tourney had an incredible average of 43,235 spectators per match (most as doubleheaders.)

The American women were world champions in soccer; the year before, the men had qualified for their first World Cup tournament in forty years. However, back home only family and a tiny number of fans were aware of the tournament and the significance of their win in China. Bora Miluntinovic, the coach of the U.S. men's team, led about a dozen people to JFK airport in New York to meet the squad when they returned from Asia. Michelle Akers reflected back on the event: "We'd gone through this incredible experience, played our hearts out, achieved this incredible thing, and we come home and it's like the 'Twilight Zone.' Nobody knew what was going on. I didn't quite know what to expect. We'd received a lot of attention from the international media, but nobody from the States was interested. It was kind of my introduction to how long a road women's soccer really had to go."

In the years between the first two World Cups, the team played only twice in 1992 but then seventeen times in 1993, thirteen in 1994, and fourteen in 1995. About 40 percent of these games were at home, with most drawing in the three- to six-thousand range. In 1994 Dorrance stepped down as coach to return to the Tar Heels full time, replaced by Tony DiCicco, his assistant since 1991. Dorrance is still the women's head coach at UNC, and in 2009 had won twenty NCAA titles in twenty-seven seasons, finishing second on three occasions. Dorrance remains an iconic figure for the development of the women's game. Aaron Heifetz summed up his impact when he said, "Anson's made soccer hip. A teenage women's soccer player is a cool thing to be. Soccer players are the most popular girls, the prettiest girls, the most social, the most athletic; and all of that started in Chapel Hill. Our sport needed a Chicago Bulls and that was UNC, and we needed a Michael Jordan and that was Mia Hamm. Anson created all that."

Before the 2005 World Cup in Sweden, U.S. Soccer provided a six-month residency training camp in Florida with pay and, though the salaries were at subsistence levels, with it the players had more stability in their personal lives than ever before. The Swedish tournament itself was a very low-key affair with an average attendance of 4,316 a game, far below what China achieved. Everything about this event had a dampening influence: the weather was cold and rainy, the crowds were tiny and largely unenthusiastic, and the U.S. team played below expectations. The United States had lost key players Jennings and Heinrichs through retirement. The positive news was ESPN's decision to broadcast all of the American's games live. Again, Norway and the United States were the class of the tournament, but Norwegian coach Even Pellerud (later the successful women's coach of Canada) and his squad won out, defeating the United States 1–0 in a hard-fought semifinal. After the game, the Norwegians replicated the New Zealand rugby team's celebratory crawl on the field in which each player grabbed the ankles of the woman in front of her and scooted on her knees. Bizarre as it was, it steamed the Americans and provided constant motivation in their battles with the Norwegians for years to come. Norway won the title in a 2–0 win over Germany while the United States eclipsed China by the same score for third.

Star forward Tiffeny Milbrett said, "It wasn't our tournament to win. I really believe that. I think Norway was a better team than we were. I see '95 as part of this team's evolution, I think it was necessary to lose that tournament in order to solve some problems, work some things out. Everybody needed to go through a soul check, a gut check, a heart check. Had we won, I don't believe we would have won the Olympics in 1996." The 1995 World Cup experience thus became an inspiration to step up their individual and team preparation for what would follow; the 1996 Olympics and the 1999 World Cup. During the second half of the decade, the national team members would receive unprecedented attention for female athletes; the speed at which that happened would take *everyone* by surprise and would forever change the landscape for not only women's soccer but the game of soccer in general, as well as all of women's sports.

2

U.S. National Team, 1996–1999

"Welcome to Our Party"

Two U.S.-based events took place in a four-year period that would forever change the direction of women's soccer both domestically and globally: the 1996 Olympic Games and the 1999 Women's World Cup. The latter tournament in particular would cement the U.S. National Team into the American consciousness in a way that went way beyond even the players' wildest dreams.

1996 Olympic Games

The Atlanta, Georgia, Olympic Games were significant because the International Olympic Committee (IOC) added more women's sports to the agenda, including high-profile sports such as basketball, softball, and tennis, in an attempt to equalize the number of men and women participants. At first it looked like women's soccer would miss out, but Marilyn Childress, a Georgia soccer leader and adult soccer player, led a two-year-long grass-roots lobbying effort of FIFA, the IOC, and the Atlanta Organizing Committee. The IOC relented under the pressure, adding a limited format for the sport with only eight teams (half of the men's total): the United States as hosts and the seven highest finishers from the 1995 World Cup.

Childress's efforts were a monumental achievement for the local soccer community, particularly given the contentious ongoing relationship between FIFA and the IOC. For most other sports, the Olympics are seen as world championships. FIFA has bent over backwards to make sure that this is not the case in soccer, worried this would deemphasize its own World Cup, for which it fully controls ticket, sponsorship, television rights, and advertising revenue. The World Cup was FIFA's sole operating funding source every four years. On the men's soccer side, the Olympics have always been viewed as an exhibition tournament of sorts. The IOC usually acquiesces to FIFA's wishes because of soccer's global popularity. Even though full national teams rarely compete, by pricing tickets relatively inexpensively, the IOC could still count on large crowds, as tickets were easier to come by than for other popular sports like swimming and diving. Before 1992 the games were limited to amateurs, though many athletes from Communist nations were sarcastically called *shamateurs*. The IOC ignored the fact that eastern European athletes were usually highly compensated within a communist system. Showing up on work rolls of a government or industrial organization obscured the fact that they worked full time at their athletic craft.

Since 1992 the Olympic men's tournament has been a hybrid under-23 (U-23) age group tournament with teams permitted to field three older players. Some teams utilized these exceptions to bring in stars, while others treated the tourney as an inconsequential development exercise. Among those sharing that view in '96 was New England Revolution's Irish coach Pat Stapleton, who responded to his player Alexi Lalas's request to miss a few Rev games because of the Olympics with a profanity-filled tirade, the gist of which was that Stapleton felt that the tournament was an unimportant nuisance. Fortunately, the women didn't have the political baggage of their brothers; they didn't have age or amateur issues, and the best players came to compete in the Olympics, just like in softball, swimming, and track and field.

It was hard to get over the feeling that the women's games were an afterthought, a late throw-in from soccer parlance, and very much a test case with future participation anything but guaranteed.

The games were condensed into an eleven-day period with only one day of rest between them, with rosters limited to sixteen players. The financial risk was mitigated by hosting the first-round games as doubleheaders with the men—outside of Georgia. Some organizers were concerned that, despite soccer's popularity in most other countries, higher-profile sports would pull U.S. fans away from the early games. Outsourcing games to "non-Olympic venues" was successfully implemented for men's soccer games during both the Montreal 1976 and Los Angeles 1984 Olympics. For 1996, games were held in Washington DC, Miami and Orlando, Florida, and Birmingham, Alabama. Fans in these markets could be a part of the Olympic experience and still be home for dinner. Besides the hardcore soccer fans, there was very much the feeling that some came only to say they had attended the Olympics; if it wasn't soccer, they'd watch kayaking if that was close by. The drawback with the scheduling was that only the semifinals and finals were in the host state, but even then, they weren't held in Atlanta but in Athens, a college town sixty miles up the road with a large American football stadium.

The U.S. team, stung by its World Cup semifinal loss to Norway the year before, put full effort into preparing for the Olympics, going into a full-time residence camp in the months before the tourney. U.S. Soccer spent five times more on the women's team than the men's, in part because of the women's odds-on chances to make the final. There was a disruption early on when the players held out for a better contract, and nine players missed a month of training—not the team's last conflict with U.S. Soccer over the following few years. The local soccer community lived up to Marilyn Childress's promises; tickets went fast, especially for the semifinal and finals. Everything was set for a memorable eleven days.

The U.S. women beat Denmark 3–0 in Orlando before 25,303 on July 21, and then Sweden 2–1 on July 23 in front of 28,000 in the same venue. Two days later they held China to a scoreless tie before 43,525 in Miami. Qualifying easily for the semifinals, the United States then won a thrilling match versus Norway 2–1 on

July 28 in overtime with 64,196 watching in Athens. On August 1, they bested China 2–1 for their sport's first ever Olympic Gold Medal in front of 76,489. Over 140,000 had watched their semifinal and final matches in Athens, when only three years before, the record attendance for a U.S. women's international had been 6,120 in rural Mansfield, Ohio (June 15, 1993.)

The women's games were tremendous events, and the home team's success helped to create momentum at the gate. There was one glaring negative; there was virtually no television coverage. Other than an occasional score mention or brief highlight, NBC kept the team out of its broadcasts; cynics suspected it was a retort to soccer-friendly rival ABC/ESPN/ESPN2, which had carried the 1994 Men's World Cup games. NBC prioritized other sports that they felt would drive ratings and ignored a tremendous moment in the sport's history. U.S. Soccer President Alan Rothenberg referred to NBC's coverage as "a disgrace," adding, "NBC stinks, plain and simple."

1999 Women's World Cup: The Set-Up

The '96 Olympics directly benefited the 1999 World Cup, providing a crucial platform for it to become the most successful women's sports event of all time. The large crowds gave World Cup organizers the opportunity to recast the marketing model that FIFA had encouraged shortly after the 1995 World Cup in Sweden, which was lower key than a carnival barker with laryngitis. Sweden's tournament averaged 4,300 a game in stadiums holding 5,000–10,000, except for the final. FIFA envisioned games in smaller stadiums on the populous U.S. Eastern Seaboard; in other words, a small, manageable regional event that wouldn't lose lots of money. Led by U.S. Soccer president Alan Rothernberg and organizing head and fellow lawyer Marla Messing, both veteran senior executives of the Men's World Cup in 1994, they successfully convinced FIFA that the Olympic attendances could be duplicated if the games were held across the country in large stadiums supported by large scale promotional efforts. FIFA finally agreed to take the risk of a more expensive event (doubling the budget from $15 million to $30 million) and set the stage for what would be the most astounding three weeks in the history of the sport in the United States, men's or women's.

FIFA helped by making some changes to the format they used in 1996, upping roster sizes per team from sixteen to twenty, and increasing rest days between first-round games from 1 to 2.5 days on average. Both changes would help improve the quality of the competition.

U.S. Soccer went to work on the marketing side, leveraging databases built for World Cup 1994 to sell advance tickets. FIFA women's football committee member Per Ravn Omdal said he'd be "extremely happy" with 20,000 per game or 340,000 total: "That would be a real breakthrough for women's soccer." The response from the U.S. buying public was tremendous, forcing the organizing committee to revise its attendance targets upward, first from 312,000 to 400,000, then to 475,000 two months before the games, topping off just before the start in July at 500,000, or 30,000 for each of the seventeen game dates of doubleheaders. This was close to double the post-Olympic U.S. National Team record crowd of 17,358 versus England on May 9, 1997, in San Jose.

A few months before the games, the Organizing Committee started a general marketing and awareness campaign to further drive ticket sales and publicize the event to a mass audience. One whimsical television advertisement spot, set in a dentist's office, depicted midfielder Julie Foudy waiting to have two fillings. As an irreverent spoof on teamwork, Tiffeny Milbrett and Tisha Venturini declared that they would "have two fillings" as well. "Two fillings," became an overnight buzz phrase. Then late-night television talk show host David Letterman got involved, talking continually about the players after Brandi Chastain's pre-Cup appearance on his CBS show. Letterman anointed them with a *nom de guerre* that summer that helped make them national icons, declaring that, "The U.S. team . . . is Babe City, ladies and gentlemen. *Babe City!*"

Letterman's attention highlighted an aspect of women's team sports heretofore avoided or actually suppressed: an image of femininity and wholesome sexual appeal. The team, rather than being insulted, accepted it quite willingly, seeing it as a message "that women can be both athletic and feminine in an endeavor that, in many countries, still carries the stigma that women who play are somehow unwomanly." Team co-captain Julie Foudy said of the focus on the team's beauty, "It makes me laugh. It makes me think, 'God, are we not beyond that?' Ask the 70,000 plus here why they came to watch us play and they wouldn't say, 'It's because that Tisha Venturini is a hot babe.'" The players endeared themselves to Americans with their light, fun-loving attitude. Foudy joked to ESPN's *The Magazine* that her ideal World Cup uniform would be "little pink teddies."

Gatorade released a commercial starring Mia Hamm that was a huge success. She was shown beating basketball icon and fellow University of North Carolina Tar Heel alum Michael Jordan at tennis, soccer, fencing, and other sports to the Irving Berlin song refrain, "Anything you can do, I can do better." The press also focused on the true "soccer mom" angle on the team, as Joy Fawcett had two daughters and Carla Overbeck was raising a son.

The team went into residency as they had before the Olympics. Labor strife again came into play over stipends for housing, massage equipment, and support staffing. Ten Olympic gold medalists boycotted a camp before a December 1998 friendly with Ukraine. This time, players were out for only three days. "Everything's been resolved," U.S. Soccer secretary general Hank Steinbrecher said. "We are about one goal, winning the World Cup. There were certain issues that they felt would help them."

Though U.S. Soccer's contracts with the women had ballooned since 1991, players still struggled to survive while training full time and making public appearances. In 1991 each player earned $1,000 a month in salary from the federation, which was doubled four years later. Their Olympic-year contract paid them a salary that increased each year after and peaked at $3,150 per month in 1999.

The contract included escalating performance bonuses for winning friendlies and major tournaments. The team members would receive a $250,000 bonus to share from U.S. Soccer for winning the World Cup or $150,000 for second—$13,158 and $7,895 respectively per each of the nineteen professional players. U.S. Soccer budgeted $3.1 million in 1999 for the women's effort. The figure included bonuses, salaries, housing, and a nanny for Carla Overbeck's and Joy Fawcett's children. Critics focused on what the U.S. men would earn if they had won the 1998 World Cup—$400,000. The men had received $20,000 for making the World Cup roster the year before compared to only $2,500 for the women. Steinbrecher explained, "The fact is the women aren't getting paid what they're worth. But there's very little that I can do if I'm not making any money. It's an anomaly in the United States, we have such a great team. But sponsorships have been difficult to come by. We average only 9,000 [attendance] a match outside of the World Cup or the Olympics. So it's still a very, very difficult equation."

For those involved in the event, this World Cup wasn't about the money but rather increasing acceptance for the sport and women athletics. World Cup CEO Marla Messing wrote in the FIFA WWC '99 *Official Program*, "The Women's World Cup has grown into more than a sporting event. It will be a mark in time signaling the great changes in the lives of girls of the past generations and set the sights high for those to come." The key to this acceptance was the relationship the team had always had with their fans, which they never took for granted. Defender Brandi Chastain explained, "It's really a relationship of unconditional love. And I think it's significant, what we're doing out here. It gives these kids a point of reference: You can be part of something this big. . . . It's been a part of our foundation from the beginning. . . . We want people to know they're important to us." Mia Hamm summed it up best in a speech after the World Cup, "We have a responsibility that men's sports don't have. We have the responsibility of having women's sports succeed. We all know men's sports are expected to succeed. We all know people expect us to fail."

Members of the squad relished the opportunity to be role models for kids. Throughout the 1990s they would spend hours signing autographs, attending youth camps and games, and making numerous public appearances. World Cup Board of Directors member Donna De Varona won two gold medals at the 1964 Tokyo Olympics in swimming and remembered, "There was no vision, no future [in women's sports at that time]. Women weren't coaches, they weren't administrators, they weren't television commentators. . . . Things have changed [in the United States], and what I love most is young girls and young boys just accept that this is the way it should be." The team approached the public with a missionary zeal, and Marla Messing felt that their impact had global implications: "Sports is certainly a leading factor in the cultural evolution of women all around the world. We seem to accept women as athletes before we accept them, perhaps, in a business environment or a political environment. As there are increased opportunities for women in athletics, particularly in soccer, and they are given recognition as soccer players, we can slowly bring them into other parts of our society." A lot was riding on this opportunity, and the U.S. women delivered, on the field and off.

Women's World Cup 1999: The Tournament

The U.S. team was potent and focused for a run at a second title. They posted a 22–1–2 record in 1998, with 15 games on home soil. Seven players returned from the 1991 and 1995 World Cup teams; Michele "Mufasa" Akers, Joy Fawcett, Julie Foudy, Kristine Lilly, Mia Hamm, and Carla Overbeck all started in '91 and '95, while Brandi Chastain was a substitute forward in 1991.

The one concern leading up to the opening game was the team's weakness as a television draw. The ratings for the first three U.S. women's games in 1999 declined each time, from a 0.30 rating on ESPN on January 30 versus Portugal in Ft. Lauderdale to a 0.22 rating for the Finland match in Tampa on ESPN2 a few weeks later (one single rating point represents 1 percent of viewers in the surveyed market area at the time of an event). By comparison, the men's Major League Soccer games averaged 0.44 in 1998 on ESPN/ESPN2.

In the U.S. team's first game, on June 19 in Giants Stadium versus Denmark, the Americans overcame opening-game nerves and delivered a competent 3–0 win. Amazingly, they attracted 79,972 fans, more than had attended an NFL playoff game at the same venue five months earlier. TV ratings on ABC were a respectable 2.2 and 6 share overnight. Soccer veterans who were there commented on the tremendously passionate crowd and took notice of the "ponytail hooligans," large numbers of teenage and adolescent girls (and some boys too) who brought homemade signs, painted their faces, and wore jerseys of their women heroes—particularly Mia Hamm. Julie Foudy said afterwards, "It was a great atmosphere [at the Olympics] to play soccer but this is our event. In the locker room, we were saying, 'This is our party. Welcome to our party.'"

The United States' second game drew 65,080 in Chicago's Soldier Field to see the home side thrash Nigeria 7–1. In their final game of the first round, the Americans sent North Korea home with a 3–0 victory before 50,484 in Foxboro Stadium. Even the non-U.S. games were bringing in respectable crowds, such as the 22,109 for the Germany–Brazil and Nigeria–Denmark doubleheader on June 27 in Landover, Maryland; 34,296 in Chicago the day before for Norway–Japan and Ghana–Sweden; and 29,401 in Giants Stadium the same day for China–Australia and Canada–Russia. The media attention increased with each American win, with the national outlets unable to get enough. "We are zoo animals, that's what we are," Tiffeny Milbrett whimsically assessed the commotion surrounding the team since the tournament started. "We are the circus freaks. We're fish in a fishbowl. People are looking in, so curious, 'Oh, oh, they moved! They're feeding now! Look!'"

The United States finished a hard fought quarterfinal with Germany as 3–2 victors in Landover, Maryland in front of 54,642, including President Bill Clinton. On ABC, the game drew a palatable 2.19 rating for 1.7 million households. Television ratings for WWC on ESPN overall were higher (1.05) through the quarterfinals than for the men's '98 World Cup in France (0.90 for 27 games), and almost double National Hockey League regular season telecasts (0.59). Though these were good numbers, they paled compared to what was to follow in the Americans' last two matches of the tournament.

It was a phenomenon nobody saw coming, not least the U.S. women, who always had been confident they would capture America's imagination, just nowhere near to the extent they did. "Who knew, huh?" says Milbrett. "The only way we've experienced anything like this is if we were watching the Men's World Cup, sitting in the stands with all the festivals and atmosphere. You never could have predicted this. It's shocking." It was simply a team of girls next door—bright, intelligent women who cared about each other, their fans, and the sport—but reporters and analysts struggled to understand why they suddenly rivaled rock stars. Observers had never seen so many high-profile athletes give so much time to the children who adored them. "This is the most important thing we do," co-captain Foudy explained.

Long-time women soccer followers saw the sport itself changing compared to previous events. The teams played with more sophistication, particularly in defense, but without the niggling bending of rules seen from Italy's men in virtually any World Cup. Most squads played a zonal defense with a flat back four. Back in '95, some teams played some variation of zone combined with woman-to-woman marking. A few, like the United States, still played with a sweeper and two marking backs. But teams had to adjust their defensive schemes with so many speedy forwards emerging like Australia's Julie Murray, China's Sun Wen, Norway's Marianne Pettersen, and Brazil's Pretina. Teams added quick outside backs who could also push forward, which the United States had done well with former forward Brandi Chastain or Joy Fawcett. Now, players like Brazil's right beck Nene, Norway's Brit Sandaune, and China's Bai Jie and Wang Liping could make threatening forays on goal. U.S. assistant coach Lauren Gregg explained, "It was because of the increase in athletes that are playing the game and because of improvement of the tactical nature and the speed of the women's game."

U.S. Soccer chartered a plane to fly the team from Maryland to California for the semifinal. They clinched a spot in the final with a 2–0 triumph over Brazil in front of 73,123 supporters at Stanford. The frenzy around the team continued unabated. Two days before the final against China, Oscar winning actor Karl Malden was among 2,000 who attended a practice at Pomona-Pitzer College. "That's more than watched our games in the early '80s," observed Kristine Lilly.

ESPN had hyped the final in spoof advertisements questioning if President Clinton would attend, before he finally announced that he would fly across the country on short notice to be at Pasadena's Rose Bowl. Singer Jennifer Lopez was brought in at the last minute at considerable expense to entertain the sell-out crowd between games, again emphasizing that this was a premier event. Attendance was 90,185, the largest crowd for a women's sporting event ever. Both the United States and China were tired by the final, but the astounding crowd atmosphere more than compensated. Both sides knew each other well and each developed a strategy to offset the other's strengths. In the semifinals, China destroyed Norway 5–0, while the United States had looked "slow and inconsistent," according to *Soccer America*'s Scott French, in defeating Brazil 2–0. U.S. Coach Tony DiCicco tried to offset China's blistering pace by placing his forwards wide to funnel the Chinese into the middle of the field so that wing backs Wang Liping and Bai Jie couldn't attack down the sidelines. Defenders Fawcett and Chastain also stayed in their defensive end, taking away space for the Chinese to create attacks, but also forgoing some goal-scoring opportunities. Coach DiCicco noted, "We had to make sure their outside backs didn't become attacking personalities. We had our wingers stay wide and not pinch in, and we basically said, 'Okay, they have two center backs [Fan Yunjie and Wen Lirong], let them play with the ball, let them try to find central options, let's not let their outside backs into the game.' For most of the game the strategy worked beauti-fully." Chinese coach Ma Yuanan opted for a cautious approach because of the 100 degree heat, to better conserve the energy of his tired players. While the Americans had the advantage in ball possession time, their offense was stopped cold by an ultra-mobile and cluttered Chinese midfield, which focused on defense first and then looked for counterattacking options.

ABC News reporter Robin Roberts interviewed President Clinton live during halftime of the second match. The commander-in-chief joked that he met ESPN's challenge to come to the Rose Bowl but talked seriously about the World Cup's legacy: "In some ways, it's the biggest sporting event of the last decade. It's new and exciting for the United States. It will have a very far-reaching impact, not only for the United States, but for the world."

With the match scoreless at the end of regulation time, it looked like the fairytale would end badly in overtime when Fan Yunjie's header from Liu Ying's corner kick in the 100th minute flashed past goalkeeper Briana Scurry, but Kristine Lilly, positioned correctly on the back post, headed it clear just before it crossed the line. A player guarding a post never leaves until her goalkeeper releases her; Lilly's play was textbook perfect. Scurry admitted that she was beaten but Lilly saved the day: "Lil is a workhorse and she's one of the best players in the world. There's no one I would trust more on that post than Kristine Lilly." As the clock pushed 6:00 p.m. Eastern time, ABC's *World News Tonight* was due to start. Unlike countless times in the past, a network did not cut away from the game. Lead soccer announcer J. P. Dellacamera proclaimed that they were not going to *World News Tonight* because they had world news they were covering there, again emphasizing that the tournament would have a lasting affect on soccer's perception in the United States.

The game went to penalty kicks. Soccer purists aren't fond of that method of deciding ties, because it's seen as artificial and not part of the game. Everything was different though for this World Cup. As the crowd of ninety thousand roared on, no one complained about the penalty kick solution, then or later, no doubt in large part because the home team won. Brandi Chastain made her spot kick after Chinese midfielder Liu Ying had her shot saved controversially by Briana Scurry, who admitted she moved forward before the shot, an illegal move. (A goalie can only move along her goal line before a shot and cannot cross the line.) Chastain tore off her shirt in celebration. Some criticized the disrobing, seeing it as a publicity ploy for the Nike prototype sports bra that she wore. Chastain explained that her shirt shedding was "momentary insanity." She further said, "I don't know, I kind of lost my mind. I thought, 'This is the greatest moment of my life on the soccer field.' And I lost control." Instead of flak, most people accepted her defense as genuine and it became one of the most memorable moments in sports history—still shown today on the iconic intro-duction of ABC's *Wide World of Sports*. Chastain was the most soccer-mad player on the team, constantly watching men's soccer. She saw men celebrate that way, and in the passion of the moment, imitated that behavior without thinking about it.

Women's World Cup 1999 — The Aftermath

The team celebrated amid extraordinary media and fan acclaim. The next day the victory was the lead news story, not just in sports sections, but all across the nation. ABC's *Nightline* raved about the U.S. women, calling them "the team that may have changed women's sports forever." The team was featured on the covers of *People, Time, Newsweek*, and *Sports Illustrated*, highlighting that it was more than a sports story. The team members went to Disneyland for a parade, the White House for accolades from President Clinton, and to Niketown in Manhattan for a rally. Akers, Chastain, Hamm, Lilly, and Scurry were featured on five special-edition Wheaties boxes, another first for soccer, not just women's soccer. *Soccer America*'s Paul Kennedy summed up the impact of the World Cup when he wrote, "Our little world of American soccer has been turned upside down and may never be the same."

The acclaim and tributes continued through the end of the year. The World Cup Champions were named *Sports Illustrated*'s "Sportswomen of the Year," marking the first time soccer had been honored by the national sports magazine. They were named the Associated Press Story of the Year, and the U.S. team was voted Female Athletes of the Year, the first time a team won the award. Mia Hamm said about the latter award, "This is a great honor for us. One of the things we were most excited about with the World Cup was the media support that we had. . . . Everyone kind of really got excited about and appreciated the fact that it was such a wonderful event. Soccer's not covered that much, especially the women's side of the game. But they came out and took the time and it gave us an opportunity to show them what we're all about. We're just so thankful for that, and we're so honored with this award."

After the immediate euphoria of the win, discussion turned to the long-term effects of "The Babes of Summer." Colleen Hacker, psychologist for the U.S. team and a title-winning college soccer coach, said, "This is a coming of age for women, like Title IX, the right to vote, and Sally Ride as the first female astronaut. The true essence is something you can't grab, touch or quantify. Because a little girl in a third-world country saw strong, independent and capable women playing soccer these past few weeks, she'll realize that she's not crazy for wanting to do something out of the ordinary. She'll say to herself, 'If they can play soccer, then I can be a veterinarian in Rwanda.'" Brandi Chastain said, "[The World Cup] was my vehicle for empowering other women, on the soccer field, in the home and the workplace. It was so amazing to look into the Rose Bowl stands and see the faces of thousands of little girls and women. I wanted to shout, 'We're doing this together!'"

Scott French, who covered women's soccer for many years for *Soccer America*, wrote, "Never before has a female team sport received so much attention and interest as the third Women's World Cup. The way the world looks at women's sports will never be the same after this summer's tournament." Lynn Berling Manual, the editor in chief of *Soccer America* at the time wrote,

Women's World Cup '99 was a brilliant show. It's been astonishing how so many elements came together at one time: a U.S.-hosted event; an 18-month grass-roots ticket-selling campaign; a winning team; the "babe factor" of attractive, well-spoken, well-behaved athletes; the Letterman factor (with David Letterman clearly entranced with the "babe factor"); 25th anniversary of Title IX; a nation clearly ready to clutch the team to its bosom. Even the disappointing penalty-kick finale turned into a plus because it was a simple yet dramatic conclusion to the game that didn't require any soccer knowledge to appreciate. It continues to astonish me how the team, some of its players and a few notable moments (such as the bra-baring victory cheer by Brandi Chastain) have quickly moved into our cultural fabric.

It was the best time to be a soccer supporter in the United States. The soccer bashers were largely quieted, though there was still some criticism, if not of the team—which would have bordered on heresy—then of the way the media hyped it. Noted author and *Detroit Free Press* columnist Mitch Albom commented on ESPN's *Sports Reporters*, "The American media behaved shamefully and irresponsibly [in hyping the final]. It is our job to report on it. It is not our job to get in front of the parade and [wave] the baton."

There was a tendency to view '99 as a one-off, a perfect storm of approachable players, lack of competitive alternatives for fans and media, and savvy marketing. However, the sport's development in North America had been iterative, through stops and starts, and was a culmination of many efforts to farm the soccer fields in America over the past four decades. It never would have happened without the large crowds at the 1996 Olympics, Title IX, and the successful marketing effort of the Men's World Cup 1994, which left a large surplus of funds to fuel further growth in constructing and connecting a soccer community. Clay Berling, who founded *Soccer America* in 1971, talked about how important the soccer community was for the event, "Soccer people really made it happen and they showed how powerful a group they are. It was the soccer people who first bought tickets. When they filled Giants Stadium to 79,000, the tournament got the nation's attention and the media jumped aboard. If the soccer people hadn't put butts in the seats early on, you wouldn't have seen the media attention that followed, the subsequent increase in TV ratings and the surge in ticket sales to the general public."

The "ponytailed hooligans" were icing on the cake and a tremendous opportunity for future growth. Clay Berling felt the roots of the success reached back all the way to the North America Soccer League's evangelical efforts from 1967 to 1984 in a country that didn't know soccer at all, because they marketed to families. Girls and women became familiar with the sport and then sought out opportunities to play. With the explosion of female soccer players in the late 1980s and 1990s, professional game promoters realized that women from ages eight to forty were a key target audience. One promoter commented to me at a Men's World Cup game in 1994 in Washington DC, that future events had to draw in the large number of young women who were in attendance that day.

The final tally on WWC '99 attendance was 638,225 for seventeen events (an average of 37,543) comprising thirty-two matches, more than double the original target and better than some past men's tournaments. This led the way to a FIFA first—the 1999 Women's World Cup actually made a profit of approximately $2 million—something that only the Men's World Cup had previously generated. Profits left over went to the U.S. Soccer Foundation, which supported the organizers with a $2.5 million loan. Organizing Committee president Marla Messing told reporters late in the tournament, "This is the truth—and you guys don't like to hear this—but we really are not out to make money. We are going to make money, but it just wasn't an objective of the event."

A grateful U.S. Soccer Federation rewarded the team with $1 million in bonuses, up from $250,000, which amounted to about $50,000 a player, acknowledging their crucial role in the success of the tournament. The players were stunned, given their tough negotiations with their federation in the past, but appreciative. U.S. Soccer president Bob Contigulia acknowledged what a closely run thing the financials were when he pointed out that, "If the women had not made the final, [WC99] would have lost money."

The topping on the cake came when the final TV numbers came in. For the championship game, ABC posted a rating of 11.4 and 31 share nationally, with 40 million people watching the game. In terms of individual markets, Los Angeles posted an incredible 21.7 rating, with Washington DC, close behind at 19.8. Women's soccer usually earned 0.30 range ratings on ESPN and ESPN2. The game beat out other big summer events in viewing numbers, such as the NBA finals, Kentucky Derby, Indy 500, and the Masters golf tournament. Soccer television writer Jim Murphy observed, "Some will say that you could televise the 'USA vs. the World' in horseshoes and get a big number, but for an event that six weeks ago was barely in the public consciousness and featured women athletes, this is an impressive achievement."

As everyone caught their breath after the initial celebrations, officials started to think about future World Cups. WWC '99's professional organization facilitated their phenomenal mass media coverage. However, could any future host possibly match that standard? Messing offered this advice a few days before the final game: "I think the most important thing for the next country that's going to stage the Women's World Cup is to believe in it the same way we believed in it. This is a world-class event and it needs to be treated as such. We invested resources in the event, we took risks, and it paid off. . . . For this event to continue to build into the next millennium, other countries and FIFA need to continue to invest in it and to take those kinds of risks." Norway's Per Ravn Omdal, chairman of FIFA's Women's Football Committee said, "We have to take from this all the positive things U.S. Soccer had provided into the game, in terms of event management, selling, marketing, [promoting its players as] role models, including sponsors in the promotion of the game."

The '99 World Cup changed the dynamic and general acceptance for the sport of soccer in general. Soccer fans in the United States had been waiting for myriad men's events to help elevate the sport to mainline acceptance: the North American Soccer League; Pele's three years with the Cosmos; high-profile exhibitions with Real Madrid, Manchester United, and other international teams; qualifying for World Cup 1990 and 1998; hosting World Cup 1994; Major League Soccer's launch in 1996; and so on. Then a group of women, whose nucleus had already won two major international titles but had plied their trade in relative anonymity for years, came along and rocketed the sport to unforseen levels in three short weeks. The '99 wwc Final *is still* the most watched soccer game on television in the United States *ever*. The game was the pinnacle of years of effort to popularize the sport by introducing females to the game. The sport had been introduced to potential new followers of both the men's and women's game. The men's game, though making progress, seems to fall into obscurity at times; the women added adrenaline and new vitality to the sport. The sport of soccer would be much the poorer and much different without the women's game. For that, true fans of the sport will be forever grateful to the "Babes of Summer."

3

Professional Women's Soccer and the WUSA

"The Best Three Years of My Life"

July 10, 1999, was, in many ways, the pinnacle event for soccer in its history in the United States, not just the women's game. How could you surpass 40 million U.S. viewers watching on television on a hot Saturday afternoon in July while 91,000 baked in the Rose Bowl, including President Clinton? Despite earning their second world title, filling stadiums, attracting mainstream media attention, gaining widespread acceptance as top-class athletes, and being acclaimed as role models to the country's youth, the national team players did what elite athletes do—they immediately set another goal. They wanted what their male counterparts had in most major markets around the world: a professional league to hone their skills and spur the further development of the sport. World Cup 1999 was the big bang; now they needed daily competition and an ongoing vehicle to continue to market the sport. However, the '99 tournament was not the initial stimulus for the launch of a professional league. World Cup 1999 was an important trigger, but work on the new league actually began shortly after the team's previous major international title, the Olympic Games Gold Medal in Georgia in 1996.

National Soccer Alliance (NSA)

Some of the same elements of the 1999 World Cup success were present in 1996 at the Atlanta Olympics, including fervent support by soccer playing youth and packed stadiums cheering on the successful home team. However, the Olympic soccer competition was shorter (eleven days vs. World Cup's three weeks), only eight teams competed, twenty-five other sports competed for attention, and women's soccer had next to no television coverage. Still, the Olympic crowds and the resounding success of the women caught one promoter's attention and became a base to build a league upon.

After the Olympic Games were finished, Harvard MBA graduate and sports marketer Jennifer Rottenberg began an effort to launch a women's professional soccer league, naming her prospective entity the National Soccer Alliance (NSA). In September 1997, she announced that the league planned to start a twenty-game, ten-week schedule in an April to July window in 1998 with eight teams:

Boston (Natick MA)
Dallas (Duncanville TX)
Los Angeles (Fullerton CA)
New York–New Jersey (Piscataway NJ)
Raleigh NC
San Jose CA
Seattle WA
Washington DC (Bethesda MD)

Rottenberg's model was to utilize high school and college stadiums that had seating for about 5,000–6,000. Her capitalization plans for $12 million would handle three years of league operations, breaking even after the first year with an average attendance of only 2,750 per game. The investment capital was meant to cover cash flow gaps, since the league was designed to be self-sustaining. League player salaries would range between $15,000 and $30,000 for the season. U.S. National Team player Tisha Venturini gave a player's perspective on the value of the league, "This [NSA] is extremely important. Other countries have leagues and are getting an edge every day of the year, in practice five days a week, competing, where we have two games a month." Besides Venturini, other American stars such as Mia Hamm, Michelle Akers, and Kristine Lilly committed to the league. NSA also received strong interest from top players in other countries. Anson Dorrance, coach of the U.S. World Championship team in 1991, was on the NSA advisory committee.

As Rottenberg was exploring high school stadiums for a Washington DC, area franchise, she received a call from John Hendricks, the founder and CEO of Discovery Communications, who broached the idea of using a larger venue, University of Maryland's Byrd Stadium (with capacity for 35,000 at the time). Hendricks ran a successful multichannel cable television conglomerate with over thirty networks including Animal Planet, Discovery Health, the Learning Channel, and its flagship, the Discovery Channel. He had a science background in school and started the networks as a conduit for informative documentaries and thoughtful programming. Hendricks also had a keen entrepreneurial mind. He gave reality television superstar producer Mark Burnett a visible platform for his adventure race series *Eco-Challenge* before Burnett sold *Survivor* and then *The Apprentice* to major networks. Hendricks became a soccer fan through his children, and became known as Saint John among the U.S. National Team players, thanks to his passion and support of their game.

The budget and operations model for NSA seemed achievable, attendance projections were realistic, and strong investors led the way, but the effort ran aground over U.S. Soccer's sanctioning for professional leagues in February of 1998. Looking back, Jen Rottenberg said, "[When starting this effort] I was not aware of the Division I status. It was political. The fact you had to get approval wasn't on my radar screen. The players wanted in; we just needed investors." She wanted to leverage the relationship that the players had built with their fans, adding, "I'm a huge fan of the pioneers of the national team, what they did, building presence and role models." The U.S. Soccer Federation's mission is to promote the game at all levels. However, the timing of NSA's effort was problematic for them, as beginning a year before World Cup 1999 could potentially cost them sponsorship and advertising dollars for the FIFA tournament that they had a sizeable financial stake in.

To outsiders, the U.S. Soccer Federation organization can seem confusing, particularly since it is a nonprofit entity with three major units: the professional, the amateur, and the youth divisions. The professional organizations (Major League Soccer and the minor leagues falling under the United Soccer Leagues) controlled a third of the general assembly vote, even though they only had a few hundred fully professional players compared to the youth division's 3 million registered players at the time. The youth division, famous for its fractionalization, comprises many different constituents with their own agendas, many of whom only care about their son's or daughter's team. Soccer is recreational to them and they see no tie-in or benefit from the professional or global game; it really is inconsequential to them.

U.S. Soccer in turn is a member of the global governing body for the sport, Federation Internationale de Football, based in Zurich Switzerland. FIFA's charge is to promote and manage the sport globally, primarily through its 208 member national associations, more than belong to the United Nations (192). FIFA has divided the world into six regional confederations to oversee the associations, which in turn register players, assign referees, and protect the interests of the game. FIFA usually sides with the local federation in all jurisdictional disputes, and has the power to even mandate that members cannot take other members to civil court, but must work through FIFA's procedures for settling disputes. If U.S. Soccer didn't sanction the NSA, then FIFA wouldn't either, and players in the league could face sanctions from their national soccer federations, including bans from playing for their national teams.

The NSA leadership unexpectedly faced some rules that the American federation had implemented to avoid a situation that it faced in the late 1960s when three men's soccer leagues tried to start at the same time, almost committing hara-kiri on the professional game. In 1967, the federation, known then as the United

States Soccer Football Association (USSFA), was a weak organization and totally unprepared for the sudden interest in starting professional soccer, spurred by the live televising of the 1966 World Cup final from England. One group, the United Soccer Association (USA) was given USSFA's blessing to operate, which meant that they could recruit FIFA-affiliated players from all over the world. The other two leagues had merged to form the National Professional Soccer League (NPSL), which was decreed an "outlaw league" but surprisingly managed to recruit enough players who risked suspension from FIFA in their home countries. The most troubling thing to federation officials was that the "unofficial" NPSL was able to sign a national television contract with CBS. The two leagues eventually merged into one entity, the NASL, after the first season, but FIFA and the American federation had learned its lesson. After the NASL's demise in March of 1985, U.S. Soccer, perhaps feeling a bit over-officious and with too much time on their hands, developed professional and amateur league standards for Division I, II, and III levels for both men and women, based on salient attributes such as coverage across their four regions, budgets, stadium capacity, and operating standards. The only problem was there were no Division I men's or women's leagues at the time.

So the NSA came along and seemingly fit the criteria, but U.S. Soccer officials were concerned about the new league negatively affecting the 1999 World Cup, both financially and taxing players with too many high level games. To Rottenberg, the start date was nonnegotiable; she reasoned that if they started the year before the World Cup, she could then reduce the schedule of games to accommodate the 1999 World Cup and 2000 Olympics. She explained, "We would have a baseline established even if they didn't win [in 1999.] If 1999 came and went and they didn't win the World Cup, what do you start with, the fourth best players?" Some hypothesized that Major League Soccer (MLS) had some influence on the final outcome; the nascent men's league was struggling to build a fan base and could be severely weakened if the women siphoned off even a thousand fans a game. This concern was premature, though

MLS would definitely play a role in WUSA's similar sanctioning woes a few years later. In the end, U.S. Soccer had the power to dictate, and Rottenberg gave up her effort.

Women's United Soccer Association (WUSA)

After the NSA was rebuffed, John Hendricks didn't give up on the idea of a professional league and kept working behind the scenes, quickly taking over Rottenberg's leadership mantle when she walked away. With the widespread acclaim and phenomenal success of the World Cup in the summer of 1999, Hendricks was ready and moved quickly. He locked up U.S. National Team player contracts in order to drive investors, television contracts, and sponsors his way. All of the U.S. World Cup champions (with the exception of collegian Lorrie Fair) signed on as "founder members." Hendricks would ultimately set a team salary cap of $800,000 (double U.S. Soccer's Division I requirement), guaranteeing that the lowest paid players made close to what their MLS counterparts made—about $25,000 a year. The WUSA clearly intended to pull in all the talent so that another league, if one was able to start, would be seen as minor in comparison.

Hendricks, like Rottenberg before him, was new to American soccer's political minefield and ignored U.S. Soccer's sanctioning requirement, even though it could have been his undoing. World Cup team members felt they had substantial power with their success, as national team midfielder and clubhouse spokesperson Julie Foudy explained, "Talking with the whole team, they all say the same thing. We will only play for WUSA. We feel with all the qualities they have, all the standards they've exceeded, [U.S. Soccer approval is] going to happen. We're hoping the Federation sees it in the same light. We can't control it, of course, but our loyalty and commitment are to the WUSA."

It was another ramification of the players' difficult relationship with the federation. Competing without sanctions had high risks for the athletes; U.S. players could forfeit their right to play internationally by signing with the WUSA. There was also the concern that the federation would take a hard line to prove a point against their employees. Hendricks just continued signing players, focusing on the best international players, at one point claiming to have over one hundred letters of intent or oral commitments from players around the world. Without U.S. Soccer approval, FIFA could stop these internationals from joining the league.

There were grave concerns with whether the concept of a women's pro league would succeed at all. Burton Haimes, the chairperson of a U.S. Soccer Federation committee formed back in 1991 to investigate the feasibility of launching a Division I women's pro league, defended U.S. Soccer's cautiousness in not immediately giving the new league its blessing. Haimes said in 1999, "The idea is to launch a league not just based on World Cup results. People are not going to invest [only] as a statement for women. In the end, they want to make money." U.S. Soccer's secretary general, Hank Steinbrecher, said, "It's a very difficult business. Americans love a big event. But the women average less than 9,000 a game when not playing in an Olympics or World Cup." Others were skeptical as well. *Soccer America*'s editor, Paul Kennedy, felt that a women's pro league had to overcome soccer's poor past, plus "the unproved track record of women's pro sports." At least the MLS had hard core ethnic fans, particularly among Latinos, but the fans of the women's national team were a much different audience. "A women's pro league will blaze a new trail if it can thrive on a core market of teenage girls, the primary target audience for USA '99," Kennedy reasoned.

U.S. Soccer, often depicted as slower than your average everyday glacier, did not immediately approve the WUSA even though it more than met its minimum requirements. While the federation dithered, Major League Soccer showed an active interest in starting a women's league. U.S. Soccer and Hendricks finally agreed to both contribute a hundred thousand dollars for Mark Abbott, who had designed MLS's business plan, to create three business models for a women's league. More politics: Abbott was still on the men's league payroll, as chief operating officer. Two of the plans explicitly defined a relationship between the WUSA and the MLS, but WUSA investors preferred the third model, which would make the women's league completely independent. Hendricks publicly declared that the WUSA was going its own way, forcing the men's league into a corner. The MLS could stand by as Hendricks's group nabbed a potentially major portion of the soccer marketplace, or it could try to protect its turf. There really was no option for the four-year-old league, which was struggling for a niche in the U.S. sports world. On March 30, 2000, the MLS announced it would submit a bid for a Women's Major League Soccer. Hendricks didn't appear fazed, carrying on with announcements about his investor group, claiming he had $40 million in committed funds, not far short of the $50 million that MLS had when it started. Hendricks leveraged his media relationships to form his investor group, selling the league to other cable companies as content. The group included Cox Communications, Comcast Corporation, and Time-Warner Cable. Amos Hostetter Jr., the chair of Pilot House Associates and cable pioneer of Continental Cablevision (which as MediaOne became the third-largest U.S. broadband communication provider), joined Hendricks as an individual investor.

Hendricks announced the eight charter franchises in February of 2000:

Atlanta Beat
Bay Area CyberRays (San Jose CA)
Boston Breakers
New York Power
Orlando Tempest
Philadelphia Charge
San Diego Spirit
Washington DC Freedom

Chicago, Dallas, Los Angeles, Portland, and Seattle missed out on the launch list. Besides the usual measures of suitable stadiums and soccer support, one unique key criterion used to select cities was "substantial cable television distribution by one or more of the investors." Time-Warner controlled the New York and Orlando franchises, Cox operated clubs in Atlanta and San Diego, Philadelphia was run by Comcast, and Hostetter ran Boston. Two franchises were equal partnerships among the investors; DC with Hendricks and Comcast, while Hendricks and Hostetter ran the San Jose (Bay Area) club. By the third season, Hendricks would be the sole director of the Freedom.

Tony DiCicco, who resigned as U.S. women's national team head coach by the end of 1999 to spend more time with his family, joined the WUSA in an executive position. Well respected by federation officials, he clearly understood American soccer politics and knew what was at stake when he said, "For U.S. Soccer and for the soccer community to turn their backs on the potential of this investor group would be the biggest folly in the history of soccer in this country, in my opinion. They have the resources and ability to pen avenues to media we have been dreaming about our whole lives."

A third group added to the confusion in April of 2000 by announcing its intent to seek U.S. Soccer sanctioning as a Division I professional league. The Women's Soccer Association was a South Texas–based entity that planned for twelve teams with "charter franchises" in Richmond, Virgina; Pennsylvania's Lehigh Valley; and Flagstaff, Arizona. Not surprisingly, given their small markets, it soon dropped out with money problems.

Full proposals were due to U.S. Soccer by May 1, with a decision due in the summer of 2000. Behind the scenes, U.S. Soccer wanted the WUSA and the MLS to join forces. Hendricks would have no part of it. The WUSA did submit a cooperation agreement to the MLS that addressed ways in which the outfits could work together, essentially on marketing, promotion, scheduling, and stadium development. Hendricks explained his reasoning: "It's extremely difficult [for the groups to operate the league together]. It could mean one of the controlling groups has two priorities, the men's game and the women's game. We think this is very important, that there be an investor group fully behind the women's league, with the women's league being the sole priority. It doesn't mean we can't have a co-operative agreement."

The gender war in soccer, a new version of the long history of fractious American soccer leagues, was finally averted when the two groups signed an agreement to work together in late May. Both league leaders seemed sincerely pleased; MLS commissioner Don Garber explained, "We came very close, we had our application ready to go. At the 11th hour, John and I and the investors were able to get together and have a meeting of the minds that made sense. It's something that we are very excited about. We feel that today's announcement will result in a relationship that is best for the growth of soccer at all levels, not just the men's and women's league but at youth levels."

John Hendricks won his argument of a league focused on women, "We think this is a break-through in league cooperation in this country. We're excited that this plan develops a cooperation both in the immediate future and is also very forward-looking." The players, supportive of the WUSA all along, were ecstatic about the results, "Obviously, as we've seen from other sports, having two leagues wouldn't have been best for the game," said U.S. captain Carla Overbeck.

As part of the agreement, the MLS and the WUSA discussed operating expansion teams in each other's territories. Five of the new WUSA's eight markets also had an MLS franchise: Boston, New York, Orlando-Tampa, San Francisco Bay Area, and Washington DC, though the WUSA's Orlando franchise would relocate to Raleigh-Durham to become the Carolina Courage before the first game, after Time-Warner couldn't finalize a stadium lease contract. Under their new cooperative relationship, if the WUSA wanted to start a team in a city that the MLS had a team in, that franchise would be operated by the MLS or its investors in that city, as was the case in Los Angeles. From the men's league perspective, WUSA franchises Philadelphia (Comcast) and Atlanta (Cox) had attractive investors in potential MLS expansion sites. In theory, both leagues gained: the MLS received the added exposure from the WUSA's major cable operators, and the WUSA got the benefit of the experience that the MLS had in the American soccer market.

With all barriers now gone, in August 2000 U.S. Soccer anticlimactically granted the WUSA its official approval as a Division I pro league. U.S. National Team defender Kate Sobrero said, "Finally many women can make a living playing the sport they love. The WUSA will provide a wonderful training environment to help ensure we remain the best soccer team in the world." Mia Hamm succinctly said, "This is a wonderful time for soccer in this country."

WUSA's business plan called for losses of $37 million, with the break-even point coming in year 4 or 5. The ownership group committed to $40 million for league expenses plus an additional $24 million for venue development. Hendricks said, "With this investor group, if we got into a fifth year and said, 'Hey, we need another $20 million,' everyone would be willing to fund this, whatever amount it would take." They set a target of an average attendance of 6,500 but then raised it to 7,500 per game for the 2001 season.

The investors believed that they were involved in launching more than just a league, that they would leave a mark in furthering the development of strong values for America's youth. Investor Amos Hostetter wrote in the inaugural WUSA media guide, "Something magical happened in the Summer of 1999 that touched the heart of America. We were all captivated by the determination, competitive drive and wholesome appeal of the U.S. women who took on the world and won. This is a wonderful venture that will add a valuable new dimension to the sports landscape."

Even the large media conglomerates were caught up by the illustrious moment the U.S. National Team created in 1999. Joseph J. Collins, chairman and CEO of Time-Warner Cable said, "At Time-Warner Cable we look for opportunities that offer our cable customers something special. Through our participation in creating the WUSA league, we will give them not only something special, but something to cheer about. America has fallen in love with women's soccer. Here at Time-Warner Cable, we intend to keep the romance alive." Brian Roberts, president and CEO of Comcast echoed the sentiment: "There is a powerful appetite in America for sports programming and at Comcast we have been delighted to make investments that provide our customers with exciting sports entertainment. . . . We are proud to be in a position to both serve our viewers and to help create this opportunity for these remarkable young women who continue to inspire us." Despite the nice legacy messages, Collins and Roberts were very clear: their companies were buying media content. The social dimension was laudable, but only as it supported the visibility and viability of the product.

The television rights were purchased by Turner Network Television, who paid $3 million to carry fifteen games in 2001. Turner Sports President Mark Lazarus said, "Given the national promotion, the local promotion, the push the operators will put on, and what the league will put together, we think we can draw somewhere in the neighborhood of a 2.0 rating with this programming." Hendricks agreed that a projection of 2.0 "is reasonable at this point." These forecasts were based on the 11.4 the women drew for the 1999 World Cup Final, not the 0.4 MLS average on ESPN/ESPN2.

Similar to Major League Soccer and other leagues during the 1990s, the WUSA had a single-entity business structure, established as a limited liability company. Investors operated clubs but owned shares in the league, not individual teams. The league negotiated all player contracts and set strict salary cap guidelines. The model neutralizes the ability of teams in larger markets to spend more than those in smaller markets; even sponsorships are leveraged across the teams as well. Equalized spending by teams is also designed to promote parity of play, preventing team dominance on the field solely through having a bigger wallet. The single entity model essentially was developed to protect owners against themselves while conveniently eliminating player leverage in individual team negotiations. One unique aspect of the WUSA's Board of Governors made it different from all other existing sports leagues: Julie Foudy sat on the league's Board of Governors, the first active player in the history of American professional sports to do so. Also, the WUSA founding players were considered shareholders in the league, taking an equity stake in lieu of higher salaries. Uniquely empowered, they felt that they could influence the direction of the league.

The teams put together front offices, gathered coaching staffs, and began building their rosters. The wusa allocated three players to each team from the founders list, based on three things: where the players wanted to go, where they were from, and competitive balance (see tables 2 and 3 in the appendix).

Next, the wusa held an allocation draft of sixteen global stars signed from seven different countries. Finally, a league-wide draft was held to supplement the founding and international allocation players. Teams could field up to four internationals; six alone came from China's '99 World Cup silver medalists, including the top four picks in the supplemental draft, once the Chinese government gave their approval for their national team stars to play. The wusa seemed to have all the right pieces in place leading up to their April 2001 start: a realistic business plan, committed corporate investors with deep pockets, television broadcasters as a major focus (never soccer's strong suit in America), and the best players in the world.

WUSA — Season 1

On April 14, 2001, the wusa officially kicked off with a bang in front of an enthusiastic crowd of 34,148 at rfk Stadium in Washington dc. The promotional hype was dc Freedom's Mia Hamm vs. the Bay Area CyberRays' Brandi Chastain, but the game really was a celebration of the growth of women's sports. The CyberRays fell by a single goal in a choppy, uneven match but this didn't upset a buoyant Chastain in postgame interviews when she said, "[The loss] doesn't diminish the fact that we are a part of history and we've changed American culture for young girls. People asked me this week, 'What would make this league a success?' and I said, 'We've already been successful. We started a league.'" TNT's rating for the game was 0.5 for 393,087 households, better than two mls games on espn and espn2. Not only that, soccer followers noticed that the 34,000 crowd outdrew every mls game that weekend.

The impressive opening day helped get the league off to a rousing start. After forty-seven games of the eighty-four-game regular season schedule, average attendance reached 8,657 per game, well ahead of expectations. League publications cited possible expansion markets as Chicago, Columbus, Detroit, Los Angeles, Miami, Portland, and St. Louis. The MLS had teams in Chicago, Columbus, and Los Angeles, but sources in Columbus said that, despite the agreement between the two leagues, no talks had transpired between the MLS's Columbus Crew team to bring the WUSA into the Ohio capital. Furthermore, the Crew's management had no interest in the idea. Both leagues monitored stadium development efforts in Denver, Houston, and Milwaukee.

Meanwhile, sloppy play on the field improved somewhat as the season wore on; the players became more comfortable with one another and improved with daily high-level training sessions. The teams had taken very different approaches in selecting head coaches, ranging from a few former men's professional coaches (DC's Jim Gabarra and Boston's Jay Hoffman), ex-women's coaches at the collegiate level (Philadelphia's Mark Kriokorian and New York's Pat Farmer), a women's club coach (Tom Stone in Atlanta), a federation staff coach (San Diego's Carlos Juarez) and even a former women's coach at the University of California–Berkeley who had been pursuing a professional golf career for the past few years (Bay Area's Ian Sawyers.) Significantly, there was only one woman head coach, Marcia McDermott in Carolina, a former collegiate soccer coach at Northwestern, Arkansas, and Maryland. After winning the championship game the second year (following a bottom of the table finish in 2001), McDermott reflected on the inaugural year: "[In year 1] the first thing that happened was I didn't have enough familiarity with the players in the draft and with professional soccer. In putting the team together, we pursued talent and had ideas, but we didn't have a cohesive enough plan, and the talent we organized wasn't cohesive enough. That was my mistake. That was a problem. I assumed too much about the professionalism. No one knew enough about professionalism."

One thing that the league seemed to be clear on was who their target audience was since the successful attendance figures centered on attracting six- to eighteen-year-olds to their stadiums. Even the founding players thought it was part of their charge to try to reach young boy and girl players, particularly the famed pony-tailed hooligans from 1999. At times, it seemed the WUSA's marketing effort came down to one word: *Mia*. Mia Hamm was the touchstone, the face of the league to the youth market and the one person that league survival hinged on. Hamm's DC Freedom averaged 14,421 at home and 11,227 on the road that first season to pull the league average up to 8,116, which without Freedom games home and away would have slid to 6,558. Atlanta Beat general manager Lynn Morgan explained how Mia's team was a marketing gem to the league: "We use Mia Hamm in our advertising. We promote her name and her team. We're crazy if we don't leverage our assets."

There was a problem though, and you could see it in Hamm's play; there were so many marketing demands on her that it was taking a toll on her on-field job. As her game suffered, so did DC's prospects, and ultimately the marquis franchise finished tied for last with Carolina, winning only six times in twenty-one games. The top four teams in the single division format made the playoffs, which were all one-game affairs. All three playoff matches were thrilling, high scoring contests. Atlanta topped Philadelphia, and Bay Area disposed of New York by identical 3–2 scores. Atlanta and Bay Area met in the final—fittingly, the two teams that tied for first in the regular season standings—and went to penalty kicks before Bay Area won 4–3 before 21,078 at Foxboro Stadium in Boston (see table 4 in the appendix).

The most positive aspect to the first season from a league standpoint was the average attendance of 8,116 for regular season games (8,307 with the three playoff games added), which was 10 percent above the revised target of 7,500 a game. DC Freedom (14,421) and Atlanta Beat (11,092) finished well above the mean, while Boston (8,012) finished just under. Bay Area/San Jose (7,692) and Philadelphia (7,541) posted strong numbers, while Carolina

(5,255), New York (5,742), and San Diego (5,714) lagged behind. Fans enjoyed the in-stadium experience, with all teams staging lots of activities primarily geared for children. Unfortunately, the attendance numbers didn't translate to the TNT viewing figures. The first year ratings averaged 0.36; the low ratings socked the television company owners in their root business. For the second year, games were moved to the PAX network, which guaranteed a consistent spot on Saturday afternoons . . . at the exact time as MLS games on ESPN/ESPN2; so much for the cooperative agreement! Another problem was that PAX was not widely available by local cable providers throughout the United States and had low name recognition.

The clincher in the bad news department was that the five-year investment cushion of $40 million was gone before the playoffs. The league reported income of only $5.5 million. John Hendricks dismissed concerns by saying, "The amount of investment in the WUSA, more than $60 million, is relatively small change to the companies involved. You have to realize this is at a level in Discovery (cable network) terms of three documentaries a year. For some of the other companies, this is a small investment." Despite the astounding amount of money that was burned through in a matter of months, the investors were still committed and positive. "We couldn't be happier," said Fred Dressler, who directed Time-Warner Cable's interests in the league. "This has been one of the best things that we've done in a long time. Anybody's who's been around the games, around the players, knows this is a unique opportunity."

Further complicating the ledger sheet was that the WUSA generated far less revenue in sponsorships than it had anticipated; a strong point of WWC '99. Advertisers didn't see the connection beyond the noble goal of helping a cause and their business objectives. With no business rationale of assisting with their key goals such as brand-building or increasing sales, sponsorships fell into another business line item: the charitable donation category. The trouble with WUSA's link with the women's movement is that, compelling though it was, the league now competed against United Way contributions, company sports tickets, and the like. WUSA became a "nice to have" for organizations, but these are also the first things cut when times are bad. League brass believed, to their detriment, that the WUSA's primary weapon in generating sponsorship dollars was the connection the teams and players had made in their communities, which bred fierce fan loyalty. "The sponsors see this as a special audience and a captive audience that they can attack in a different way than normal sponsorships work," Time Warner's Dressler said. Attracting sponsors was to be a lasting problem for the WUSA, however. The market unfortunately simply did not respond to the intangibles that were created by the existence of a professional women's sports league.

WUSA — Season 2

The league made some big changes for 2002. League headquarters moved from New York City to Atlanta, eerily exactly the same shift the NASL effected three decades earlier, following its first season after league membership fell from seventeen to five. Fortunately, no WUSA franchises folded or moved. Cox Communication owned 25 percent of the league through its Atlanta and San Diego set-ups and provided legal, technological, marketing, public relations, and administrative support from its corporate offices. In the process, the league cut permanent staff from twenty-six to seventeen, and more than half the latter figure included new hires. CEO Barbara Allen was jettisoned and replaced by Lynn Morgan, who oversaw both Cox franchises in 2001. Allen, a long-time executive of Quaker Oats, an Internet provider, and an office supply company, said more than once she didn't realize what she was getting herself into when she joined the new league. Morgan was a good choice; she had worked at Cox for ten years, handling Olympic tie-ins for the company. She had a top-level sports background, having played collegiate tennis at the University of Georgia. Before year 2, she said, "We feel we have a better handle, now having gone through a season, on what resources to commit, on our business model. . . . We've got some work to do, but, no question, it's a reasonable goal and, I think, an achievable goal." Atlanta and Carolina moved into new facilities, while San Diego's and Philadelphia's were upgraded. The Bay Area CyberRays became the San Jose CyberRays, branding itself after its home community, which was a historical hotbed for professional soccer in the United States.

On the field, the second year brought better parity among the teams (with the notable exception of the New York Power, who fell apart due to numerous injury victims and listless play from the survivors, ending with a league record low three victories out of twenty-one games). The league welcomed some new impact players, including German National Team striker Brigit Prinz, Norwegian midfield star Unni Lehn (both Carolina), China's Zhou Lihong (Philadelphia), and U.S. National Teamers Danielle Slaton (Carolina) and Abby Wambach (DC). The two poorest performing teams the year before, Carolina and DC, made complete turn-arounds to snatch playoff spots. Carolina waived eleven players from their inaugural roster and increased their talent base, while Mia Hamm superbly led DC, revitalizing her career by becoming a super sub after missing some early games. Carolina defeated Atlanta 2–1 in an engaging semifinal, while DC outlasted Philadelphia 1–0. Carolina bested Hamm's Freedom 3–2 in another superb advertisement for the women's game before 15,321 in Atlanta's Herndon Stadium (see table 5 in the appendix).

In the fall of 2002 the operation post-ops were worrisome, and league officials worked hard to reassure fans, players, and sponsors, all the while bailing out the red ink that poured into the entity. The big positive of the first year, average attendance, was no longer such a bright point, falling from 8,307 to 7,196 per game, a 15 percent decline and way off the 8,500 target. Washington DC (9,297) and Atlanta (6,784) showed the largest drop-offs from 2001 by almost 5,000 fans a game, while Boston showed a huge gain to 8,120, the second-highest total. The Mia factor was still important to the other teams but less so at home; the Freedom drew almost the same number to every road game (9,191) as they did at home (9,297).

TV ratings plummeted as well, from 0.4 on TNT to 0.1 on PAX. The financials were frightening; the league spent $29 million in

2002, down from $40 million, and while expenses did drop, revenues were a paltry $9 million. The WUSA had spent close to $70 million in two seasons, offset by income of about $15 million. Despite a deficit that would seem to warrant World Bank assistance, league officials remained positive. Former U.S. National Team player Kevin Crow, who left an executive position with San Diego Spirit to become the league's new chief operating officer, said confidently, "If you've ever sat at the league meetings, ever been to a board meeting with investors, it would be impossible to come out with this thought process [that the league is struggling to survive]. Do you think I'd be moving across the country [from San Diego to Atlanta] if I thought this was a risky proposition?"

Crow joined the league office to handle the eight team general managers, freeing up President Morgan to focus on marketing and sales. Morgan tried to reassure everyone that WUSA wasn't in panic mode: "I think people read into the fact that we blew through [our five-year funding plan] the first year. They draw the analogy: 'Oh, they must be in trouble.' Our investors are so committed, our sponsors are very committed, we're not holding on by a thread. We're doing the right things, and I have the ability to do them at a pace that makes sense. I don't have this tremendous pressure right now to suddenly become profitable."

Founder John Hendricks continued to feel that the WUSA would be profitable by 2007: "Our expectations are that at some magical moment in time, probably between the fourth year and the sixth year, the revenues will exceed the expenses. And we know we have a successful business for the long term." Others were not as optimistic; two coaches turned down the San Diego Spirit job for the security of their college positions, including Santa Clara's 2002 NCAA champion coach Jerry Smith, who also happened to be Brandi Chastain's husband. The job went to Omid Namazi, a professional men's indoor coach with virtually no experience coaching women, though Namazi turned out to be a revelation. A sore point to some is that the league made no progress in developing and promoting women as head coaches. The only female coach during the first two years, Marcie McDermott, strangely resigned after winning a title with Carolina Courage, reportedly tired of repeated battles with her general manager, Jerome Ramsey. Ramsey was a lawyer and Time-Warner executive who came with absolutely no sports management experience. McDermott returned to the Courage front office after Ramsey was let go a few months later. Swede Pia Sundhage became the lone woman coach in year 3 when she joined Boston Breakers. Sundhage, well respected in international circles, had made 146 appearances and scored 71 goals in a twenty-one-year international career for Sweden, retiring in 1996. She was an inspired hiring and would have a colossal impact on the Breakers' season. Sundhage would later lead the U.S. National Team to an Olympic Gold Medal as head coach in 2008.

WUSA – Season 3

Despite the bravado statements from the league chiefs, the money troubles began to manifest themselves publicly when the WUSA slashed the player budgets for year 3 to help reduce expenses. The founding players took pay cuts from $80,000–$85,000 down to $60,000, with the team salary cap of $834,500 in year 1 falling by almost 30 percent to $595,750. The league average salary dropped from $46,631 to $37,234. Rosters were cut to sixteen full-timers (down from twenty in 2001 and eighteen in 2002), two reserves, and a new cheaper "developmental player" classification who would suit up only when full-time players were unavailable. The U.S. Soccer Foundation funded one reserve spot per team starting in 2002. It was not a good signal that the foundation, charged with distributing grants to develop the game earned from interest income on the $40 million principal in profits from World Cup 1994, would invest only about $150,000 in the venture.

John Hendricks's deep-pocketed investors had put up $40 million to start the league, another $20 million at the end of 2001, and $40 million during the second season. Hendricks admitted in retrospect, "By the start of 2003 it was clear we were running out of finances." In June 2003, this author had a long discussion with a women's soccer coach with strong contacts in the league who argued that the WUSA's objective as television content was an unmitigated disaster. He felt that the league would expire, most likely during or after its fourth season in 2004. It turned out the desperation was far worse than most followers imagined.

As things were tanking, the league blindly continued its focus on marketing to youth. A unique league-sponsored multimedia production became available in 2003 titled: *Girl's Guide to Soccer Life by the Stars of the WUSA*. It was a combination of a book and DVD, with chapters containing quotes and inspirational stories from forty-some players, focused on topics such as: "Dealing with Obstacles," "Daring to Dream," "Finding Success," and "How to Organize Training on Your Own." CEO Lynn Morgan wrote in the book's foreword, "While WUSA players have the opportunity to play the game they love and make a living doing so, they also realize they can bring positive change to the youth of America. Being a role model and positively influencing children is something that the WUSA and its players see as a remarkable opportunity. Community service and charity is something that the league—including every player, team, and general manager—treats as a top priority."

The league never wavered from their focus on marketing to youth, which again was socially important, but wasn't driving the gate receipts or sponsorship dollars. The low television ratings put pressure on investors like Time-Warner and Comcast, who had created programming that people weren't watching and advertisers weren't buying. Hendricks later felt the league needed to target older teens and "soccer dads," but it was too late.

Ironically, 2003 was an important year for women's soccer, as the fourth edition of the Women's World Cup was set for China in September, shortly after the WUSA season concluded. Some connected with the league expressed the giddy thought that the World Cup and the U.S. Women's National Team's quest for a third world title would again enrapture America; a replay, muted perhaps, of the galvanizing 1999 tournament. This line of thought concluded that the World Cup publicity would inevitably help the WUSA, since as many as fifty players were shortlisted for the World Cup. This included most of the U.S. team and key players from Australia, Brazil, Canada, China, France, Germany, Japan, and Norway. League Chief Morgan said, "We're really trying to find a way to recapture the lightning that came out in 1999; [we're] looking for ways to make that association with what people remember about 1999 and the excitement that event grabbed. Kind of remind them how they felt after that event, and use the season as our platform [to connect with them]." In May, early in the WUSA season, came the news that the Women's World Cup was being transferred to the United States on short notice. An epidemic of a virulent form of pneumonia known as Severe Acute Respiratory Syndrome (SARS) had been discovered in Guangdong province a few months before and spread throughout Asia. FIFA granted China the hosting rights to the 2007 event in compensation, and U.S. Soccer stepped in at short notice to host the tournament. This news further inflated hopes within the WUSA ranks that the World Cup would raise the profile of the game and the league would benefit, particularly with sponsors and prospective investors. Through attracting solid crowds in six cities and leaving U.S. Soccer and FIFA with a sizable profit, the 2003 World Cup was a positive event for the sport in the United States and abroad. However, by staging the games in September and competing against football and baseball, the cup never had a chance to reignite the iconic mega-event of 1999. The 2003 Women's World Cup and the WUSA will forever be linked, but in a way that no one expected.

On the field, some exciting additions to the league included Canadian National Team forward Christine Latham and U.S. National Team midfield ace Aly Wagner (both San Diego), German National Teamers Conny Pohlers at forward (Atlanta) and Sandra Minnert in midfield (DC), Australian forwards Cheryl Salisbury and Joanne Peters (both New York), striker Maribel Dominguez of Mexico (Atlanta), and midfielder Stephanie Mugneret-Beghe of France (Boston). San Diego's new coach, Omid Namazi, led a renewed Spirit team to their first playoff spot. The Beat and Freedom made the semifinals again, but the real surprise was Pia Sundhage's Boston. They posted a league best ten wins and thirty-seven standing points (three points for a win and one for a tie). The postseason debutants were dismissed by DC while Atlanta's Beat eliminated the Spirit. The Freedom beat Atlanta in the Founders Cup by 2–1 in overtime in San Diego on two Abby Wambach goals. The Beat was the only team to make the playoffs all three seasons while losing in two championship finals. Unfortunately, they would not have another title chance, nor would anyone else (see table 6 in the appendix).

The End of the Dream

Five days before the start of Women's World Cup 2003, John Hendricks overshadowed the event with his announcement, on September 15, that the WUSA was suspending operations immediately. "A shortfall in sponsorship revenue and insufficient revenue from other core areas of the business proved to be the hurdles which the WUSA could not overcome in time for planning the 2004 season," Hendricks said. Time-Warner, which operated the New York Power and Carolina Courage, and Comcast, which ran the Philadelphia Charge, bailed out after the season ended. "In August, it was pretty critical, getting down to running out of [money]," Hendricks said. "We were in jeopardy that if we didn't shut down [when we did], we would not have a good [employee] severance plan, and it would likely force us into bankruptcy."

The budget tightening and reduced salaries had cut the gap between expenses and revenues by $4 million from $20 million in 2002, but the $16 million difference and approximately $100 million spent in three years left them with too much of a hole to fill. "We didn't see any immediate impact that could bridge the funding problem," said Hendricks. "We tried as a last resort to look around the country to see if there were any alliances that we could make . . . piggyback on the infrastructure of other sports teams [and leagues]. That was just too challenging. There were very few opportunities where we could tackle this." Philip Anschutz, who controlled up to six MLS franchises at one time and built the soccer-specific Home Depot Center in Carson, California, was solicited, but he passed at the start of September. This summed up the value of the treaty the WUSA had signed with the MLS three years before. The most visible aspect of their working relationship were double-headers with the MLS and WUSA franchises in DC. Otherwise, the MLS seemed to keep its distance so the WUSA lacked the guidance of a league that had started less than seven years before.

The WUSA's inability to attract sponsorships, a problem since the beginning, was the death knell for the league. Going into the 2002 season they needed to find eight companies (four each in 2002 and 2003) to pay $2.5 million a year for exclusive sponsorship rights within a category such as automotive, sportswear, technology, and so forth. Only Hyundai and Johnson & Johnson joined, at $2 million each. Hendricks admitted, "I was intoxicated by what I witnessed during the '99 World Cup, and all the sponsors surrounding that event." Lynn Berling-Manuel, then editor-in-chief of *Soccer America* wrote, "Our sport is still challenged, both for women and men, to turn the millions of soccer players in the United States into fans. Butts in seats and TV ratings are how a sports success is judged. Sponsors are being pointed to as the culprits that didn't support women's pro soccer, but the reality is that those companies have many, many choices of avenues—both sport and non-sport—to speak to female customers. With modest attendance figures, microscopic television ratings and a tough economy, the WUSA was a difficult choice for them to make."

The falloff in average attendance—from 8,116 in 2001, to 7,116 in 2002, and to 6,667 in 2003 (an 18 percent slide in two years)—indicated that the product wasn't even resonating with those who had gone to a game. In year 3, DC still led in attendance (9,928), followed by Philadelphia (7,245), Atlanta (6,958), Boston (6,931), and San Jose (6,781) above the average. Carolina (5,737), San Diego (5,635), and New York (4,249) dragged the total down. The Freedom still led in away attendance (8,445), but clearly the Mia affect on the league had worn off, as DC only had a slight advantage over the surprising New York Power (7,957), who drew 87 percent more on the road for every game than at home. Perhaps New York should have played *all* their games on the road, as there were whispers that their abysmal home attendance figures were inflated. Apparently, some fans came to their games dressed as empty seats. By comparison, the MLS's attendance during those three years averaged 14,961 in 2001, 15,821 in 2002, and 14,899 in 2003 (See table 7 in the appendix). Hendricks would admit in September of 2003, "I mistakenly assumed ['99 World Cup support] would flow over to the league."

U.S. Soccer President Bob Contigula told the author in 2007, "The '99 World Cup brought tremendous attention to the women's game and women's causes. Players interpreted it that they could accomplish anything. Expectations were overestimated in terms of a pro league. We learned a successful event does not equate to a successful league. They believed their own press releases. Players did it as a cause; they didn't do it as a business." Even John Hendricks had trouble at the end separating the sponsor's needs from the mission: "It's a discouraging thing to read about huge deals to sponsor one athlete in the tens of millions of dollars," he said, referring to Nike's $90 million deal with then high school basketball star LeBron James. Even though Nike was one of Mia Hamm's sponsors and had even named the largest building on their Oregon campus after her, they refused to do more for WUSA beyond outfitting three teams. Hendricks added with some frustration, "Some minor NFL stars sign $2.5 million deals. Why not do one less shoe deal and spread that $2.5 million to 160 players, support women's professional soccer and allow little girls the chance to dream that maybe they can play professional sports. That's something all of us guys got—[professional sports] was always a dream, regardless of whether we could do it." Berling-Manuel further commented, "It's amazing the coverage that WUSA's demise is getting. Happening days before the opening of the Women's World Cup is certainly part of that, but it also makes clear that the WUSA is still considered as much a social story as it is a sports story." Freedom coach Jim Gabarra years later commented on the WUSA's counterproductive salary structure, which contributed to its demise: "Teams kind of landed like an alien ship in their markets, and they didn't have grass-roots support. From the players' point of view, the WUSA was a nice gig. They worked six or seven months and got paid for twelve. It didn't make economic sense." *Soccer America*'s Mike Woitalla felt that, for a sport that had only infiltrated mainstream consciousness beginning in 1996, it was "terribly over-optimistic" to expect the league to thrive.

The WUSA provided an extremely high level of soccer, a family atmosphere, and role models whom youth could look up to. It clearly was not enough. The WUSA became confused early on between their missionary zeal to teenage and pre-teen girls and marketing. Professional soccer executives have long joked that if kids could drive, they would have no attendance worries whatsoever. The WUSA took this notion way too far in confusing the players' role as aspiration figures for youth and their key target audience. The WUSA overemphasized young girls and their families, while failing to capture a fan base of adults and men. Some criticized the atmosphere at WUSA games, including fun zones, contests, and "girl-power music" that was great for kids but not appealing to older teens or to adults. In some cases, adult males felt the atmosphere demeaned both the game and the women who played it, while simultaneously making them feel unwelcome.

After Hendricks's announcement, there were natural expressions of shock among the WUSA's corps of executives, front-office employees, and players, common after any sport team or league fails, but there was a difference this time. There was an absence of vitriolic comments blaming the league's investors or management. Something rang odd there. Hendricks was still referred to as "Saint John," which, after all he had done for the women's game, was justified. The players didn't seem to accept that the world's best women's league was finished; couching the situation as *it had taken a break now*. It quickly became clear that the leading lights of the league, Chastain, Foudy, and Hamm, were talking up the possibility of the league coming back to life. The overwhelming theme again was that sponsors should support women's sports because it is "the right thing to do and they definitely *have to do it now* to save the league." Board member and San Diego Spirit midfielder Julie Foudy passionately argued, "The positive impact our sport has had on youth players, both boys and girls, and their perception of women as athletes, has been inspiring to experience first hand, it is empowering for kids to have role models like the players of the WUSA." Besides being self aggrandizing, it was not the best lead slide in a sales presentation to a Fortune 500 company. Hendricks had to dispel a conspiracy rumor that intimated that the announcement to shut down, right before the World Cup, was really a last ditch ploy to convince prospective sponsors that the league would die immediately unless they stepped up to support it. These theories became more difficult to fight off as, within hours of the announcement, such support was said to be materializing, led as always by the never shy Foudy. The U.S. National Team captain proclaimed, "People are coming out of the woodwork. People are saying, 'What's the deficit? Sixteen million dollars? That's it? We should have done something?'" Not only did her efforts fail to reflect marketplace reality, it built up false hopes for players and fans. Press coverage shifted from the World Cup games to an analysis of the WUSA's demise and efforts to rise from the dead.

Unwilling or unable to fully give up, league officials gave intellectual property rights—names, logos, and such—to the Players Association chief John Langel, who headed a committee of a few ex-WUSA executives, Foudy, and noted women's sports advocates Billie Jean King and Donna Lopiano of the Women's Sports Foundation. This group worked to revamp the business plan, tried to attract new sponsors, and started a "Keep the Dream Alive" ticket initiative fundraising campaign. During the summer of 2004, WUSA staged three festivals aimed at keeping their brand in front of their audience while impressing potential sponsors and investors. They lined up five sponsors: Coca-Cola, McDonalds,

Deutsche Bank, athletic apparel company Under Armour, plus Adidas in an equipment arrangement. A number of communities were interested in hosting the exhibitions, including all the former WUSA markets as well as Los Angeles/Carson, California; Chicago; Cincinnati; Cleveland; Columbus; Dallas; Denver; Ft. Lauderdale, Florida; Hampton Roads, Virginia; Houston; Minneapolis/St. Paul; Portland, Oregon; and Rochester, New York.

Though it wasn't publicized that way, the relaunching of the WUSA hinged on the success of the festivals. Officials were banking on the games to bring in some much needed gate receipts and sponsorship dollars since the "Keep the Dream Alive" campaign had fallen far short of its $2.5 million goal. It was designed to raise a $1,000 annual commitment from 2,500 clubs, organizations, and businesses, but had brought in only $135,000, mostly from individuals. Games were played over two weekends at the National Sports Center in Blaine, Minnesota, and as a doubleheader at the Home Depot Center in Carson, California. In Minnesota, the New York Power tied the Atlanta Beat 2–2 on June 18 in front of only 2,017. The following day, the Washington Freedom drew with the Boston Breakers 3–3 before 5,017 in a stadium seating about 6,500. Stars like Mia Hamm, Marinette Pichon, Abby Wambach, Charmaine Hooper, Maribel Dominguez, and Shannon Box all played, but the rosters resembled all-star teams rather than team lineups from 2003.

The third event took place on June 27. In the first game, the San Diego Spirit defeated the Carolina Courage 2–1 and then the Philadelphia Charge shut out the San Jose CyberRays 2–0. The gate receipts showed that 7,123 fans showed up. The festivals financially were miserable failures. As was consistent with the WUSA since its beginning, that fact was less important to the players than other issues. U.S. National Team member Angela Hucles gushed, "The memories just rushed over again, how great it was when we had it. I think we all appreciated it when we did have it, but this is just another reminder of why this [the WUSA] is so important." American star Shannon Box said, "I see the league coming back.

This is the beginning of it, not the end. We're rebuilding, and this is the start of it." Teammate Aly Wagner pondered, "How can the WUSA not exist when you have that kind of fervor, that kind of passion from little girls?" Again, the emotional and social aspect blinded the players, but the realistic aspect screamed, *19,000 empty seats at Home Depot Center!* Business-wise, again it was another devastating setback for the women's professional game.

The WUSA professionalized the women's game for the first time, and the media company involvement was unprecedented for the sport at any level. For the players, as three-year Atlanta Beat veteran Nancy Augustyniak said wistfully to this author a few years later, playing in the league was "the best three years of my life." With the failure of the festivals and the "Keep the Dream Alive" fundraising campaign, it was time to scrap the WUSA baggage and start over.

4

Women's Professional Soccer

With the WUSA's demise, more than 150 players suddenly had to look elsewhere for their livelihood, and the failed enterprise took an emotional toll on many. "I couldn't hold back the tears," said Heather Mitts, who played for the Philadelphia Charge. "I was devastated because we had the right product and people who loved the league, but the right business plan was not there." Former Atlanta Beat defender Julie Augustyniak said, "After the [WUSA] ended, I was definitely in shock for awhile."

Picking Up the Pieces from WUSA

U.S. Soccer kept its national team players busy with an expanded schedule of friendly games. For the other professionals, their play was bound to atrophy as they gravitated back into the amateur leagues in the United States and overseas. Many landed in the United Soccer League's Women's League (w-League) and the Women's Premier Soccer League (WPSL), the two top-level amateur leagues in North America. The w-League began with a brief exhibition in 1994 and launched a full season in 1995 with nineteen teams spread nationwide. By 2008 the w-League had grown to forty-one teams in the United States and Canada. The WPSL began in 1998 in California with seven teams and by 2009 had over fifty teams all across the United States. In both leagues, the ex-WUSA players found that some of their teammates were current college and even high school players. This led to vastly uneven quality due to a team's philosophy. The w-League's Vancouver Whitecaps, one of the most committed organizations to women's soccer in the world, routinely fielded sides full of Canadian internationals mixed with a few top-level American imports. Other teams, such as the Real Colorado Cougars, were essentially a high school side, utilizing graduates of their younger age-group teams, mixed in with a few college and older local players. In addition to the quality drop, players saw huge cuts in their salaries, as the amateur leagues could only reimburse expenses so they wouldn't run afoul of NCAA restrictions.

Other players found spots on teams in foreign leagues. In 2005 U.S. National Team pool players Hope Solo, Aly Wagner, Danielle Slaton, Christie Welsh, and Lorrie Fair signed with Lyon in the French women's league, while others went to Sweden. A few took college coaching positions, hoping that professional soccer would return quickly.

Many international players went back home to semiprofessional soccer. Marinette Pichon became the best-known player in France after playing in the WUSA in 2002 and 2003 while leading France to the Women's World Cup finals for the first time. She lamented the loss of the WUSA: "I made 7,000 Euros [$9,000] a month in the WUSA and finished training at 2 o'clock. I had a house. I rented an SUV. Here, I live in an apartment and make 1,200 Euros [$1,500] a month as an administrative assistant for the Essonne sports council."

Some players had to make a decision whether to continue to put their working and personal lives on hold, waiting for the WUSA to return. Lisa Krzykowski, twenty-seven, made the league-minimum salary in 2003 in San Diego after two seasons with the Beat. When the WUSA shut down, she reflected, "If there's not a season in 2004, I can't stay in shape for 2005. I don't know if I want to. I feel I've done a lot in my soccer career. I haven't really gotten a taste of anything other than soccer for a long time. I've got a degree I'm sitting on, that I'm just about ready to put into use. You get to a point where you're tired of [the uncertainty]. I love playing, I especially love playing professionally, but I'm to the point where I need to settle down and move on. I want to get engaged soon (with her boyfriend). I'm closer to 30 than 20, which means eventually, I want to think about kids." It became harder for players to put off family and career decisions as the prospects of a new league looked more and more unlikely as time went on. Family and friends would ask how they could possibly justify the sacrifices of training for something that might not ever return.

Women's Soccer Initiative Inc.

Shortly after the failed WUSA summer festivals, a new business plan was drafted for re-launching pro soccer in 2006, two summers off. A new nonprofit entity, Women's Soccer Initiative Inc. (WSII), was established to carry this to fruition, with seed money coming from the U.S. Soccer Foundation and the Federation. The driving force behind this rebirth was Tonya Antonucci, a former Stanford and WPSL player and a business executive in the information technology sector. For several months, players, reporters, and fans speculated about the 2006 scheduled date; rumors would leak but there weren't many encouraging words.

The launch was finally pushed back, first to 2007 and then to 2008. In February 2007, Antonucci announced six lead investment groups who had committed to five markets—Chicago/Bridgeview, Illinois; Dallas; Los Angeles; St. Louis; and Washington DC—with one owner group still deciding on a market. Two months later, New York/New Jersey and Boston came on board. Then, just a few weeks before the 2007 China World Cup, the start was delayed again to 2009—after the owners split on when to start. Michael Stoller, managing partner for Boston's team explained, "The first [reason] was being sure that we have longevity in our league and we overwhelmingly believe that starting in 2009 will assure the long-term success of each and every team. And most importantly our sport has two critical events during 2007 and 2008, namely the FIFA Women's World Cup starting in several weeks and the

Olympics next summer. We did not want to impact the various national teams between these two events and we did not want our league to take the focus away from these two great events for our players or our fans."

Taking fans' focus from two events held halfway around the world (China) was a red herring; the reality was the league didn't have the number of teams or investors set to move ahead. The rights to an eighth team were held by an entity called Soccer Initiative LLC, which the *San Diego Union-Tribune* later identified as led by John Moores, owner of Major League Baseball's San Diego Padres, but they dropped out, as did the underfunded Dallas group, quickly replaced by San Francisco/San Jose.

The WSII used a different ownership paradigm than the single entity approach of the WUSA and MLS. Each franchise had individual investors, and Antonucci felt strongly that there would be value in each owner defining revenue potential and expenses based on their particular market's potential. She reasoned that these owner groups would have the business acumen to construct a quality team based on their market reality, without the self-controlling and sometimes inhibiting model of league-controlled budgets.

Team owners included some strong business leaders mixed with soccer entrepreneurs. Philip Murphy, the national finance chair for the Democratic National Committee and former managing director of securities firm Goldman Sachs, was behind the New Jersey Sky Blue. Boston's lead investor was Harrah's Casino CEO and chairman Gary Loveman. Many soccer fans would recognize John Hendricks's name; the WUSA founder led Freedom Soccer LLC of Washington DC. Though no longer in a lead role for the league enterprise, his backing of DC showed his commitment to women's soccer as well as his home market.

The WSII reached out to the MLS in ways the WUSA never did. Antonucci wanted to avoid "'stand alone' women's soccer franchises." Soccer United Marketing (SUM), the marketing arm of the MLS and the federation that also controlled the men's and women's World Cup broadcast rights for the United States, handled the new league's sponsorship development efforts, including television contract negotiations. One of the investors behind the Los Angeles franchise was the Anschutz Entertainment Group (AEG), owner of the MLS's Los Angeles Galaxy and the Home Depot Center, among other sports enterprises. Two other new teams shared stadiums with MLS teams: the Chicago Red Stars rented the Chicago Fire's Toyota Park and FC Gold Pride shared Santa Clara University's Buck Shaw Stadium with the MLS San Jose Earthquakes. DC Freedom did a couple of doubleheaders with DC United at their RFK Stadium.

Women's Professional Soccer (WPS) — The Dream Returns

In January 2008 WSII officially became Women's Professional Soccer (WPS) and announced that they would start a twenty-game schedule in April 2009. Individual team budgets would be approximately $1.5 to $2 million, on top of a franchise fee of $1.5 million. Salaries would be much more realistic than in WUSA. The salary cap for eighteen full-roster players was $565,000, with an average of around $30,000. U.S. National Team players were paid around $40,000, negotiated by their union.

The team line up was:

Boston Breakers
Chicago Red Stars
FC Gold Pride (San Jose/San Francisco)
Los Angeles Sol
St. Louis Athletica
Sky Blue FC (New Jersey/New York)
Washington DC Freedom

Players were excited at the prospect to play professionally, even at salaries below WUSA levels. Tiffany Wiemer, a top pro prospect at Penn State when WUSA folded, regularly had to justify the sacrifice of training and working inconsistently: "Some people might say that I need to grow up and face reality, but to that I say I'm 'putting the adult world on hold' and 'pursuing my life goals', also known as 'living the dream' in order to play at the highest level possible, but that's the fun of it all." In 2008 to prepare for WPS, Weimer played in WPSL, then Finland and Brazil before signing for WPS's FC Gold Pride in 2009 and the Boston Breakers for 2010.

Former U.S. Soccer president Bob Contigulia felt that if the league followed its conservative plan and was patient, it had a good chance to succeed. The key was to focus on five-year sustainability. He cautioned that if the league didn't make it, "it would be a cataclysmic failure and a huge setback [for the women's game] globally."

Soccer versus Careers . . . or Both

WPS teams started to attract players, holding four combines in the last half of 2008 for over three hundred prospects and a series of drafts for international and domestic players. Two dozen WUSA players returned to WPS rosters, including some who had become college coaches. Lindsay Massengale gave up a full-time assistant coaching position at Idaho State University in Pocatello, where she had been on staff for three years, to try out with FC Gold Pride. Massengale explained her decision to leave a secure environment with no guarantee of a contract: "It's great getting to do what you love every day and play in something you're passionate about." She made the team as a development player but played only four games for a total of 193 minutes. Massengale was released at the end of the season.

Keri Sanchez won four consecutive titles at the University of North Carolina, and played eleven times for the U.S. National Team and three years in the WUSA. She never stopped playing and hoped to continue whenever the new league started. To help make ends meet, she became the head women's coach at Claremont-McKenna-Mudd-Scripps College in southern California, "I think the first couple of years you keep playing hoping that the league comes back," she said. "I think probably in the last couple of years I was just playing because I enjoy playing. I think it helps my coaching as well." Sanchez wasn't drafted, figuring her age (thirty-six) worked against her with coaches preferring to develop younger players. The soccer mom to a ten-year-old son stepped into the LA Sol defense as a free agent late in the season after the Sol had a string of injuries. She was able to retain her coaching job as the WPS ended before the college season: "Playing always helps with my coaching so if anything being back and able to play is just going to help me be a better coach." In the fall of 2009, Sanchez led her college team to a 16–3–2 record and the second round of the NCAA Division III tournament.

Mary-Frances Monroe was another WUSA veteran who juggled WPS with her head coaching position at the University of Albany: "Now that I coach I find that there are things that I'll tell my players that I have to do now myself," she said. "It's a great experience to be able to coach and play at the same time. I definitely think I understand the game a little bit better." Monroe returned to Albany and led her team to their first America East playoff berth with an 8–7–1 record, their first winning season since joining NCAA Division I in 1999. Monroe said, "Making the playoffs for the first time was one of our goals this season and they did it. Their dedication and commitment each and every day helped us achieve that goal." Though her Breakers did not make the playoffs, Monroe had one assist in five games from her midfield spot but was released during the 2010 training camp.

Others gave up or postponed careers in other fields. Former National Team forward Christie Welsh worked for eighteen months for National Geographic's television show *Wild Chronicles*. Megan Schnur completed her internship for a master's degree in physical therapy and put off joining the "real" world. Her classmates prepared for job interviews while she focused on training for the WPS. She explained before she was drafted, "I've thought about [what happens if this opportunity doesn't pan out], but at the same time, I don't want to think about it, because right now, for me, I know I want to pursue soccer. . . . I want to see where I can go. I mean, we don't get to play soccer forever; we don't get to chase our dreams forever." It panned out! Schnur played every regular season and playoff game for Sky Blue, was called into the U.S. National Team for the first time after the season, and had her contract renewed for 2010.

Maggie Tomecka took a break from her residency program at the University of North Carolina School of Medicine to play in the WPS. She was a senior at UNC when the WUSA folded. She hadn't received any national team looks, so she gave up the sport and went to medical school. "The first six months were easy," she said. "I was able to let some lingering injuries heal, and for the first time in years was able to walk around without any pain in my legs. I was enjoying putting all my focus on school." As the WPS made plans, she had "an insuppressible urge to play again." Before Tomecka began the internship, she discussed her desire to play professionally with the hospital administrators: "They were more supportive of me than I could possibly have imagined. I am so thankful to have found a program which understands why I need to play and how important it is for me to achieve my personal goals." She balanced training with an eighty-hour-a-week internship schedule. She set herself a two year window to play in WPS and then she would review her options after the 2010 season. She played eleven games, starting six for the Boston Breakers, and had her contract renewed for 2010.

Chicago Red Star's Nikki Krysik put off her last semester at the University of Virginia and entering law school to go pro, explaining, "I don't necessarily want to be a lawyer but I would really like to further my education." Others combined their new careers with the WPS. As a vice president at Tenant Consulting, a Washington DC commercial real estate brokerage firm, Joanna Lohman, twenty-six, had already established a successful business career. Lohman's accomplishments have shown other players the possibilities that exist in combining a professional sports career with a traditional business position. She explained, "As a professional athlete, you're goal oriented, you have leadership capabilities and you're used to not winning every game and coming back. . . . You have the desire and ambition to make it to a higher level. And I think that works really well in the business world." Lohman, a Penn State grad with degrees in mathematics and business, helped out in the Freedom's corporate offices before joining Philadelphia in 2010.

Natalie Spilger left soccer after a subpar 10–9–2 senior season and first round playoff exit at Stanford. Spilger explained that it was "a frustrating year. I kind of was done with soccer. I feel like I had a bad breakup with soccer after my senior year." She went on for a masters in construction engineering management and worked in the energy field but was inspired to return after watching the 2006 Men's World Cup. She combined her two passions and founded GreenLaces in 2008. As a nonprofit organization, GreenLaces' purpose was to engage the global athletic community to improve the planet with specific actions (that are published online.) GreenLaces works with youth athletic leagues and after-school programs to teach children the importance of recycling and eco-friendly lifestyles to promote "a greener generation." Spilger says, "The effort has been received extremely well. Athletes are realizing that as role models we can use our presence to inspire those around us to get involved in environmental causes that affect everyone on the planet. . . . I decided I didn't just want green buildings. I wanted green minds." Spilger and her GreenLaces athletes made promises to improve the environment and wore recycled green shoelaces to demonstrate their commitment. Spilger worked hard on both efforts, "By the time I finish with all [Chicago Red Stars] activities each day I go home and work on GreenLaces until about 10 at night. . . . It's important work and it keeps me very busy. . . . I feel like I have two full-time jobs." Spilger played in seventeen games, started thirteen, and had her contract renewed for 2010.

The league attracted many top internationals, helping its credibility, but none were more important for global recognition than Brazilian superstar Marta, who left Umeå of Sweden for the LA Sol. Marta explained her move to the United States: "The United States is known to be the center of women's soccer. . . . If we can really help this league go to a new level, I'm positive other countries will follow the model that is being done in the United States." She was the equivalent of the MLS' acquisition of David Beckham in 2007, providing instant press and credibility; Los Angeles Lakers star Kobe Bryant even came to watch her practice. Though receiving a women's soccer record salary commonly reported to be about five hundred thousand dollars a year, Marta actually was the third pick in the International Draft, so that she could go to LA, where AEG could leverage their other promotional units on her behalf.

Other top talent came to join the league. Boston Breakers signed England's Kelly Smith, one of the best strikers in the world, with 100 goals in 112 games with English top side Arsenal Ladies. She previously had played in WUSA with Philadelphia and explained her return to the United States: "A four-year contract adds longevity to my career. I couldn't earn anywhere near to what I'll be getting in WPS if I stayed in this country [England]. But it's not just about money. It's about playing with and against the best players in the world, training every day, and everything else that goes with being a professional footballer." Brazil sent the most internationals (nine), followed by Canada (six, with two more added later in the season), Australia (five), England (five), Sweden (four), Japan (three), and two unheralded midfielders from France, both of whom would have profound impacts on their teams. Two-time reigning World Cup Champions Germany encouraged their national team players to stay home ahead of the 2011 Women's World Cup, since they were hosts. The international stars brought different styles, entertainment, and legitimacy for the WPS' claim as the world's best women's league.

It wasn't just top player talent that was being recruited from overseas. The WPS named Mary Harvey as chief operating officer, bringing her in from FIFA in Switzerland, where she had been the director of development for five years, overseeing a staff of twenty along with fifty consultants. At FIFA, she had been instrumental in the development of the women's game globally. Harvey previously worked at global consultants Deloitte and Accenture and was a World Cup (1991) and Olympic Champion (1996) as a goalkeeper for the United States. Harvey was an inspired addition to the league office, bringing international credibility and the ability to understand player issues. Early in the season there were a number of red cards for violent play, and she worked with U.S. Soccer to hold team meetings between referee instructors and players to discuss recent changes in rule interpretation.

Aspirations of College Players

Future prospects, particularly those graduating in 2010 and beyond, felt that now they had a platform to continue their soccer careers at the highest level. U.S. U-20 National Team forward and North Carolina senior Casey Nogueria said in early 2009, "It's actually really exciting for all of us. A lot of us want to go to the next level and play. Before this league came out we were going to have to go overseas. But now this league will probably be the most dominate in the world." Nogueria joined Chicago Red Stars for the 2010 campaign.

WPSL Arizona Rush and University of Arizona senior defender Analisa Marquez said during WPS's first year that the new league had added to her career options: "It does keep me thinking—medical school or play pro. It sounds fun; how often do you get to say you played pro? It makes me think twice about what I want to do." Marquez had planned to take a year off before medical school. Less than nine months later, she had made the roster of the Boston Breakers, despite not being selected in the general draft. One of her Rush teammates even quit a teaching job in order to train in the fall, hoping to catch on with a WPS or European professional side.

Marketing

On the marketing side, WPS teams associated themselves with local youth programs, utilizing their players for camps in exchange for tickets. The league even started their own licensed camps program, as Antonucci explained, "as a way to reach fans that are not in WPS markets and to grow the WPS brand across the country. It is a revenue driver but it is also a brand builder." One league player would appear at each camp in fifteen cities, including Council Bluffs, Iowa, Orlando, Pittsburgh, and Reno.

One important reason for developing the WUSA was that it was seen as programming for their cable company owners. The WPS approach was radically different. They signed a three-year agreement with Fox Soccer Channel for a game of the week, but no rights fees were paid. Advertising revenue would be divided between the network and the league. Fox Soccer Channel was a good choice, because it was the home for soccer fans in the United States and Canada and had always treated the sport seriously. A regular time slot on Sunday afternoons was important to have a predictable window for viewers throughout the season. The agreement helped the WPS reach Fox Soccer's predominately male, eighteen- to forty-nine-year-old soccer savvy viewers while Fox now had programming geared to females. Mike Petruzzi, Fox Soccer Channel's vice president of marketing, explained, "We always have a great male story to tell. To be able to go out with a female product was great for us."

Some high-profile companies joined WPS as sponsors, led by equipment supplier Puma, who paid $10 million over three years. "Puma was impressed with the infrastructure and leadership of WPS," said Paul Gautier, Puma AG's international brand and marketing director. "We're confident that the league will be successful. . . . Also, no women's team sport captures the imagination of the American public like women's soccer." Other sponsors were energy drink manufacturer Advocare, nasal spray flu vaccine FluMist, flavored water maker Hint, biologics company MedImmune, and the U.S. Coast Guard. The severe recession in the United States that started in late 2008, the worst since the Depression in the 1930s affected sponsorship particularly at the team level. The Boston Breakers had targeted sponsorship revenue of $600,000, cut that to $300,000 but only raised about $250,000 in year 1. "Scary isn't the right word," Mary Harvey said when asked about the economy's impact on the league. Harvey felt that the launch was "a long pregnancy, but we were prepared [for the effects of the recession].

We're adjusting as necessary like everybody else is, trying to be as nimble as possible." Harvey did enjoy signing off on every player contract, "Because this league exists . . . we're creating 200 jobs."

Though an obvious target market, the league was cognizant that youth players and their parents alone would not provide the gate revenue the league needed to survive. They weren't dependable as regular attendees, since they can become "soccered out" after youth team practices and games all week. The last thing a lot of parents (or players) want to do is sit through another ninety minutes of soccer, no matter who is playing. "Success at the gate has to have a tribal following and not just a van of soccer-playing kids who come to one game a year," says Doug Logan, former Major League Soccer commissioner who was involved in earlier women's pro league investigations. Logan added, "If your business model depends on youth soccer, it won't be enough."

The WPS budgeted for a realistic average attendance goal of four to six thousand per game. The league purposely stayed away from promoting the cause of supporting women's sports because it is "the right thing to do" as the WUSA mistakenly did. "We're branding to everyone. It could be the 35-year-old guy who plays twice a week," Commissioner Antonucci acknowledged. "For all those young girls and young women, we're creating heroes. But this is also the sports and entertainment business. This is not a cause, this is not a charity. This is a value proposition for sports fans that we really can entertain people." Andy Crossley, the Boston Breakers director of business development and later general manager agreed, "We need to get out of the ghetto of being a role model for girls. You can't make dads feel like they're visiting Chuck E. Cheese's." The WPS focused on the quality of their players and the games. As they stated on their website, "Our mission is to be the premier women's soccer league in the world and the global standard by which women's professional sports are measured."

Tonya Antonucci felt that a focus on the game was warranted and possible this time: "We need the dialogue in the media to move beyond 'Isn't it great and it's socially important they come back,' to a discourse about the X's and O's of the sport. I think it's important to make sure that we move from message to sport in terms of how we have coverage in the media. . . . Our message needs to reflect what's going on on the field in terms of sport." This is the Holy Grail for the growth of women's soccer in North America as well as internationally: convincing fans and media to discuss the sport solely based on game strategy and play. At the Women's World Cup finals in 2007, a female reporter interviewing players after a game focused mostly on the players' off-field clothing preferences, including the astounding question, "I love that blouse you have on; is that your favorite?" The reporter admitted later that she didn't really understand the sport, federation politics, or contractual issues, so she stayed away from questions about their game. It does the sport a disservice: rather than providing readers with informative descriptions about the sport, they get tangential drivel.

The wps was closely watched by promoters and supporters of other women's sports leagues (softball, ice hockey, and basketball). The standard bearer for women's pro sports is the WNBA, started in 1997 by NBA owners. Unable to attract many new investors, in 2009 NBA team owners still retained eight of the thirteen franchises. Rick Welts, chief executive officer for the NBA Phoenix Suns and two-time WNBA champion Phoenix Mercury said, "If this was just an economic decision, we [in Phoenix] would have been out of the WNBA business a long time ago. We think because of our NBA ownership, it's strategic and promotes basketball year-round. We operate U.S. Airways Center on behalf of the city, and it's terrific programming for our suite holders and fans. But it's not a commitment that could go on forever if we don't improve the economics." If there is a decision between spending money on a men's or women's team, the men's team will win out on revenue potential alone. Sports consultant Mark Gains, who works with prospective basketball investors, said, "The social aspect [of women's basketball] is wonderful. But in times of recession, tough business decisions must be made. Teams are saving money in many ways, and one is staffing. If you have a choice where to put your marketing staff effort, it's on the NBA team, not the WNBA team. . . . You hope, given enough time, the WNBA would develop a following and its own sponsors. We should all hope the recession does not short circuit that amount of time."

What is troubling for all women's pro sports is that after more than a decade and the deep pockets of the NBA, the WNBA still has not developed its own following and sponsorship dollars to stand alone. The WNBA has done a better job of attracting women viewers, around 40 percent for ESPN games, while less than a third of women's soccer viewers are females. David Sternberg, the chief operating officer of Fox Cable Networks, said that the largest group for their WPS games was males who also watched men's games on the network. The WPS is working with the MLS much more cooperatively than the WUSA ever did, but not to the level of a Women's Major League Soccer. The WPS shares a focus with the MLS on the growing *Soccer Nation* while still controlling their destiny, unlike the WNBA; the downside is they don't have the financial backing of a well-off parent.

2009 Season Review

The WPS kicked off its inaugural game in Los Angeles at the Home Depot Center, ironic given that the last official WUSA games in 2004, held to try to keep the league afloat, drew only 7,123. The WPS inaugural drew more than twice that figure, but a few complained that the 14,832 crowd was twenty thousand fewer than the WUSA's first game in Washington. The comparison was not fair, because this was *not* a WUSA relaunch; the WPS was a different league, with different executives, a different operating model, and, most importantly, a much more realistic business plan. WPS officials were clearly pleased with the crowd, given their mantra that realistic objectives equal long-term sustainability. The Sol won the game (2–0) and the positive fan experience gave the WPS some early momentum (see table 8 in the appendix).

The WPS first-year average game attendance was 4,493 during the regular season, which fell within its four- to six-thousand target. Los Angeles led the league with 6,299 per game, followed by Chicago (4,941), Boston (4,665), and Washington (4,597). Marta, the league MVP, had an effect off the field as well as on; Sol road games averaged 1,300 more than other teams away from home. Sky Blue FC (3,651), FC Gold Pride (3,667), and St. Louis (3,833) fell below the target minimum.

With the U.S. economic meltdown limiting sponsorship dollars, each team reportedly lost in the $1 to $2 million range (though LA Sol's loss was rumored to be closer to $3 million), but the league's careful management guidance set them up nicely for future growth, as other sports teams and even a league folded. (Individual teams in the WNBA, the National Lacrosse League, and minor league hockey, as well as the twenty-two-year-old Arena Football League shut down.) Two expansion franchises in 2010, Atlanta Beat and Philadelphia Independence, put the league in markets that were strong for the WUSA, while bringing in about $3 million in expansion franchise fees.

Aside from the financial side, the first year was deemed a success on a number of levels. The league received notice for how it embraced new technology, particularly Twitter. The WPS was the first league that allowed a few nonstarters to post messages during games. By early 2010 they had more than two hundred thousand followers on Twitter, trailing only the big four of the NBA, NFL, NHL, and Major League Baseball in followers. Director of New Media Karyn Lush said, "We are proud of the growth of our social media initiatives and continue to use it as an important and efficient medium to engage with our fan base in meaningful, compelling ways." Even COO Mary Harvey posts to a blog, because "the community that likes us is very much engaged in social media and they enjoy blogging and tweeting, talking to each other and sharing their points of view. And I interact with them online. . . . We're not at the mercy of mainstream media anymore because we're the wrong sport or women, or whatever."

On the field, the quality was well received, and well ahead of the WUSA's first year, when teams looked quite disorganized for much of the season. One reason for the difference was the continued growth of youth soccer and more w-League and WPSL teams, about double from when the WUSA was active. Tiffeny Milbrett played for FC Gold Pride after spending three years with the WUSA New York Power, and felt that "where we left off in '03 with the WUSA, I think the players are even two and three levels above 2003. The younger that they are, the better they are getting." Breakers coach Tony DiCicco emphasized the importance of the growth of the amateur leagues in general and the w-League in particular: "It has been absolutely vital. The w-League allows players to continue to play and develop. Most female players don't reach their peak in their early 20s. It is important they continue their development for when they do reach that peak in the later 20s. The w-League is a very competitive environment because of the former professionals and internationals in the league." DiCicco also pointed out that the expansion of the U.S. youth national team program (U-18, U-17, U-15) created a far deeper pool of players with international experience. The high level of play in the WPS should further enhance elite player development, ultimately benefiting the U.S. National Teams program for years to come.

An adjective commonly applied to describe the entire WPS season was "parity," and generally in a positive way. Every team had talent and was a threat to win any game. All seven teams were in the race for playoff spots up to the penultimate round. One area that did need improving was the goal-scoring rate. Forty-one percent of WPS games had either only one goal or ended scoreless. Only Washington (thirty-two total for the season) and Los Angeles (twenty-seven) averaged more than a goal a game; the others were below. The WPS's depressed scoring average of 2.14 goals a game (1.67 in playoffs) compared unfavorably with Sweden's women's league at 3.33 for its 2009 season. Major League Soccer had its lowest goals per game average in its fourteen years (2.54) during its 2009 season but still finished ahead of the WPS. For the future, more offense should help to excite and build the fan base.

At the individual team level, the two championship game participants, LA Sol and Sky Blue FC, took much different paths to the title game, presenting interesting subplots. The Sol was the flagship team in the league, winning the regular season title and with it a direct pass to the championship game and hosting rights. An eleven-game unbeaten run midseason allowed them to pull away from the other teams, despite a 1–2–1 record in their last four games. Their young defensive players, U.S. National Team player Stephanie Cox and rookies Allison Falk of Stanford and Brittany Bock of Notre Dame, were superb; they were backed by long-time Canadian National Team keeper Karina LeBlanc, who led the league in goals against average (0.53). Relatively unknown French international Camille Abily was a revelation in midfield, contributing eight goals. Up front, Marta dazzled with her speed and tricks in the penalty box to lead the league in goalscoring with ten.

Sky Blue FC squeaked into the last playoff berth, more from the Boston Breakers' lassitude than their own efforts. Playing at Rutgers University in Piscataway, New Jersey, Sky Blue had a surreal season in 2009. Head Coach Ian Sawyers, who won the inaugural WUSA title with San Jose in 2001, was 1–3–2 after six games when he was suspended and then fired the next week. His management style was described by people within the organization as "abusive" and "dictatorial." President and CEO Thomas Hofstetter felt Sawyer's style didn't fit the culture he wanted, explaining, "We all work so hard on a daily basis. You can't be good if you don't have fun in what you're doing. . . . There has to be a culture of trust and openness to collaborate. We all believe in that. I think we're back on track for that."

Assistant coach and ex-WUSA player Kelly Lindsey took over from Sawyers. Though the team environment seemed more positive, things were still turbulent and inconsistent on the field. Australian Sarah Walsh was exchanged for former Notre Dame scoring star Kerri Hanks of Athletica, and little-used defender Christie Shaner was sent to Los Angeles for a 2010 draft pick. Sky Blue struggled with injuries to goalkeeper Jenni Branam, forward Natasha Kai, and Australian midfielder Collete McCallum. Several national team call-ups midseason also contributed to a lack of continuity. Lindsey's team was 5–4–3 and in the playoff hunt when she unexpectedly quit, peeved that her assistant Joe Dorini was suspended by management. Hofstetter again explained, "Kelly was challenged. Being a college coach and professional coach are two different things. At the end, she was not there yet and it showed. She struggled with it. I don't want to say she did a bad job, but she needed to grow into the job." Hoffstetter added that it had been unlikely that she would remain in the position in 2010, which may have played a role in her decision to leave.

With two games left in the regular season, coach number 3 entered. U.S. National Team captain Christie Rampone took over while continuing as a player, assisted by long time local coach Mick Kelly. Everyone was clear that this was a temporary appointment to finish the season. Rampone said after her first game, a 2–0 win over FC Gold Pride, "I think it's definitely a little different as a coach. You're thinking about some changes you're going to make as well as playing my role and making sure everyone's playing with confidence and trying to decide what formation we might have to change into if things aren't working out but I think we weathered the storm in the first half." The Sky Blue then lost away to Washington 3–1 but clinched the last playoff spot when Boston failed to beat the Sol the next day. As the fourth-place team, no one expected the Sky Blue to win a game, but Rampone had other plans, encouraging the team to "Pack for LA," before their first playoff game in DC, to get them to focus on winning the two road games it would take to make the final.

Of the three teams who missed the playoffs, Boston was the biggest disappointment. Seemingly, they had everything: a former U.S. National Team World Cup, Olympic title, and U-20 World Cup–winning coach in Tony DiCicco; all-time international caps leader Kristine Lilly returning from maternity leave; dynamic British imports Kelly Smith and Alex Scott; and veteran keeper Kristin Luckenbill in goal. To top it off, they had the first pick in the general draft and chose Olympic Gold medalist and NCAA College Cup winner Amy Rodriguez from the University of Southern California. Early on, they looked a potent threat to the Sol after a 3–2–0 start that included the Sol's first defeat. The Breakers then tied three of their next four and ended the season winless in their last quartet, including the 2–1 loss to LA at home when a win would have put them in the playoffs. Smith was slowed with injuries but still scored six goals. Rodriguez, however, was a bust, scoring only one goal and so out of sorts that DiCicco sent her on as a substitute late in the season in the sixty-second minute and then pulled her off after fifteen minutes for another forward. "She just was not working hard enough," DiCicco explained on his rare substitution of a substitution. "I didn't want to take her out. I mean, I basically wasted a sub putting her in. Before I put her in, I said, 'Are you going to work hard?' And I don't think she worked hard enough." DiCicco left Rodriguez at home for their last road trip. In September she was traded to the expansion Philadelphia Independence along with the fifth overall pick in the 2010 general draft in exchange for Philadelphia's second and eleventh pick of the draft. An uncharacteristically shaky Kristen Luckenbill, who won a WUSA title with the Carolina Courage in 2002, lost her goalkeeper job midseason to Ali Lipsher, a Hawaiian native and Duke graduate, who went undrafted and made the team through open tryouts. Lipsher finished the season with a 0.58 goals against average (GAA) in ten starts, the second best in the league, and lowered the team's average by almost one goal per game.

Chicago Red Stars' and FC Gold Pride's inability to score condemned them to the bottom of the standings, though at times both played exciting and attractive soccer. For Chicago, Brazilian superstar forward Cristiane and U.S. National Team midfielder Carli Lloyd were disappointments. Lloyd as an allocation scored only two goals with one assist and though Cristiane had seven goals— including the season's only hat trick against FC Gold Pride—she arrived clearly out of shape. For Gold Pride, a disappointing last place campaign was mainly attributable to two factors: defender Kandace Wilson's season-ending injury and their inability to score goals. Over one-third of their goals (six of seventeen) came in two games. They were shut out eight times, with all but one ending in losses. Canadian Christine Sinclair (six goals) and former U.S. international Tiffeny Milbrett (four goals) accounted for 60 percent of Gold Pride's scoring. A ten-game winless streak left them at the bottom of the standings. Cynics referred to the team as FC Old Slide, as they preferred veteran talent, signing Milbrett (age thirty-six), the legendary Brandi Chastain (age forty-one) and former Brazilian star Sissi (age forty-two). Only Milbrett had her contract extended for 2010.

A common problem for the playoff qualifiers, which was known going into the season, was that the European Championships in August would prevent many of the WPS's top internationals from helping their teams after the regular season. Nine WPS players were called up, six from playoff teams:

England: Eniola Aluko (St. Louis), Anita Asante (Sky Blue FC), Karen Bardsley (Sky Blue FC), Karen Carney (Chicago), Alex Scott, and Kelly Smith (both Boston)
France: Camille Abily (Los Angeles) and Sonia Bompastor (Washington)
Sweden: Sara Larsson (St. Louis).

St. Louis and Sky Blue each lost two players while DC and LA both gave up one. The league has said it will strive to avoid key international tournaments, particularly those that disrupt the playoffs, in the future. Approaching the third- vs. fourth-place game, the Washington Freedom was in top form, winning four of their last five matches. Heavily favored over Sky Blue, the hosts were a solid 5–2–3 at home, with the second-best record in the league. WPS team scoring leaders Washington Freedom had Abby Wambach (eight goals), Australian Lisa DeVanna (six goals), and French National Team midfielder Sonia Bompastor (four goals) as their main sparkplugs. They also had the leakiest defense in the league, conceding the same number they scored (thirty-two). The midseason arrival of Canadian international goalkeeper Erin McLeod solidified the defense, while their offensive strike force was always dangerous, scoring three or more goals on six occasions. The most important of these was their final regular season match versus Sky Blue (3–1), where a loss and other results could have left them out of the playoffs.

The Freedom was expected to do well in the WPS, as they were the lone WUSA franchise to remain active after the league folded. The Freedom played as a club team and competed in the minor W-League, winning the title in 2007. Several players stayed with the franchise through the years, giving the Freedom continuity and chemistry unmatched by other teams in the WPS. Twelve of the twenty-two roster players in 2009 played for the Freedom in the W-League or WUSA. Head coach Jim Gabarra and assistant Clyde Watson guided the team since it began in 2001. Gabarra modeled the organization after the European club system, in which teams maintain developmental and other lower-level teams. He called it a "pyramid," with the Freedom at the top, the W-League amateur team just below and youth league programs in Maryland and Virginia below that; all the teams played the same style. Gabarra explained, "We provide the avenue for the player who wants to play professionally, to kind of walk up the steps of the pyramid." Owners John and Maureen Hendricks provided the stability off the field, donating $6 million to the Maryland Soccerplex in suburban Montgomery County. Surrounded by twenty-four fields used by youth and adult teams, the stadium capacity was increased to 5,200 for the WPS season.

Sky Blue shocked the Freedom by stealing a 2–1 victory, with player-coach Christie Rampone stamping her mark on the team with two second half substitutions. Natasha Kai was nursing a shoulder injury, so she rested during the first half, and little used Brazilian Franciella came on late and both scored.

Sky Blue next traveled to meet the second-placed team in the regular season, St. Louis Athletica. Led by former Brazilian National Team coach Jorge Barcellos, Athletica turned around from a scoreless and lethargic 0–2–1 start. Despite losing Brazilian star midfielder Daniela for the season with damaged knee ligaments, they steadily made their way up the table, led by the bright play of English import Eniola Aluko, who finished with six goals and four assists. Despite their propensity for 1–0 wins (seven of their ten victories) they claimed second place with six wins and two ties in their last nine games. Sky Blue once more emerged triumphant on an opportunistic goal by defender Keeley Dowling. Aluko's loss to England's National Team hurt the Athletica dearly, as she had been such a positive offensive force. Despite the raiding Australian Sara Walsh (former Sky Blue starter) and Christie Welsh (acquired from LA midseason) up front, Athletica looked like they wouldn't score until Armageddon.

Now a definitive phenomenon, Sky Blue kept traveling west as the championship match was only three days later. Many wrote them off, assuming they would tire early against the rested Sol, who could start the explosive Marta and the best defense in the league. Rampone was a master of utilizing her squad however, starting Kai, who had subbed into the previous two games. Franciella also started and controlled central midfield with fellow Brazilian Rosana. With strong wing play from Heather O'Reilly on the right and Kacey White on the left—a constant, inventive force throughout the season—Sky Blue's midfield possession game blunted the Sol's speed and power. O'Reilly scored an early goal, in the sixteenth minute, but the key event of the game happened eleven minutes later, when Sol defender Allison Falk was red carded for tripping U.S. Olympic Gold Medalist Kai on a breakaway about thirty yards from goal. It seemed harsh, and Sol Head Coach Abner Rogers complained, "I didn't feel it was a red card. It was a poor decision. [Left back] Stephanie Cox was a covering player, it wasn't a last defender [call], and there wasn't a blatant tackle. . . . It was a clumsy tackle, and it was a questionable yellow [card]." Goalkeeper Jenni Branam, who played with San Diego in the WUSA, described by Rampone as "a warrior in the back," played flawlessly against the Sol. Besides the home team losing, the crowd of 7,218 was less than half the inaugural's crowd (so much for an extra week's preparation or, in the Sol's case, an extra month to sell the final).

The event was very professionally staged and the game a true reflection of the WPS's quality on the field.

When asked after the game whether, since she had won four of five games as head coach and secured the first WPS championship, she had second thoughts about giving up her coaching position and returning as a player, Rampone said, "I still want to play the game. I think I can do a better job being on the field and maybe helping the head coach next year, but I definitely put my time in, and I'm retiring as coach for now until I'm done playing." On top of everything else, Rampone also had an ovarian cyst removed in an emergency operation in July while away on national team duty. She revealed after the championship game that she was three months pregnant, but hadn't told her teammates or the media because she didn't want to distract them during their playoff run. Rampone, universally respected as a calm, stable influence as the team captain during the 2008 Olympic Games, put herself onto a different level with her visionary leadership of Sky Blue. Thanks to her planning and game management, a team that was in constant turmoil all season will be forever remembered as the first WPS champions. When Rampone is done playing, there should be a long line of teams wanting her to return to coaching.

Interestingly, Sky Blue general manager Gerry Marrone signed an experienced female coach for 2010, Finland's Pauliina Miettinen, who had played and coached in her home country and in the United States. Marrone explained, "We decided our goal was to have a female coach since we are a female team in a female league. Pauliina is an experienced player at the highest level. . . . What's more; she is a great communicator with a dynamic personality, supplemented by her training in psychology." Though Rampone would play without a coaching role after returning from maternity leave in mid-2010, Miettinen reached out to Rampone's assistant Mick Lyons, asking him to stay on to help her in New Jersey.

Midfielder Kacey White reflected on the title a week later in a telephone interview and emphasized the league's parity: "As time goes on I've become even more proud of the team and the effort everyone put in. To win the inaugural WPS championship is a big deal all of us are extremely excited about and also very proud that we were able to pull it together at the end. . . . We don't want to take for granted that we're going to be there [title game] next year. If it showed anything this year in WPS, each team had their ups and downs and it was pretty unpredictable, we know we're going to put in a lot of work and keep improving ourselves as individuals and as a team to try to get back there next year."

The week after the final, the WPS staged an All-Star Game in St. Louis with Swedish league power Umeå, Marta's former team. The All-Stars added to the lore of year 1 with an exciting come-from-behind 4–2 victory over Umeå, who had won the European title twice and finished runners-up on four other occasions in eight years. About 4,100 fans saw Umeå take a quick 2–0 lead within fifteen minutes with goals by Madeline Edlund and Sofia Jakobsson. Kristine Lilly and Marta replied for WPS before the break. In the second half, the All-Stars kept up the pressure with two goals from Christine Sinclair, outpacing Umeå, who had only one substitute available and tired quickly in the second stanza. Umeå was hurt since a number of their players were at the European Finals in Finland, and Swiss international star Ramona Bachmann had to stay at the hotel in St. Louis due to the flu. A few weeks later Bachmann was drafted by the expansion Atlanta Beat, and goal-scorer Edlund signed with Athletica. The 4–2 win helped to further emphasize, albeit in a small way, that the WPS was the top women's league in the world.

Preparing for Year 2

There were wholesale roster changes after the season, driven in part by many contracts ending at the end of August and the expansion draft for Atlanta and Philadelphia. Surprisingly, even the playoff teams discarded about half their roster. Notable players released were U.S. internationals Heather Mitts (Boston), Carli Lloyd (Chicago), and Leslie Osborne (FC Gold Pride). All three were quickly signed by other sides—Mitts by Philadelphia, Lloyd with Sky Blue FC, and Osborne by Boston. Los Angeles dumped midfielder and 2008 Olympic Gold Medalist Aly Wagner, who later retired. International stars let go included China's Han Duan (Los Angeles), Canada's Melissa Tancredi (St. Louis), and Brazil's Fabiana (Boston). Other top-quality internationals took their places, including 2010 European Championships star Daphne Koster of the Netherlands (Sky Blue FC) and England's Katie Chapman (Chicago Red Stars). Opening game rosters had players from nineteen countries, up from twelve the previous year, with Finland, Iceland, Denmark, Germany, Norway, the Netherlands, and New Zealand represented for the first time.

The top stories in season 2 focused on the widely different fortunes of the two expansion teams, the demise of three franchises, FC Gold Pride's stellar season, a late expansion team for 2011 with a championship pedigree, and the owners taking control and minimizing the role of the league office, coinciding with Commissioner Tonya Antonucci's departure. The latter situation soon brought fiscal losses to a head and severe concerns about the league's ability to survive in 2011 and beyond.

FC Gold Pride went from last place in 2009 to first place, dominating the regular season with only three losses and five ties in twenty-four games for fifty-three points. The team acquired Marta when the Los Angeles Sol folded in January, and Head Coach Albertin Montoya used a core of players from the first year, including goalkeeper Nicole Barnhart, defender Rachel Buehler, and forwards Christine Sinclair and Tiffeny Milbrett. In addition, he integrated two rookies to good effect from nearby Stanford: left back Ali Riley, who plays internationally for New Zealand (her father's birthplace); and forward Kelley O'Hara. Montoya added U.S. National Team holding midfielder Shannon Boxx midseason, and the team scored nine more goals during the season (forty-six) than second-place Philadelphia (thirty-seven). They scored four goals on three occasions and tallied six versus Atlanta. They set a new record for consecutive games without a loss with thirteen in the regular season, eclipsing the Sol's mark of twelve. Marta led the league in goal scoring during the regular season with nineteen and repeated as league MVP. Nicole Barnhart won the goalkeeper of the year award and recorded the lowest GAA with 0.77 and most shutouts with eight. Ali Riley was named Rookie of the Year. Canadian international striker Christine Sinclair led the league in assists with nine and also had ten goals (fifth in the league).

Boston Breakers' second-place finish was nothing short of miraculous, considering they were left for dead around the midseason All-Star Game, with only one win in ten games. A run of seven wins and one tie in their next nine games meshed with a scoring run of seven goals from English international Kelly Smith and the inspired play of rookie Jordan Angeli from Santa Clara University, who finished the season with seven goals and three assists. Rookie goalkeeper Alyssa Naeher, who played for head coach Tony DiCicco when the United States won the U-20 World Championships in 2008, took over midseason from Allison Lipsher and helped solidify the defense. Amy Le Pellibert was again named as WPS Defensive Player of the Year. Boston finished at 10–8–6 for thirty-six points, after narrowly missing the playoffs the previous year.

Philadelphia Independence was a revelation, and Paul Riley was named WPS Coach of the Year for the masterful way that he used discarded players Amy Rodriguez and Heather Mitts from Boston, along with midfielders Joanna Lohman (five goals) and Lori Lindsey (second in the league in assists with eight) from Washington. Rodriguez was third in the league in goals with twelve, after only scoring one with Boston in 2009. Goalkeeper was such a strength with two ex-Sol players—2009 record setter Karina Le Blanc and Val Henderson each started at least ten games—that LeBlanc was shipped to Chicago after the season finished in exchange for 2011 draft picks. The Independence finished with a 10–10–4 record for thirty-four points, two points behind Boston.

Washington Freedom slipped into the playoffs with an 8–9–7 record and thirty-one points. Abby Wambach was second in the league in goals (thirteen) and in assists (eight). The Freedom overcame some turmoil late in the season as long-time assistant

Clyde Watson was let go as rumors circulated that head Coach Jim Gabarra would follow him, which indeed took place after the playoffs.

Sky Blue FC, the defending champions, just missed the playoffs with a 7–10–7 record for twenty-eight points. Sky Blue continued its reputation as a graveyard for coaches, dumping Finnish coach Pauliina Miettinen when the team was in third place, replacing her on an interim basis with assistant coach Rick Stainton, who did his long-term prospects with Sky Blue no good by going 2–4–4 in the final ten games. After the season, Sky Blue hired their sixth coach in two years, former Freedom coach Jim Gabarra. Sky Blue, hurt all season with injuries to key players, never overcame the loss of goalkeeper Karen Bardsley, who had a stellar season ended by a practice ground injury while at the All-Star game.

Chicago Red Stars started off slowly once again and fired head coach Emma Hayes in June. She was replaced by Omid Namazi, who had primarily coached men's indoor teams, though he had coached San Diego in the last year of the WUSA. Brazilian superstar Cristiane was an overpaid disappointment, finishing with three goals. Ella Masar was a bright spot with eight goals, as was rookie Casey Nogueira with her three goals and four assists primarily as a substitute, and goalkeeper Jillian Loyden, who joined from St. Louis during the off season. Loyden finished second in GAA at 1.17 and shutouts with six, and was selected to the U.S. National Team for her play.

Atlanta Beat was a stellar addition off the field. Led by a vivacious and visionary owner, T. Fitz Johnson, the Beat opened the first purpose-built stadium for a women's professional soccer team, in conjunction with Kennesaw State University. The 8,200 seat KSU soccer stadium is a landmark, a crown jewel for the women's game. On the field, the Beat was an unmitigated nightmare. They started the season with one win in eight matches. The international forwards that head coach Gareth O'Sullivan brought in were ineffective and not up to the level of WPS play. Switzerland's Ramona Bachmann and Germany's Shelley Thompson had one goal between them and Mexican National Team veteran Monica Ocampo only scored three times in seventeen games. Things improved marginally when five Athletica players—including English international Eniola Aluko and U.S. stalwarts Hope Solo and Lori Chalupny—were signed after their team folded in May; the Beat quickly were dubbed Atlantica. A three-game winning streak in July was not enough to make the playoffs and they finished last with twenty-one points from five wins, six ties, and thirteen losses. Atlanta scored a league low twenty goals in twenty-four games (tied with Sky Blue FC) and allowed forty goals, the most in the league. Coach O'Sullivan didn't make it to the end of the season, replaced by relatively unknown academy coach James Galanis. The Beat released or traded most of their squad ahead of the 2011 season (see table 9 in the appendix).

A highlight was the All-Star Game, which Atlanta hosted at the end of June. In front of 4,610, the top vote getters from fans, media, and coaches—Marta and Abby Wambach—were named captains and selected their starters in a playground, "pick them" format. In an entertaining game, Marta's XI won 5–2 with two goals from Marta, and one each from Gold Pride teammate Christine Sinclair, Atlanta's Aya Miyama, and Philadelphia's Amy Rodriguez. Atlanta's Eniola Aluko and Boston's Lauren Cheney replied for Abby's XI.

St. Louis Athletica made it through only a quarter of the season before folding because of a lack of funds. Owner Jeff Cooper reportedly lost $2 million during the 2009 season and brought in additional investors from the U.K., brothers Sanjeev and Heemal Vaid. Cooper, a lawyer, apparently didn't fully vet his partners, and they quickly stopped funding the team in May, along with a new men's Division II side that Cooper also owned; operations head Heemal hopped a flight home, leaving Cooper with about $1 million in debts. The men's side finished the season because U.S. Soccer, which ran the league, required a $350,000 bond for each team. The WPS had no such fallback. League Commissioner Tonya Antonucci explained that the finances didn't justify the WPS funding Athletica through the rest of the season. The WPS would require team bonds for 2011, which brought a unique set of issues, discussed below.

In the first round of the playoffs, Washington Freedom battled host Philadelphia Independence even until the last minute of overtime as penalty kicks loomed before a paltry crowd of 2,378. Outstanding Freedom rookie forward/defender Nikki Marshall turned the ball over in her own half while trying to dribble out of trouble, and Tina DiMartino fed Amy Rodriguez, who buried the ball past Freedom goalkeeper Ashlyn Harris.

Philadelphia again won the semifinal in overtime, defeating the Boston Breakers on a Thursday night before only 2,676 at Harvard. Danesha Adams scored the winner from another Tina DiMartino assist after 103 minutes. A tired and worn out Independence flew out to the Bay Area to play FC Gold Pride on two days rest and were overrun 4–0 on two goals by Christine Sinclair and single tallies from Marta and Kandace Wilson. The Gold Pride added the championship title to their regular season crown before a near sellout crowd of 5,228. Coach Albertin Montoya felt that playing Philadelphia and Boston in their last two regular season matches—both wins at home—helped them avoid the championship game lethargy that the Sol encountered after they clinched the 2009 regular season crown and a bye into the final.

During the game, the WPS announced that Western New York was joining the league for 2011. The news was a financial boost to the league, with the existing team owners sharing a rumored entry fee around $1.25 million. The new franchise was led by Joe Sahlen of Buffalo, who also owned a well-known regional meat producer, the W-League Flash and an indoor soccer and arena sports complex. The team announced they would split their games between the thirteen-thousand-seat Marina Auto Stadium in Rochester and the much smaller Niagara University Field in Lewiston, New York, just outside Buffalo. Niagara's soccer field was dedicated to soccer and lacrosse but only accommodated about a thousand fans. The Western New York ownership group was in discussions with the university to add another two to three thousand seats, at the team's expense, for WPS matches.

Rochester/Buffalo/Southwestern Ontario was a good move for

the league. Rochester in particular is a phenomenal soccer city, where the people have long understood the sport and supported it. The Rochester Lancers were long-time members of the NASL, and their move in 1970 from a minor league, along with the Washington DC Darts, probably saved the NASL from folding at that time. The Rochester Rhinos of the USL, begun in 1996, were a tremendous success story in the USL for many years, drawing around 10,000 fans a game when the league average hovered around 3,500. They have also shown strong support for the women's game. A crowd of 7,662 braved the rain to watch a WUSA exhibition between New York and Washington at Rochester's Frontier Field in 2003. Marina Auto Stadium, a soccer-specific stadium opened in 2006, has hosted the U.S. National Women's Team in the past, including a 2009 game in which 8,443 saw Rochester native Abby Wambach score her 100th goal. One question surrounding this franchise is whether Rochester fans will support "half-of-a-franchise." Rochester does support top quality soccer, and if they back the WPS franchise as expected, attendance could be near the top of the league. What about Buffalo then? In 2010 the W-League Flash only averaged 236 fans a game for their six matches, below the league average of 336 and well behind leading Vancouver Whitecaps FC Women (1,513) and Atlanta Silverbacks (1,200). In Buffalo, despite the on-the-field success of the Flash, who won the 2010 USL W-League title in August, the team would have more of a selling effort for the sport than they would in Rochester. The Flash would finally sign to play all their 2011 WPS games in Rochester, and the Sahlen's meat products company purchased naming rights for the stadium.

The Flash was able to begin play much faster than other ex-pansion franchises because they had been a professional outfit for the previous two years in the W-League, paying salaries well above the other teams in the league. Sahlen expected to draw from his pool of 2010 champions—all of whom were free agents—in order to be competitive immediately in WPS. Sahlen said, "We want to keep some continuity [with last year]. If they are WPS caliber, we will look at them." He felt that realistically up to half of the team would have a shot at moving up. Midfielder and league MVP Kelly Parker joined Sky Blue FC after the W-League championships, and Veronique Boquette made a strong impact with the Chicago Red Stars at the end of their season. Mele French played briefly in WPS in 2009 and then in Germany. Local defender Alex Sahlen, goalkeeper Pamela Tajona-Alonso and midfielder Jenny Anderson-Hammond are others who would seem to have a good chance of making the team for 2011. As Joe Sahlen said, "The more who come from this year's team, the better." A successful season on the field in 2011 should help the Flash draw fans from both cities.

This good news of expansion was offset by the team owners' decision to pare back the league support structures, in order to eliminate the contributions they made to fund the league office. This move reduced the San Francisco–based offices from about ten staffers to effectively one—the league general counsel Anne-Marie Eileraas. They lost founder and CEO Tonya Antonucci, COO Mary Harvey, and other key staffers. Harvey had tremendous international contacts from her years at FIFA and was widely respected in U.S. soccer circles. As for Antonucci, her vision and drive reconstructed a professional league after the demise of the WUSA, when many thought it couldn't be done. Antonucci brought in investors and ownership groups, created marketing and television agreements, sold sponsorships, and was instrumental in attracting the top American and international players in the world to the new league. She also instituted the financial model that allowed the league to start and expand during the Great Recession. Atlanta Beat owner T. Fitz Johnson, who doubles as the chairman of the league's Board of Governors, said about Antonucci: "No other person did more to bring this league from idea to fruition over the past six years than she did. WPS would not be here without Tonya Antonucci and without her tireless work and unending passion for launching this league."

Antonucci herself was positive about the league's future despite the loss of the Los Angeles Sol and St. Louis Athletica, as well as a 20 percent decline in attendance from the first year. Antonucci said, "There is still a lot of work to be done, but we have laid the groundwork from which the owners can continue to build towards a long-term and sustainable league. I'm leaving this in the hands of some incredibly passionate people who are doing everything they can to grow the league and ensure its success. But we absolutely need support from grass-roots soccer fans and young female players." Still, one was left with an uneasy feeling that the owners made a cost-savings move that sacrificed the future in gutting the league of some of the key people who brought it into existence. Elieraas replaced Antonucci as CEO, while retaining her legal responsibilities, and reporting to the team owners.

Attendance was a letdown in 2010, as it fell by 20 percent, from 4,518 in 2009 to 3,600 in 2010 (including playoffs). The Men's World Cup in South Africa did not provide a surge in attendance as league officials hoped, but in fact did more damage during the soccer-saturated summer. Average attendance before the World Cup started was 4,010, fell to 3,219 during the tournament, and climbed slightly to 3,412 afterward.

Only Boston increased attendance from their first year, gaining 7 percent, with 4,490 attending in 2010 compared with 4,183 in 2009. The Chicago Red Stars were the only other team to average over 4,000 (4,025). Washington (3,825), Atlanta (3,690), and Sky Blue FC (3,320) were in the middle, with the champion FC Gold Pride (3,027) and expansion Philadelphia (2,938) bringing up the rear. Gold Pride's and the Freedom's attendance fell 20 percent from the year before.

It was just weeks after the championship final in late September that the dreaded "the league is folding" cries started. The league had set a performance bond for each team for 2011—rumored to be around $250,000—that the league could draw on so they could run a bankrupt franchise through the season, to avoid another St. Louis Athletica meltdown. FC Gold Pride and Washington Freedom announced that they needed more time beyond the November 15 deadline, as they were trying to locate more investors. Gold Pride's problems were not a surprise—they had moved thirty minutes north from San Jose to Hayward—and despite a phenomenal team, attendances were disappointing. The team's general manager Ilisa Kessler didn't give any reason for optimism when she said, "We're looking under every rock we can to find somebody who is interested. . . . It doesn't look likely." Kessler lamented that "we put the best player in the world in our market [Marta] and we had a great record, every game was a wonderful show and it still didn't translate into ticket sales. What does the public want? Or do they want it at all?"

Washington was an entirely different matter. Led by John and Maureen Hendricks, the Freedom had continued after the WUSA folded in 2003. No family had been more supportive of the women's game, so the fact that the Hendrickses were looking for new investors was disconcerting. The WPS successfully launched and expanded during a devastating economy. However, finding investors and sponsors on relatively short notice as businesses still struggled was another thing altogether. It was eerily similar to the "Buy now or it may be gone" tactic that the WUSA was accused of using in 2003 and 2004 as it sought new investors and sponsors, which did nothing to save the league.

Further adding to the confusion was that the Chicago Red Stars and Boston Breakers had not put forward their bonds either. The Red Stars, paying exorbitant rents in MLS' Toyota Park for two years, also was looking for additional investors. Chicago put out a self-serving statement, implying that the other teams' struggles were badly hurting their own search for investors and sponsors: "The Chicago owners continue to fund the team, but the Washington and Bay Area news has affected some of the Red Stars' planned partnerships. Thus, we continue to seek additional investors and long-term economic partners and hope to close on both current prospects and new prospects that may come to light soon." Boston was simply waiting on the others to commit for 2011. With the league postponing the expansion draft, some wondered if Western New York would back out. The media speculated as to just how few franchises the league needed to continue (league sources who would comment said six). In late November, FC Gold Pride announced that they were folding, after efforts to move them to Los Angeles fell through. Washington stayed in, but Hendricks sold the franchise to Dan Borislow, who moved the team to Boca Raton, Florida, and renamed it after his company's telecommunications device, magicJack. Chicago missed the deadline and ultimately took a leave of absence for 2011, intending to return in 2012. One has to wonder if it was merely a coincidence that these problems emerged just weeks after Tonya Antonucci's departure and a sign that the owner-driven league was doomed to failure without the guidance of the league office.

The WPS reduced its league schedule from twenty-four to eighteen games in 2011 with no All-Star Game and a two week break for the first two weeks of the Women's World Cup, which began June 26. Gold Pride and Red Star players were free agents, along with a number of other players who had been on two-year deals. The lineup for 2012 included Atlanta Beat, Boston Breakers, magic-Jack, New Jersey's Sky Blue FC, Philadelphia Independence, and Western New York Flash. One of Tonya Antonucci's key planks in starting the WPS was to have a national scope; for 2011, the league will be only on the Eastern Seaboard, which means that media in other regions are not likely to pay attention to it, and it will be difficult for WPS to sell national sponsorships. Future years will tell how much the two months of uncertainty in 2010 held back future investors, markets and sponsors.

Expanding to Atlanta and Philadelphia was a good move in 2010, though Philadelphia—a strong WUSA market—needs to improve its crowds moving forward—and Western New York's entry may have saved the league, but the WPS needs to consider some other good soccer markets. There are three cities that did not house WUSA teams but deserve serious consideration in the future: Portland, Seattle, and Vancouver BC.

A prime market is Portland, Oregon, which was once known as Soccer City, when the Portland Timbers played in the NASL from 1975 to 1982; Portland supports the men's and women's game without hesitation. Portland drew 23,325 for a U.S. Women's National Team exhibition with Canada on June 6, 1999, just before the start of the World Cup. Four years later they topped that with a sellout crowd of 27,623 for the 2003 World Cup semifinals. Like Rochester, Portland had exposure to the WUSA, hosting the September 2002 All-Star game in front of 14,208 fans at PGE Park. Portland Timbers are moving up from Division II soccer to Major League Soccer for 2011.

Seattle is another strong market dating back to its NASL inaugural season of 1974, and then subsequently as a lynchpin of the USL A-League/First Division. The city is a primary market for touring British teams, and its MLS expansion side averaged over thirty thousand fans a game in 2009 and 2010. Seattle has hosted CONCACAF (Confederation of North, Central America and Caribbean Association Football) women's Gold Cup games in the past.

The third key market, 2010 Winter Olympics host Vancouver, had a long run in the NASL (1974–84) like its Pacific Northwest rivals to the south, but it has been its acceptance and commitment to the women's game that is particularly salient. The W-League Whitecaps have shown how to develop a women's team fan base while working within the parent men's side organization. Between the WUSA and WPS years, Vancouver's average was higher than all other women's amateur and professional clubs in the world, even Umeå of Sweden. In 2005 the Whitecap Women attracted 3,697 per game with one crowd of almost six thousand. In 2006, average attendance grew to 3,941, over six times the W-League average of 597 (see table 10 in the appendix). Former Whitecaps Women's and Canadian U-20 National Team head coach Bob Birarda described the city's support for the women's game: "It's a pretty unique situation; we have a place where the players can go and actually be a part of a fan base. They get to play in front of people who care about the game in Vancouver, which is pretty cool."

Vancouver is an example of a proven soccer market that has embraced the women's game. As a traditionally strong USL men's organization, they added the women's side and then supported it so that it became an important component of the club, leveraging strengths rather than fighting for limited resources. Birarda said, "All the people that work at the club really support having the [women's] program, and they treat it with complete respect all the time. It's been really good for the program to be attached to a club that's become a really professional structured franchise." Vancouver entered MLS for 2011, and it will be interesting to see if they make a similar move for their women's program into the WPS.

Other viable options for the WPS could be smaller markets that support soccer but where the team won't be lost by media coverage of local NBA, NFL, baseball teams, and so forth. This could include suburban areas of larger cities—much like St. Louis Athletica's home in suburban Fenton, Missouri, or a market like Louisville, Raleigh-Durham, or Salt Lake City. As the Sky Blue FC's midfielder Kacey White said, "As we expand, more cities will be involved and more communities will be aware of the league and what's going on and that will help in the next two to three years." Expansion by the league is important; it brings in additional fees to the current league members, and a larger league will attract more media and sponsorship attention. But the choice of locations and new owners is crucial to future stability and growth. The WPS has planned to have twelve teams by the 2012 season. After the turmoil of the 2010/2011 off-season, attracting new teams may be harder, but this is still important for survival to 2012 and beyond.

The WPS, with careful planning and realistic objectives, launched and expanded despite a devastating economy. As the business environment improves, they hope that sponsorship revenues will as well. The WPS needs to make it five years before most will consider it beyond embryonic stage, especially with the WUSA's history. Marilyn Childress, who led the quest to add women's soccer to the Atlanta Olympics, once said about the WPS: "The women's league only has one shot. If it fails, there won't be another women's league for 10–20 years."

TWO

Challenges in the Middle East, Africa, and Latin America

5

The State of the Game in the Middle East

A quick glance at Islamic and Arabic countries of the Middle East and North Africa, members of FIFA's Asian Football Confederation (AFC) or Confederation Africane de Football (CAF), including Iran, Iraq, Oman, Palestine, Pakistan, Saudi Arabia, Tunisia, and Yemen, could cause one to forever write off any hope for the success of the women's game in the region. Many of these countries have rigid views of women's roles in society, such as ingrained perceptions of girls and women as second-class citizens, as well as proscriptions severely limiting communication between men and women. When you mix in rampant poverty and overlay religious restrictions affecting women's activities that even determine unique rules of dress for sports, the barriers seem too great to overcome. Women players have faced verbal and physical abuse, prohibitions on their sport, and pressure to abandon the game—including from family members. Is it really worth the effort in these countries? The answer, according to those active within the game in the region, is an overwhelming yes. Despite the daunting obstacles, the potential in these countries is sizable but requires a different measurement standard than that used in North America or Europe.

FIFA's latest global survey of players (The Big Count), conducted by Lamprecht & Stamm SFB AG, a Zurich-based research agency, shows that of the 265 million players in 2006 among its then 207 member countries, around 10 percent or 26 million are girls and women (see table 11 in the appendix). Of registered players, the figure is 4.1 million women (more than double the figure just six years ago) compared with 34.2 million men. Looking at the two confederations of the CAF and AFC, both record a lower percentage of females who play than the overall average; 6 percent for the Asian Confederation and 2.9 percent for the Africans. Upon closer inspection, the AFC number is driven by East Asian countries where the women's game has a substantial history, such as China (7.3 percent), Japan (6.3 percent) and even North Korea (13.1 percent).

When we look at individual countries in North Africa and the Middle East, twelve countries out of a combined ninety-nine in Africa and Asia had no formal soccer opportunities for women or girls in 2006, including Kuwait, Libya, Oman, Pakistan, Saudi Arabia, Sudan, Syria, and the United Arab Emirates. In Afghanistan 526,000 males play the game on a regular basis compared with only 340 females. Only fifteen female soccer teams registered with Egypt's association, compared with hundreds of men's teams, even though half of its population of 62 million people are women. In Lebanon there are only one hundred females, or 0.03 percent of the three hundred thousand plus active members. However, people active in the sport's development say that women's soccer exists throughout the region—it might not be formal or eleven-a-side, but females are playing and need encouragement.

Iran, an Islamic Republic that surprisingly has a higher percentage of women active in the game than Japan and more total players (110,000) than South Korea but with vastly different barriers to growth than the East Asian countries, is a good place to start to understand the struggles of female soccer players in the region.

Iran — Women's Soccer behind Closed Doors

Iran's conservative religious precepts and controversial definition of women's roles in society run up against Iranians' paramount passion for the game of soccer. Women actually played the sport during the 1970s when some of the major men's sides such as Taj established teams. Italy's National Women's Team, one of the early global proponents, even toured the country late in 1972 and drew 25,000 fans in Tehran for a match with Taj. The Islamic Revolution of 1979 ended women's playing efforts by establishing strict rules segregating men and women. Women were even banned from watching men's games to prevent "socializing between the sexes."

Futsal, a small-sided version of the game (four players and a goalie) played on a basketball-size court, was the route back to the game for women. *Futsal* is extremely popular in Iran and is played both outside and indoors. In 1993 interested students at Alzahra University stood up to university officials, which led to reluctant permission and the first unofficial competition for females since the Islamic Revolution. Women's football activity continued to grow until, in 1997, the physical education organization finally formed a women's *futsal* committee. Sport clubs began to encourage women's *futsal* teams throughout the country. These efforts led to an official competition held at Alzahra University in 2001 that included twelve teams from different universities.

For authorities, *futsal* was a palatable solution for women: they could play in an indoor facility where men could easily be locked out. In this way, university officials and players were not contravening Sharia law, the Islamic edicts that are derived from the Koran and the practices of the prophet Mohammed. Sharia means "the path to a watering hole" and is a religious code for how believers should live their lives (e.g., through prayers, fasting, helping the poor). Most Muslims adapt Sharia to some extent, but a few Islamic countries have used Sharia as a basis for formal laws that are thus enforceable by their judicial system. Some nations implement strict interpretations—including Iran—while others have more liberal applications, such as in Jordan. Iran's implementation of decrees that men and women should dress modestly resulted in sexual segregation and the norm that women should not have exposed skin at any time. For indoor *futsal*, the players could wear tracksuit pants to cover their legs, long-sleeved jerseys for their arms, as well as a hijab to cover their head. Farah Azwai, an athlete at American Intercontinental University in London, talked about the difficulty of playing while wearing a hijab: "I used to wear a bandanna and tried fixing my hijab in different ways but it wasn't very practical and I always had problems."

Sporting goods manufacturers continue to investigate alternatives that allow a woman to cover her head while not inhibiting her play. FIFA President Sepp Blatter, who has cemented his position as the Calvin Klein of dress in women's sport by advocating spandex and hot pants to replace shorts, at least got it right when he said that FIFA will start an indoor championship for those countries "where women cannot—by religious or social reasons—expose [their legs] in public."

The religious element guiding women's participation in sport is open to different interpretations. Sayings attributed to Mohammed recommend an active life, with running, horseback riding, swimming, and archery mentioned specifically. Islamic concern for "one's body, cleanliness, purification, and force" ultimately collides with values confining women to home and family spheres. Thirteen-year-old Reem Musa was touted as Israel's best football player and was the only Palestinian on Israel's national youth team. She started playing at age nine and was teased by the boys on her team, but that didn't last long because she competed well against them. People asked her father and mother how they could let their daughter play football—a man's sport! They also criticized her for wearing shorts when the Koran says that a girl should cover her legs. Reem's father responded that there was no mention of shorts in the Koran, but it did say that women should swim and ride horses.

Stricter interpretations of Muslim Sharia law have even resulted in the complete banning of the women's game. The governor of the northwestern state of Zamfara in Nigeria branded the activity as "unislamic." Interestingly, the men's game was unaffected in a soccer-mad country where the men qualified for the World Cups from 1994 to 2002.

Sharia law created an uneven ground on a sporting level as the women attempted to restart outdoor soccer, which had been in mothballs for close to thirty years. This was demonstrated when the

Iranian National Team was formed in 2005 in order to participate in the West Asian Football Federation Women's Championships in Amman, Jordan. They drew their players from twenty-two provincial teams who met for the first time to decide a national championship. The juxtaposition of different nations' implementation of Sharia law was apparent in the team uniforms for the final, the fully covered Iranians competed against their Jordanian opponents, who wore short-sleeved jerseys, athletic shorts, and no hijab. While Westerners may be shocked by the idea of wearing so much clothing while playing a high energy athletic event in scorching heat—sometimes in excess of 100 degrees Fahrenheit—the players insist they have no problems with wearing tracksuits and covering their heads to conform with Islamic principles.

As international teams began to travel to Iran for matches, they realized that the dress code pertained to them as well. The Iranian National Team hosted an outdoor foreign visitor for the first time since the 1970s in May 2006. Aldersimspor came from Berlin with many players of Arab, Turkish, Greek, and Korean heritage. Players on both sides had to cover their skin, and no males were allowed entry, but it still was hailed as a historic moment. Elaleh Moladost, a female referee in the Iranian women's *futsal* league, felt that the event was important beyond just the game itself. She said that it was "the birth of a new culture, with women fighting for their rights."

Women's attempts to gain access to football form only a part of a dynamic women's movement in the country, which is inevitable for any women's activity in a society where females legally have fewer rights than males. Women do not have full guardianship over their children after divorce, and they are entitled to half as much inheritance as men unless the couple had no children, in which case his estate reverts to his parents, not to his wife. The right to divorce still rests mostly with men in the Islamic Republic. Girls are considered adults at the age of nine in court and are liable to receive the death penalty for murder; boys become adults at fifteen. If a man and a woman are injured in an accident, the man gets double the punitive damages. Women can be stoned to death for adultery, whereas men can practice polygamy. Women now play significant roles in politics and the workplace in Iran. They make up around 65 percent of students entering university. But legally, they are not treated the same as men. They are prevented from some positions, such as running for president or serving as judges.

The conservative Iranian newspaper *Jomhuri-ye Eslami* said the growing interest among women for soccer "is no evidence of ethical correctness. There are a lot of people in the world who would like alcohol, drugs, and gambling, all of which are ugly, unpleasant, and forbidden habits." *Jomhuri-ye Eslami* was referring not to women on the field but in the stands. Women have of late challenged the idea that men's games are forbidden territory. When Iran qualified for the 1998 World Cup with a last-minute goal in an enthralling playoff qualifier in Melbourne, Australia, thousands of women invaded celebrations at the National Stadium in Tehran. The issue came up four years later when Iran again found itself in the final playoff for a World Cup berth, this time with Ireland. For the Tehran leg of the two-game series, the government had to make a special exception for Irish journalists, some of whom happened to be women, along with a few hundred traveling Irish supporters. A few brave Iranian women were detained by the police, protesting the irony that foreign women could cheer on their team while Iranians were not afforded the same consideration in their own country. Noted Iranian film director Jafar Panahi covered the women's efforts in his 2006 movie *Offside*, available within the country only on the black market.

Therefore, women celebrated Iranian president Mahmoud Ahmadinejad's surprising ruling in April 2006 granting them access to men's soccer games, albeit to sit in a segregated section. The new rule was meant "to improve soccer-watching manners and promote a healthy atmosphere." Peykan's home game versus Bargh in the Azadegan League, Iran's top-level league, became a notable match when females were finally permitted to watch. Only a few attended, but the precedent had been set. The rule was undone a month later by Ayatollah Ali Khamenei, the effective leader of the country, who cited a breach with the Islamic Republic's constitution. (In 2009 the United Arab Emirates allowed women to attend men's games, in part because they were hosting the next two FIFA World Club Cups and bidding to host the Men's World Cup in 2022. Separate sections were established for females and families.)

Until sport is no longer seen as an affront to religion in the same way that business, civic, and political activities are not, the growth of the game in Iran will of necessity dovetail closely with women's rights. Even though the advancement of sport has an obvious health-based focus for men and women, the social barriers need to be removed before women's soccer has any chance for significant acceptance. Iran, with its history and unbridled love of the sport of soccer, has perhaps the best chance in the region to eventually attract fans (men and women) for the game on its own merit once the social restrictions relax. Then soccer will play a new role in society, helping to promote a healthy lifestyle, teamwork, skill development, and enjoyment for its own sake.

Egypt's Example

Egypt, while not as strict religiously as Iran, has still struggled to grow the sport since its founding in 1994. Sahar El-Hawary, a dynamic and highly organized college professor, has overcome numerous obstacles in this male-dominated society to become the single most important asset for women soccer's advocacy in the Arab world. Her charming, low key, and nonflustered approach belies the impediments she has overcome in her zeal to expand the sport's popularity. Equally adept at dealing with government ministers, international sports officials, media, and rural peasants, she treats everyone with respect and doesn't hold grudges against those who have stood in her way. El-Hawary's story, shared in multiple interviews during the 2007 Women's World Cup in China, shows the growth potential of the sport in the Arab world and how it has fostered women leaders in key administrative roles.

El-Hawary was introduced to soccer by her father, who was a leading referee in Egypt. She wanted to provide girls and women the chance to play the sport in an organized fashion, something that she didn't have growing up. She became a target for opponents in the media who were derisive of women's sport in Egypt. They told her, "You are coming to occupy our fields. We don't have enough fields or equipment for men." The coach of the women's team, Ashraf Shafik, recalled that when they first began, "No one wanted to play a game perceived as solely masculine. We'd take any girl, big or small. Now we are far more selective." But first they had to cross numerous gender hurdles. Coaches had to convince girls' families of their good intentions when they "didn't want their girls to look masculine or stay away from home for long," Shafik explained. One father did not want his daughter to hear the swear words he associated with typical soccer fans. Besides paying for a manager and a coach for the girls, El-Hawary built a four-by-four pitch in her own backyard. She began to recruit players from outside Cairo and brought the poorer girls from the countryside into her own home to live, treating them like family members. She followed every lead to find more players. El-Hawary remembers, "I would hear about a girl who plays with boys or see her playing in a field with other peasants. I would go and talk to the parents and tell them that I would take the girl back to Cairo. She would live with me and I would take care of her schooling. It took time but most agreed. They knew she would be safe. People knew I was starting something. The negative media publicity actually helped me at that point: people knew who I was. I was a woman too. If I were a man, probably no . . ."

During those early years, before it was given national status, the team was derisively referred to as "Sahar's team." "I suffered a lot," she said. "Now we train women referees and add teams every year." She received international media attention in 1997 when Egypt hosted the U-20 Men's World Cup and she served as a member of the local organizing committee. FIFA officials and media members were surprised to find that she had thirty players in training and was paying for the team out of her own pocket. She was co-opted by FIFA to work on their women's football development efforts. She particularly stressed the importance of introducing quality coaching for girls and women. Just as women were assigned dirt patches to play on while men had manicured grass fields, women had coaches who weren't qualified to coach *anyone*. Her doctoral dissertation in communications analyzed how the media treated her efforts to promote the sport. She found that the negative pieces changed in Egypt after 1997 and became more positive about women's soccer. She freely admitted, "I used the media as a tool to enhance what I was doing."

Utilizing her FIFA position, she turned her attention to neighboring countries. In 2000 she formed the first Arab League Committee for Women's Football. The Arab League is based in Cairo and handles such events as the Gulf Cup for national teams on the men's side. She has also worked with specific football associations on special events and league development in Jordan, Tunisia, and the United Arab Emirates. El-Hawary found on her travels that women's football is being played in all countries throughout the Arab world, but often on an informal basis. She and other pioneers in the region are building a proper organization and infrastructure for girls and women to play, whether it is *futsal* in Iran, seven-a-side in Egypt, or full eleven-a-side teams in Jordan.

El-Hawary's impact has been felt far beyond her region. She has been relentless in lobbying within FIFA for more money and programs for women. She was instrumental in drafting FIFA's mandate that federations must dedicate a portion of the Men's World Cup profits to women, beginning with 4 percent in 2004 and increasing to 15 percent in 2007. El-Hawary represents the experienced, passionate leader that women's soccer is developing and, with her trailblazing, girls and women in more nations now have a chance to adopt the sport. Only a few years ago they would have had to play on boys' teams and face merciless ridicule.

The national team players in the United States and Canada, as well as the WPS professionals, inspire young people. They are role models for both boys and girls, presenting themselves as active, dynamic women, and boys in particular now see girls' athletic pursuits as normal. The players' hope is that as they grow up, boys will be equally welcoming to women in all types of activities, whether social, political, business, or civic. In some African and Arab countries, however, this goal is so daunting because perceptions of "appropriateness for females" begins at such a young age. In March 2006 the *New York Times* reported, "Girls' sports are still a novelty in Somali culture, so much so that the volleyball players here have been denounced by sheiks for supposed unladylike acts, like running or extending their arms in the air, and gawked at by boys unfamiliar with seeing women do much more than cooking or cleaning or carting water on their heads. 'Some people think that if girls play sports they are prostitutes,' one woman explained. 'Our parents were embarrassed. They had bad feelings about girls playing outside.'"

In Pakistan, Monika Staab, FIFA's Women's Football Specialist for Asia, found when recruiting players that "I have to convince parents, afraid that when [their daughter] plays rough and tumble football she will not find a husband, to allow the girls to play." Staab finds that the next hurdle usually is when they get married, usually in their early twenties. They are expected to stop playing because "the role of women is to stay at home, do the cooking, washing and getting babies."

Growth of the Game in the Region

There are some positive stories coming out of the region that show that progress is coming, albeit slowly. In 2004 an Arab IX women's side composed of players from Algeria, Egypt, Jordan, Libya, Morocco, Palestine, and Tunisia held London top side Chelsea FC to a 2–2 tie in the United Arab Emirates (UAE). More remarkably, a mixed gender crowd of a thousand watched the game, which was broadcast live by five television stations. The patron of this historic match was UAE government member Sheikh Mohammed al Maktoum, and the principal organizer was none other than Egyptian soccer pioneer Sahar El-Hawary. The game was held during the annual Shopping Festival in Dubai. El-Hawary explained to UAE football officials, "You invite a lot of men's foreign teams.

Why don't you have a women's team play?" Among the guests of honor was Princess Haya of Jordan, the Jordanian king's thirty-year-old sister and wife of Sheikh al Maktoum. Besides a love of the game, Princess Haya sees sports as a good avenue to further gender equity. El-Hawary commented, "We are very proud of the princess's involvement. She is an idol among Arab women as an advocate for equality. At the same time, her commitment not only assures media attention but also more acceptance. People can see not only that Arab women can play football but also that it is help-ing to break down certain traditions. When even a princess shows interest in football, then it can't be that bad."

In Bahrain, girls now play football in the island's schools. Sheikh Fawaz Mohamed Al Khalifa, the president of the General Organization of Youth and Sports in Bahrain, said in 2002 that "women's football is breaking news. . . . More than half of the girls taking part [in trial tournaments at school] were Bahraini and not, as you might expect, English or American. We are teaching teach-ers the rules so that they can coach others. Development begins at the grass roots." The first football tournament for girls was held in Bahrain the same year. Eight schools entered the event. Football was rapidly becoming a perfectly natural pastime for girls. Fawaz says, "Why wouldn't they share in the fun that the boys have every spare minute of the day? FIFA stages world championships just for women, and women's football is played at the Olympics too. In educational terms, football is just as useful for girls as it is for boys."

Sheik Fawaz selected a young female staffer from his office, Amal Al Dossari, to start an under-eighteen women's national team. Players were identified at schools. "Everything is running like clockwork and it's great fun," Al Dossari said. The emir, the country's president, is solidly behind the growth of the women's sport. German professional coach Uli Maslo, in the country coach-ing men's side Al Riffa, remembered, "The Emir asked me to give private coaching lessons to his daughter and her friends, all of whom were football crazy. And then a cluster of lively girls actually rolled up in a limousine and I gave them coaching lessons. I have seldom seen such a group of happy girls in one go."

Qatar established a women's national soccer team early into the new century. Asian Football Confederation general secretary Dato' Peter Velappan praised the decision as "a step in the right direction for women's football." The first step was a seminar to develop female coaches to lead the new program. This is a necessity in a predominantly Muslim country that adheres to traditional restrictions on fraternization between unrelated men and women, as in Iran.

Jordanian scoring sensation Stephanie Al Naber made history in late 2009 when she joined Denmark's Fortuna Hjörring to play in their semipro league while completing her business studies. The twenty-two-year-old striker has led Jordan's rise to prominence in the Gulf region, though for the 2011 World Cup they were eliminated by Myanmar in the second round of the AFC qualifying tournament.

German native Monika Staab has played or coached soccer since 1969, before the German Federation allowed organized play. After a decade coaching at club power 1FC Frankfurt, the forty-eight-year-old coach wanted a new challenge and took a position with FIFA as a Women's Football Specialist, advising on development projects. Since December 2006, Staab has been assigned to work in Asia. She has conducted coaching clinics in Bahrain (where she is also the women's national team coach), Iran, Jordan, Myanmar, Pakistan, and Sri Lanka. In a series of interviews and correspondence late in 2007, she described her role as much more eclectic than just running training sessions:

Well I probably can call myself a missionary, as most of the countries I have visited are just starting to play women's football. . . . In Pakistan they were so thankful that I came in spite of the political tension the country faces. I go in schools to try to get the interest of football to the young girls. I do have talks with the education and sport minister to try to convince them to establish football in the curriculum, to give the girls the opportunity to play football. I work very closely with the Football Federation and the women's football committee, if there is one. Of course I do a lot of training camps—like now I will go to Kashmir—a very pure area in the north of Pakistan where a few years ago they had an earthquake. I will bring them balls, bibs, cones, and shoes so they are able to do some training.

She feels that both coaches and players would take to the sport in the region if it were introduced in schools. "I do coaching classes special for teachers who don't have much knowledge of football; the main job is to get the teacher's interest in football so they will teach it in their sport lessons." In Sri Lanka this approach worked well; after starting the sport in 2002, there was now a good quality school competition and annual national championships at the U-17, U-15, and U-13 levels, and Staab had begun to establish a U-17 national team. In Pakistan, where she had been spending months at a time, she found great enthusiasm from around two hundred girls who play: "They are very keen on learning. They love football, they like to train and play." But she has found that there is no soccer in school, and the infrastructure is poor. "There are hardly any safe football fields, and the men's football is struggling, as cricket is their number 1 sport. A lot of grass-roots [work] needs to be done to develop women's football in Pakistan."

Staab believes a general problem in the region is a lack of coaches, particularly women, so developing them was a critical requirement, "There are hardly any female coaches, as they have no experience. It will take a next generation to get female coaches, as the ones who are playing now hopefully will become coaches." Again, cultural and religious prescripts come into play, as some countries do not allow men to coach women.

Coaching-wise, Staab has found that she really has to start at the very beginning with her students in many of these countries: "They have to learn a lot of technical skills before they learn any tactical skills. The other big problem is that they are not so fit, thus it takes some time to get them a certain fitness — they love the game, but they have never been taught how to do it right." She loves the fact that they are so thankful she is involved: "Especially the players appreciate that I am a woman so I have more understanding, more feelings, and of course you're like a friend to them." She is particularly proud that she has been "brave enough to go to these developing countries with all the problems they are facing and give them some support to develop women's football."

A skeptical press is another barrier to overcome throughout the region, since their agenda setting typically reinforces traditional stereotypes, making it harder for parents to accept their daughters' interest in playing. In Pakistan the first national women's football championship drew the *Pakistan Daily Times'* rebuke. The paper branded the game stereotypically as a "catfight" after it took over ten minutes to calm the teams after a penalty kick was awarded. This happens so frequently on the men's side that it is almost unremarkable.

The progress of the sport in many countries is heartening, but advancements will always involve struggles — for access to decent fields, quality equipment, compensation for time loss at work, well-organized camps, and travel arrangements — until there is real societal change with legal and social gender equity. This will not happen overnight. The advantage that the women have in the region, which is still not the case in North America, is that soccer is vastly popular on the men's side, particularly in Iran, Jordan, Qatar, and Saudi Arabia. The game of soccer itself is acceptable; it's the idea that women can play such an assertive and demanding sport that many have been reticent to accept. There are positive steps taking place every day for the introduction and growth of girls' and women's soccer, but more needs to be done.

The Future

FIFA has done a commendable job in promoting the women's game globally and is cognizant of the religious and cultural barriers that exist in this part of the world. FIFA, the CAF, and the AFC have a difficult balance here of encouraging countries to support the game while not being seen as draconian. The latter would just lead to hard feelings that government and sports officials *must* have female teams, and they could respond by putting forth the absolute minimum effort required. FIFA has supported the development of women's soccer by mandating that a certain percentage of the $1 million share of World Cup proceeds that each of the 208 member nations receives every four years must be spent on the female game (in 2008 it was raised to 15 percent.)

The most visible tournament on the calendar is the Women's World Cup, which is held every four years. In the AFC and CAF, every World Cup sees a few more countries attempting to qualify. Of the forty-six members of the Asian Football Confederation (including most of the Middle East nations, such as Iran, Jordan, Syria, and United Arab Emirates), eleven entered the preliminary rounds in 1999, fourteen in 2003, and seventeen in 2007; but significantly, none were west of India. Only sixteen entered for the 2011 qualifiers, but Jordan and Palestine debuted along with Iran, Kyrgyzstan, and Uzbekistan. At this rate, AFC won't have a full complement of members in the preliminaries until the year 2035.

It's a slightly better story for the African Confederation. For the 2007 World Cup, almost half (twenty-six) of CAF's fifty-three members entered the preliminary rounds, compared with nineteen in 2003 and fifteen in 1999. This is before multiple withdrawals before games because the federations were unable to raise the travel costs, a situation that is common on the men's side as well. Eritrea and Ethiopia participated in 2003 but not in 2007, and 2007 marked the debut of Djibouti and Algeria to international competition. The global recession contributed to only seventeen teams competing in the 2011 qualifiers, with Tunisia and Morocco entering for the first time. The long-term goal is to someday see Libya, Mauritania, and Sudan compete as well.

Realistically, it would take some time before a country from the Middle East can hope to qualify for the World Cup, but they still gain experience from playing against more accomplished teams. To help spur development, the confederations could encourage smaller regional events for national teams. The AFC and CAF both have sub-regional international events on the men's club and national team sides such as the West Asian Football Federation Championships, the West African Championships, the East and Central African Championships (CECACAF), and the Gulf Cup. If the confederations sponsor and help with expenses for these tournaments, the teams would gain more competitive experience so they could eventually have a realistic chance of making a full confederation qualification tournament for a Women's World Cup or youth event.

Specifically for North Africa, the CAF could attempt to stage the African Women's Championships outside of western and southern Africa. By taking the premier continental event to countries like Algeria, Egypt, or Tunisia (as the confederation tries to do on the men's side), they would introduce more people to the game, particularly youth; thereby increasing the number of players and the general appreciation level for women players.

FIFA also could commit to host one of its signature events for women (World Cup, U-20, or U-17 Championships) in the Middle East, North Africa, or preferably in both regions. The tournaments could be tied into a regional health initiative, linking with the United Nations, the World Health Organization, or one of FIFA's charity partners. With Emirates Airlines as a multimillion dollar sponsor of FIFA Championships, FIFA has a unique opportunity to take a youth World Cup or even the full event to the United Arab Emirates, working with Emirates Airlines' contacts and business acumen. There would certainly not be the attendance draw of a United States, Germany, or China, but the publicity would help to further the expansion of the game while presenting role models for youth in the Gulf and northern African states. After the 1999 World Cup, Keith Cooper, then FIFA Director of Communications said, "This [profitable U.S. run event] isn't the real world. . . . If we're really interested, and we are, about developing the women's game, then obviously you've got to play the missionary bit and take it around the world."

Another important development emphasis, particularly in the

Arab countries, is to introduce the game at the school level. In Europe and South America, sports clubs are the developmental model, but in the Middle East they can be built later, after the game is introduced to children and teachers via the education system. Along these lines, promoting regional youth tourneys like a Dallas Cup in the United States or the Gothia Cup in Sweden, divided by level of competition and age, would bring youth together from countries that otherwise wouldn't have the chance to travel for games.

FIFA, the CAF, and and AFC are working hard to increase the number of instructional courses for women coaches, referees, and administrators in the region. Men are not allowed to coach women in athletics in some countries. Experienced coaches and players from Europe and North America can provide inspiration and their perspective on growing the game. U.S. college coaches could be enticed with an opportunity to scout prospective national team players, and helping local players find a suitable college to study at and play for in the United States, while building their own teams. To this end the U.S. Soccer Federation, in conjunction with the U.S. State Department, sponsored an International Sports Initiative in 2006 for four-day clinics in Bahrain, Nigeria, South Africa, and Uganda. According to a press brochure, the purpose was to "educate the target audience on American values with a goal of highlighting the positive aspects of American culture." In addition, "the clinics showed that sports initiatives can help youth discover that success in athletics translates into life skills, long-term well-being, and physical health. The values of teamwork, respect and leadership were stressed as a dialog was opened through the clinics that also included an appropriate level of technical training." Men's and women's national team players and coaches participated, including former U.S. National Team assistant Lauren Gregg and former internationals Shannon MacMillan, Cindy Parlow, and Tiffany Roberts.

Monika Staab is very optimistic about the future of the sport in the region: "I hope every Muslim country, with the exception

3. U.S. National Team forward Cindy Parlow talks in Bahrain in 2006 with clinic participants who attended in a variety of playing attire. (U.S. Soccer Federation–U.S. State Department.)

of Saudi Arabia, where women's football is officially forbidden, will have a national team in five years' time. I hope I can do my contribution to this. In ten years' time, every country should have a league competition throughout the year, as most of them play a tournament once a year. In twenty years, I hope women's football is accepted in society and every girl who wishes to play football can go out in the street and play it." Arab and Islamic nations have shown some progress but still have some distance to go in introducing and building development structures for women. After a point, social change will be needed before there is vibrant girls' and women's soccer like there is in northern Europe or North America. The effort is definitely worth the investment, for the end result will be confident, fit girls and women who have fun while learning cooperation in a team environment. They will have earned invaluable life lessons even if they never play in a Women's World Cup.

6

Challenges and Successes in Africa

According to FIFA's latest Big Count survey, in Africa only 2.9 percent of its registered players are female, the lowest of any confederation and well below the global average of 9.8 percent. The sport is taking some beginning steps in countries like Rwanda, Liberia, and Namibia, but is well established in larger countries like Nigeria, Ghana, and South Africa. As in the Middle East, soccer can collide with traditional views of the role of women, but there are unique aspects as well. In some countries females can play when they're younger, but then they are urged to give up the game when they marry. Soccer, particularly at the national team level, has been distracted by money, gender identity, and recruiting foreigners. In Africa, some "promoters" of the sport also get involved for nefarious reasons.

Money Squabbles

Finding money for women's soccer in Africa always seems to be a Broadway theater production, with various characters, intrigue, and generally unhappy conclusions. Resources are spread thin for basic services, and wars and natural disasters (like famines and floods) have further depleted individual and governmental funding on a continent striving to develop economically. Throughout Africa, most sport development efforts are government supported, unlike other regions where mass supported social clubs or private ventures drive the sport. Women's soccer has to petition for funds against other nonsports initiatives, putting it into a competitive situation. Funding decisions can be capricious.

Ben Popoola, a native of Nigeria and a well respected former women's soccer head coach at Appalachian State University in Boone, North Carolina, was the assistant coach for Nigeria's 2003 Women's World Cup Team. Popoola saw firsthand the impact money issues had on the game in Africa and hindered his coaching: "In terms of how the nation [Nigerian Federation] treated the players, it needs to be better. Now they use incentives, money instead of national pride. When I played, I just wanted to represent the national team. Now, if they don't give them what they promise, even for a qualifying game, they refuse to play or perform badly because they're psychologically down." Popoola discovered that it's not just national federation officials making bonus promises; individuals or members of certain club teams or regions negotiated awards with specific players. Popoola explained, "Ministers and state officials made promises to them we didn't even know about. You couldn't tell if they would show up for practice." Popoola added, "For a coach, it was the worst nightmare."

The bonuses can add up to serious money for the players. After Nigeria's triumph in the 2006 African Championships, Nigeria's charismatic President Olusegun Obasanjo awarded each player (whom he endearingly referred to as "my daughters") nine thousand dollars. Popoola said, "In Africa, we don't have the luxury of Title IX when it comes to the women's side. It's not well funded." Men's soccer is the priority, and if there is anything left over, then it goes to the women, unless the women's agenda coincides with some personal interests of people in power. In 2006 Izetta Sombo Wesley, the president of Liberia's Football Federation, told about how the women's team suddenly became important to officials who wanted to travel to an away game: "When our national [women's] U-20 team was to play Algeria in the FIFA World Cup qualifiers, the government said they didn't have any money. But I went to FIFA and got them to fund our trip. But after we beat Algeria and then drew with Nigeria in the first leg of the last round of qualifiers, suddenly everyone wanted to be part of the trip to Nigeria. Suddenly the money became available for government officials to travel to Nigeria." However, big problems can occur when players do not receive their promised payments; sadly, a too common occurrence.

National Team vs. Club Conflicts

During the African Women's Championships in the fall of 2006, Nigerian National Team Coach Ntiero Effiom recalled three players from their Swedish top flight club Qbik of Karlstad: Faith Ikidi, Yinka Kudaisi, and Maureen Mmadu. However, Qbik did not receive the request thirty days before the event as mandated by FIFA for nondesignated international release periods on the FIFA calendar (for World Championships and other major international events). Qbik insisted that they needed the players during a relegation battle; in Sweden the last two teams in the league table are replaced by two in the Second Division, which usually results in a substantial loss of sponsorships and grants. FIFA sided with the Swedes, determining that the AWC was not an official tournament, so clubs were not obligated to release players, (a puzzling decision given that the tournament doubled as the World Cup qualifiers). The players were torn between jeopardizing their national team spots, which had initially helped them secure their club jobs, and angering their current employer. "We're just standing in the middle of this and can't really do anything," midfielder Mmadu noted. "We want to help keep Qbik in the Damallsvenskan [the Swedish Women's league], but we also want to help Nigeria. The African Championships is the qualification tournament for the 2007 World Cup, so it's really important for the country." The Nigerian FA amped up the pressure, telling the trio that they expected them to turn up at camp immediately.

Qbik chairman Lars-Inge Hallstensson acknowledged the difficult position his imports faced but also explained the club's viewpoint: "We are the ones that are paying their wages. Unless we get a FIFA decision that says otherwise, they're playing for us." Head coach Kjell Petersson added that he couldn't envision what his lineup would look like without his three Nigerian stars. He was soon to find out. After FIFA's ruling that the club could keep the players, the trio nonetheless bolted for Nigeria's camp two days later. Qbik officials found out only when the players didn't show up for training. Qbik's Hallstensson and his board ruled that the players were in breach of contract and fired them. In spite of the turmoil surrounding the club, Qbik won their last match against Mallbacken 2–0 to stay up.

Ikidi, Kudaisi, and Mmadu returned to Karlstad after the African Championships, dismayed to find they were unemployed. They tried to claim they had been given permission by Qbik's coaches and players to leave. Petersson denied their claim; though there was widespread sympathy for the Nigerians' predicament, the club's board stood by their termination decision even after meeting with them. Chairman Hallstensson said the club really had no choice, even though they were talented players, "We can't have players that just leave when we're struggling for survival." Nigeria's FA, much too late, realized the value of having the three play in a top European league ahead of the World Cup and offered to pay the player's wages for three months and have the national team play a friendly with Qbik. Hallstensson's response was a firm no: "We have left this behind us." The players were not only without professional contracts but were further disappointed with the Nigerian FA's microscopic compensation for playing in the AWC. Ikidi and Mmadu caught on with Linköpings FC in Sweden the next season, while Kudaisi played with Pelican Stars back home. Mmadu, continuing to play with top clubs in Sweden and Norway, has since boycotted the national team after the 2007 World Cup over their handling of the Qbik incident, in a way probably helping her foreign club career. The shortsided FA administrators pressured their players, who ultimately ended up losers no matter what they decided. Overseas clubs are now understandably reluctant to sign Nigerian National Team players who may disappear during the season.

2007 World Cup: Pay Disputes and "Win with the Preacher"

Nigeria's FA always seems to have payment conflicts with their players. Less than a year after the Qbik fiasco, the Nigerian FA's frugality caused a major distraction during the 2007 World Cup. Only a few hours ahead of their crucial game with the United States, which would determine if the Super Falcons would advance to the tournament quarterfinals, the players refused to train. They claimed that the FA had not paid their promised match fees of U.S.$750 for their draw with Sweden, and if they waited until after the tournament, they risked losing their leverage. Togo had done the same thing in 2006 at the Men's World Cup before FIFA intervened and paid the players out of what they owed the Togolese Federation for making the tournament. Not surprisingly, the same thing had happened a few months before at the All African Games in Algeria, when the Nigerian women threatened not to play their semifinal because they had not received their allowances and were dissatisfied with their food. After negotiations in China, the team members agreed to take $500 a person but were shocked when FA chairman Alhaji Sani Lulu Abdullahi cut the bonus to only $400. They also felt that their $30 per diem food allowance was not adequate, given that the federation had originally promised $75. NFA media officer Ademola Olajire denied the $75 figure, saying the FA had promised only $30. Olajire admitted that there was no money in the team's coffers, saying the team was operating at "zero level." As head coach Ntiero Effiom succinctly put it, "Without money, there is no chance." The Nigerians lost to the United States 1–0 in horrible conditions from an approaching typhoon on the coast of China, and Ntiero was later replaced as coach.

To add to Ntiero's World Cup woes, he blamed the Falcons' second game loss to North Korea on an "unscrupulous pastor," according to Lagos newspaper *The Guardian*. "That pastor has been collecting money from players to offer special prayers for them so that they can play well and outshine the opponent." Ntiero argued that the man of the cloth and NFA delegation member was a meddling distraction: "When players should be resting, he is there keeping them busy. I do not understand how that man could have been allowed free reign in our camp." It was a good question since the minister came not from Nigeria but from California to give spiritual comfort to the team.

Unfortunately, Nigeria's mismanagement continued in 2008. A pre-Olympics tour to the United States had to be canceled when half the players were unable to receive U.S. visas. They lost much-needed tune-ups against the U-20 National Teams of Mexico and Canada and local W-League sides. Worse still, the Nigerian Football Federation had not contacted tournament officials by the day of their first game; the tournament organizers learned the news instead from Nigerian media members who had planned to travel with them. As one team coach who came to scout commented, "They had some visa issues . . . again; it's not the first time and probably won't be the last."

Passports, Gender, and Age Checks

A common problem for both sexes on the continent is player eligibility. At CAF and other international competitions, there are regularly questions as to players' ability to play for their national team, based on citizenship, age, and even gender questions. Until eliminated, these will forever cast a pall over African teams' involvement in these tournaments, and could scare international club teams away from signing these players.

Recruiting players from other countries for the sole purpose of playing for the national team is a recent trend globally, but has increased dramatically in Africa. In order to qualify for international football, FIFA rules state that players must have been born in the territory of the relevant team, have a biological parent or grandparent from that territory, or have lived continuously in the country for at least two years. Equatorial Guinea won the African Championships at home in 2008 with a team comprising only four home-based players, with the rest coming from other West African countries and from Brazil. Many men's and women's national teams around the world have players born in other countries. The difference is when players are recruited solely to play for the national side. On the men's side, smaller African nations such as Mauritania, Rwanda, and Niger have recruited foreign players for national team duty in recent years. In the Middle East, Qatar was investigated after recruiting Brazilian footballers—including the infamous Emerson who accepted Qatari citizenship and a multimillion dollar bonus payment in order to play in World Cup qualifiers. Emerson had previously played at the youth level for Brazil, but he changed his age and used a falsified passport to convince Qatari officials that he was eligible to play for them.

Other complaints are based on gender, specifically whether transgender athletes should be competing with women. During the 2008 African Women's Championship, there were allegations that the champions Equatorial Guinea had two hermaphrodite players, with Nigeria being the most strident with their complaints. The African Confederation later agreed to institute gender testing to prevent hermaphrodite, or intersexed, players from competing in the next AWC. They were wise to act cautiously during the tournament. The traditional determinant for sex has been the sex chromosome—XX is female, XY is male, but defective enzymes can cause discrepancies in this formula. Physiologically, females can be born with male genes and even have tiny male genitalia. Others are born with external female organs and internal male organs or vice versa. There are also cases where even some individual chromosomes are XX and others XY. When the adrenal glands produce excess testosterone, individuals appear genetically female and experience menstrual periods but can also have decidedly male traits like masculine build, thicker body hair, and a deep voice. FIFA's rules necessitate menstruation as the key criterion to compete among women, even if the athlete has some combination of male and female reproductive organs. Nigeria itself experienced the situation two years earlier, with a sixteen-year-old invited to a national team camp but not allowed to compete because during her team medical exam she was found to be intersexed. Her doctor's report, released with her permission, said, "She has [a] gender identification problem. She was examined and found to have the features of female, beginning from her external appearance, voice and reaction to issues. In my opinion, she is phenotypically female and should not be discriminated against. However she requires other investigations, surgery and hormone therapy to put her in perfect condition." Despite the doctor's recommendation, the player was banned from all women's soccer, both club and national team, until she had thirteen thousand dollars worth of surgery and treatment. Aside from the disheartening idea of performing risky and expensive surgery merely to conform to societal expectations, individual rights need to be carefully weighed against competitive balance. Too many judgments on these cases are made at local levels on a snap judgment, harming the individual the most.

This issue attracted international attention in the summer of 2009 when an eighteen-year-old middle-distance runner from rural South Africa named Caster Semenya won a gold medal in the 800-meter race at the track and field World Championships in Berlin. After testing, she was said, by Australian media reports, to have external female characteristics but internal testes rather than a womb and ovaries. In July of 2010 Semenya was officially reinstated by the International Association of Athletic Federation for future meets, although the organization did not comment on the medical details of their investigation.

The Semenya case showed that all international sports bodies, working with top medical minds, must clearly set their definitions on different forms of hermaphrodites and their eligibility for competitions. Without clearly communicated standards, these athletes will face abuse from fans, hostility from players and coaches, and continual personal questions because some officials see them as a threat to competitive balance.

Another issue that comes up for both sexes in Africa as well is doubt of the players' true ages, particularly at the youth level. In some cases, it is outright falsification. One former Nigerian

National Player admitted that she was twenty-seven when she played in the U-20 World Cup. Older national team players help younger players remember that they are now three or four years younger than what their birth certificate shows, particularly when they talk with foreigners. Other cases are due to a lack of standardized birth certificates and key documents supporting an athlete's true age. No one thinks that all administrators are actively falsifying ages, but there does seem to be a lack of vigilance on the issue. Particularly at the age group level with international titles at stake, the advantage of using more mature players is clear. Multiple excuses of "sloppy record keeping" or nonexistent birth certificates can be perceived as a dodge and instantly raise questions of veracity, particularly with such an active black market of bogus documents in Nigeria in particular. At the 2006 African Women's Championship, which doubled as FIFA's Regional World Cup Qualifiers, fifteen of the eighteen players listed on FIFA.com for debutants Equatorial Guinea were born on January 1, 1990. Three years after the tournament, the roster was still on the website. Again, this issue makes international club teams wary of importing Africans who may be several years older than they claim.

It must be noted that the passport and age issues are emerging problems in other regions as well. In early 2010 the Union of European Football Associations (UEFA) suspended the U-19 National Side of Azerbaijan from its U-19 European Championships qualifying tournament as well as from the 2012 tournament after it discovered age discrepancies for several players. Furthermore, six players were suspended because they were citizens of other countries (five Russians and one Moldovan) but playing under altered names with Azerbaijani papers.

We have seen a number of issues that African women's soccer officials need to work on to improve the transparency of the game. However, we do see cases on a number of different fronts, including more women as coaches, as administrators, and on the grass-roots level, that indicate that things are improving for the women's game.

African Women Fight Cultural Barriers

Just because women's football is permitted doesn't mean it can't be abused. Two clear examples are from Uganda and South Africa. The Ugandan National Team coach, a man, was relieved of his duties in 1998 after allegations of sexual harassment of some of the players. It took two years to restart the program after that setback, but then the new administration banned married players from conjugal visits with their husbands and even barred any player from having conversations with men for two weeks ahead of an African Championships qualifier. The team did make the eight-team finals but missed the semifinals on goal difference. Interestingly, the lead administrator who instituted these controversial rules was a woman.

In South Africa, long-time coach and educator Fran Hilton-Smith discussed the difficulties she has found over the years in recruiting players due to cultural barriers among the country's many ethnic groups: "From simple things like a belief that it was unlucky for women to play before men, to more serious issues such as men starting up women's football teams because it was seen as an easy way to develop a pool of girlfriends they could use for sex and drop if the women did not comply, have all impacted on the willingness of women to play football." The South African Federation was able to largely stop the latter problem by establishing rules that there must always be a woman in a team's management, and when teams travel, men stay in one hostel building and women in another. It's ironic that in 1997, a judge had to step in and order the South African soccer body to allow women to participate in running their own sport, after males had co-opted all the leadership positions for the previous three years. However, as Hilton-Smith explains, "The main barrier to women playing in South Africa still exists, and that is, a woman's role as a wife and mother is seen as the priority, no matter how talented she is."

In Nigeria, former national team player and assistant coach Ann Onyekeynna Chiejine's parents objected to football because "they felt that football would make me so muscular that no man would want to marry me and I would end up being unable to bear children." At the 1999 World Cup, she was the only married player on Nigeria's team, with two young daughters at home. "Some feel that when you get married, that is the end of your career, and that if you play football, you won't be able to have children," Chiejine said. "I am showing that you can still play and it will not disturb you." Chiejine ended up playing while five months' pregnant at the 2000 Women's African Championship and has four children in total.

Young players ultimately have the best chance to change their parents' and other adults' opinions by explaining the benefits they gain from soccer. In Namibia, where the sport is growing since being introduced to girls at schools, Belinda Mbaindjikua, a sixteen-year-old from the capital Windhoek, credits the game with keeping her and her friends "away from clubs, drinking and smoking as well as teenage pregnancies." This statement resonates with parents of daughters around the world. In Morocco, long-time player and fan Maria Aamoud believes that soccer plays a vital role in personal growth and fulfillment: "It's a lot more fun [than other sports], builds up all-round fitness and encourages good mental character. You learn about teamwork and putting your thoughts and ideas into practice. It's really important that you make your contribution to the efforts of the team. You have to put any fear of the strength of opponents to the back of your mind and show determination to win through."

Women Coaches for Africa

Popoola believes that African players need better coaches who are in tune with women's soccer: "Men [in Africa] think they can coach [women] the same way as with men. Women don't respond to yelling. Women need to be praised first before you can point out things to do. Presentation [of ideas and criticism] has to be different." In North Africa, Morocco's Maria Aamoud concurs: "Women's football would have a better chance of developing in Morocco and elsewhere, if more qualified trainers were recruited."

The continent also needs to develop women coaches, particularly in Islamic countries. Ann Chiejine, the only female on Nigeria's coaching staff during China's Women's World Cup in 2007, talked enthusiastically about her continued involvement with the sport. She was a tall teenager who was having trouble adjusting to playing a wide midfield position on her team. She switched to goalkeeper and quickly advanced into the national team and played in the first Women's World Cup in 1991 as well as two more editions. Soccer has allowed her to see the world. By coaching the next generation of national team players, she is "thanking the people that helped me throughout my career." The African game needs more trainers like Ann Chiejine who have playing experience on the global stage.

Grass-roots Hopes

In many African nations the game is strictly amateur and will be for some time, which unfortunately tends to keep it a game for girls and teenagers and not a sport they can play in their adult years, like swimming or tennis. Talal Abdelatif coached the Moroccan Women's National Team and reflected that "the biggest problem is that women's football only receives the bare minimum of financial support in Africa, and the amateur status of our players makes it hard for them to find jobs." So when good players leave school, they are more likely to choose a traditional lifestyle of marriage or possibly a career rather than continue playing a sport with a future that is not yet charted. South Africa's Federation took the progressive step a few years ago when they started to pay women's national team players 3,000 Rand (approximately U.S. $400) per game, a significant amount to young women from disadvantaged backgrounds.

Education affects African women's soccer, not only for the personal benefits but also because it makes it easier for coaches to teach concepts. Ben Popoola explained, "Not until we push [African] high schools and colleges to have [soccer for girls/women] will we see more kids on the national team. That will help with systems of play, functional play. They need to understand concepts;

it's hard for them to grasp what we are teaching when they aren't in school. [Without school soccer] they just play street soccer."

Fred Crentsil, the head of Ghana's Women's Soccer and an FA Board member, also prioritizes his players' education: "We are now looking for more academically qualified girls to play in the national team because we have come to realize that those girls who have gone to school or university find it a lot easier to assimilate the coach's instructions. Those who don't have a proper education tend to have problems, particularly the ones who don't speak English. If we can start by educating them, even at a general level, I am sure that you will see a real improvement in the intelligence of their play on the field."

Ghana showed their commitment to developing their players' minds as well as their playing skills when they sent twenty-three-year-old striker Rumanatu Tahiru 3,500 miles to the University of Hull in England in 2007 for a three-year program. Ghana also sent their administration manager to Hull for a year-long course in business management. Crentsil explained their cooperation with Hull:

> Together with the university, we looked at ways we could collaborate and decided that it would be good to do a training program together. That's how it all started, and it was decided that we would take the team over for a couple of weeks while the students were off-campus. The girls were shown round the facilities, went through a training program, did a lot of sports science work on their stamina and endurance, and I believe the university have been doing a lot of research that can help both them and us. While we were there, we also played [English Premiership side] Leeds United, who we beat 3–2.

Ghana's creative approach is a winning situation for both sides. The university can study elite athletes and benefit from the cultural exchanges, while Tahiru gains a college education (hopefully to be joined by others) and can play top-quality club ball with Leeds United.

Across the continent on the youth side, there have also been encouraging steps forward. In Nigeria an annual tournament organized by the Amalgamated Nigeria Women Football Club Coaches brings together female footballers from all over the country. The event not only showcases new young players but provides older players the opportunity to transfer to different teams. Even some professionals abroad come home during their holidays to play. The tournament has grown to such an extent that in 2008 the semifinals and the finals were played at the National Stadium in Lagos. Basil Obeta, the chairman of the Local Organizing Committee said, "We have always used the [field] hockey pitch for all our matches, but this time, the Director-General of the National Sports Commission has approved the use of the main bowl for the semifinal and finals. This will raise the standard of the championship and even motivate some of our young players who have been dreaming of playing in the main bowl." Another plus is that the tournament has attracted players from Ghana and Benin. The first and second divisions of the Nigerian women's league (with over thirty teams) has also helped advance the sport in neighboring markets by inviting players from countries such as Cameroon, Ghana, Ivory Coast, Senegal, and Sierra Leone.

In South Africa, there was regular women's football coverage on the nation's top football TV show, *Laduma,* as well as live broadcasts of the national team's international matches. At one stage, South African women's football also had its own dedicated weekly primetime television show. The TV presence in the country exceeds some major women's soccer supporting countries in other regions.

In Zanzibar, Tanzania, after pressure from the semi-autonomous republic's Ministry of Information, Culture and Sports, the football association decided to start a women's soccer league, involving primary and secondary school players to develop prospects for representative sides. Part of the motivation seemed to be that the minister was disenchanted with the Zanzibar Football Association's poor planning, which hastened a decline in standards, particularly for the women's game.

Women in Management Positions

Women have begun to see success in the region even within the men's game. In 2003, Izetta Sombo-Wesley was appointed president of the Liberian Football Association, becoming the first woman to head an African federation. She has since been joined by Lydie Nsekera of Burundi. In South Africa, Natasia Tsihls was the chairperson of the Women's Football Committee and the only female director of the 2010 FIFA Men's World Cup Organizing Committee. Previously, she had been the owner and managing director of the top men's professional club Mamelodi Sundowns. She talked about what she faced as a woman in a very male-oriented enterprise: "To be a woman at this level of football is really something, particularly in South Africa, where women have traditionally been treated as second class citizens and even worse in football. At one stage many years ago, my life was even threatened. But the resistance has since dropped away because of what I have achieved. Under my direction, Sundowns won six Professional Soccer League [PSL] titles between 1990 and 2000, with the worst placing during this time being fourth. This is the most won by anyone, man or woman."

Good things are happening throughout Africa, and the sport is growing in numbers and acceptance. Administrators owe it to players, coaches, and fans to step up their organizational and financial commitments. Too often, money difficulties or other tangential dramas dominate the headlines of stories coming out of Africa. Focusing on growing the buoyant potential of the game should be the primary goal. Tobias Hermonn, a female coach in Namibia, believes strongly that "women have the willpower, discipline and need the encouragement to play soccer because they have potential. Nowadays we can't underestimate them." African soccer in general will be richer by encouraging and supporting the women's game, rather than subjugating it. The potential is certainly there, waiting to be taken seriously, and for attitudes toward women's societal roles to change.

7

Latin America

Fighting Machismo Attitudes

Despite the immense popularity of the sport throughout Latin America, women players struggle throughout the region against a traditional mindset of appropriate activities that don't align with playing a dynamic and physical game. Soccer has long been a man's domain, played and followed passionately, while women's soccer has been legislated against, ridiculed, and ignored. In Brazil, seen as the world's leading light for creativity, brilliant individual skills, and national team success (with five Men's World Cup wins out of nineteen tournaments from 1930 to 2010—the most of any country), the men's game is an obsession bordering on religious fervor. Women's soccer to this day struggles for funding, respect, and followers, despite producing wonderful teams and players. In 2006 females accounted for only 1 percent of the registered players throughout the country, with approximately 2.1 million registered male players compared with only 27,000 females. Until vast improvements to the support structure for women's soccer are made, Brazil's top players will continue to play abroad.

In Mexico, another fanatical soccer country whose men's professional league teams are among the richest in the hemisphere and regularly import top talent from throughout South America, women have received indifferent support, though there are signs that things are slowly starting to improve. To grow the sport in the 1990s, Mexican Federation officials had to rely on Americans of Mexican descent, some of whom couldn't even speak Spanish, and a former World Cup star who was coaching college soccer in Los Angeles. We will start with Brazil, looking at the state of the game there and why so many top players flee for clubs abroad. We will also hear from some North Americans who played professionally there, before looking at Mexico's strategy to boost the sport.

Marta and Brazil's National Team

There's a Brazilian soccer player known by one name who denotes style, creativity, panache, and pure joy for the sport, a player universally known and admired who came to the United States to help grow the game. Pele is a good guess; he made quite an impact and introduced the sport to many Americans when he joined the New York Cosmos in 1975. But the women's game also has a single-name Brazilian superstar who can transcend the game and take it to an art form with her amazing dribbling skills and jet-engine speed. Marta Vierra da Silva, better known as Marta, grew up playing soccer with boys in the streets of the western Brazilian state of Alagoas. She said about those early days, "My biggest battle was to fight against prejudice. Some kids didn't like the idea of a girl playing with them, and I got a lot of verbal abuse. But, at the same time, I was never the last pick when they were choosing teams, so that was a sign to me that I was on the right path." She left home at fourteen and rode a bus for three days to Rio de Janeiro—five hundred miles away—to try out for Vasco de Gama's women's team. She made the squad, and by age sixteen was playing for Brazil's national U-19 side.

The 2002 U-19 World Cup was really the first time soccer fans globally learned about the five-foot-three phenom; Marta guided her team to the semifinals before the host Canadians eked out a penalty kick win after a 1–1 tie in Edmonton before 35,000 fans. After an appearance in the 2003 Women's World Cup at age seventeen, Marta was soon on the road again. Hampered by a lack of support for the women's game in her home country, she landed in Umeå, Sweden, near the Arctic Circle. "Some clubs in Brazil have women's teams, but there are no regular championships, so I had to move to Europe," Marta explained. "It's a huge sacrifice to live that far away from my family, but it was my only option in order to develop my pro career." Rene Simoes, her national team coach at the time and known for leading vast underdog Jamaica to the 1998 Men's World Cup, was fully supportive of Marta's move, saying in 2004, "The professional structure at Umeå IK, the strength of the team and the quality of opposition in Sweden can only be good for her. There are not many teams here in Brazil. The few sides we have are not professional enough, so Marta would not develop here. If you want to reach the top in women's football, you have to play in a top league, like those in Europe. That's why I'm delighted that Marta is in Sweden with Umeå IK."

In Sweden, Marta was nothing short of brilliant. In 2004, her first season, Umeå finished second in the league (known as the Damallsvenskan) but won the European Club Championship (then UEFA Cup, but now Champions League) with an 8–0 aggregate (home and away) win over German power Frankfurt. Marta was top scorer in the league with twenty-two goals. In 2005 Umeå captured the league title behind her league-leading twenty-one goals. In 2006 she again was the top scorer with twenty-one goals as Umeå defended their league title. They also captured another UEFA Cup with an 11–1 aggregate win over Kolbotn FK of Norway. In 2007, they lost their European title in the final of a close affair (0–1 aggregate against Arsenal of England) but did capture the domestic cup along with their third league title in a row, not losing a game in the process. Marta's twenty-three goals were two behind Göteborg's FC Swedish international Lotta Schelin. In 2008 Umeå again won the league, and in her final game in the country, Marta scored six goals in Umeå's 11–1 demolition of Balinge to tie Malmö's Dutch striker Manon Melis for the league lead with twenty-three.

Marta's salary rose over the years in relation to her play and what she added to Umeå's side. In 2007 she reportedly made between between $75,000 and $85,000 over ten months, up from her 2006 annual salary of $55,000; sponsor Puma contributed about half that amount. With a professional league in the planning process in the United States for 2009, Umeå more than doubled Marta's salary for 2008 to $187,000, making her easily the best paid women's player in the world. Umeå realized they had a rare jewel in Marta, but even though their home attendances were three to four times the Damallsvenskan average of about nine hundred customers a game, their revenues were not enough to prevent her from eventually leaving Sweden. Umeå couldn't compete with the appeal of playing in the best league in the world and the lucrative sponsorship opportunities that could come her way in America. She joined Women's Professional Soccer's Los Angeles Sol for their inaugural season in 2009 for a reported $500,000 a year deal, guaranteed for three years. Though not solely due to Marta's departure, since Umeå had reduced their spending during the global economic crisis, Umeå finished second in the league to Linköpings FC. They were well behind newcomers Piteå in the attendance derby (1,336 vs. 1,820), dropping 30 percent from the year before, nearer the league average of 824. More of their top stars were recruited to WPS for 2010, including midfielders Mami Yamiguchi (Japan), Elaine (Brazil), and forwards Madelaine Edlund (Sweden) and Ramona Bachmann (Switzerland).

Teammates and opponents raved about Marta's play during her time in Scandinavia. Swedish star and club teammate Hanna Ljungberg called her "the best player we have ever had in Sweden." Retired international superstar Mia Hamm said, "She's electric, with an array of moves that can make foes look like you've never played soccer before. She could be the greatest of all women's players."

Playing abroad, Marta unfortunately encountered one of the common occurrences on the men's side—the tug-of-war between club and country when the latter requests releases for international events. Though not as nasty as the standoff between Qbik and Nigeria, Umeå barred Marta from participating in the FIFA U-20

Women's World Championship in Russia in August of 2004, the last year of her eligibility for the age-group event. Brazil finished third after losing to eventual champion North Korea on penalty kicks in the semifinals. Umeå did however release her for the full national team's Olympic Games participation in Greece in 2004. Marta sparkled as Brazil made the final, where the Canarinos outplayed the Americans but finally succumbed in overtime 2–1.

Brazil's Olympic team coach Rene Simoes regretted that federation support for the women's team was "almost nonexistent," not allowing him to build on the Olympic success. To prove the point, the silver medal winners sat idle for over *two years*, not playing a single competitive international. The domestic league for women was treated as an afterthought and didn't provide the skill development needed for elite athletes. Some national team players did not even have club teams to join and had to train on their own or play *futsal* (five-a-side) in the street, just as they did as kids. A few lucky ones caught on with teams in Europe, America, or Asia. The rust showed: less than a month after their first friendly games in Korea in late 2006, they lost to the much less experienced Argentina 2–0 in the final of the South American World Cup qualifying tournament, though both teams were assured spots in China. Brazil's fall from their Olympic Games form was devastating; essentially they were starting over, leading Simoes to exclaim, "We can only hope for a miracle" in the upcoming 2007 World Cup.

In preparing for the World Cup, things did not start well for coach Jorge Barcellos, who replaced Simoes. Brazil played the United States in June 2007 in New Jersey, and their losing score line of 2–0 belied how disjointed and confused they appeared. The players were unfamiliar with one another, but they also were missing Marta, who again had not been released by Umeå. A few months later, at home during the Pan American Games in Rio de Janeiro—having had some practice time together, along with Marta coming aboard—Brazil went undefeated and shut out their opponents in six matches. Against some of the best teams in the hemisphere, they lit up their opponents for thirty-three goals, with

Marta alone scoring twelve. Most encouragingly, Brazil captured the Pan American Games Gold Medal in front of 67,788 fans at the famed Maracana Stadium, trouncing the United States U-20 National Team 5–0. Marta scored twice from the penalty spot and provided two assists and was the first woman to leave her footprints in the Maracana's Hall of Fame, along with famous Brazilian men's players like Pele, Didi, Zico, and Romario, and German great Franz Beckenbauer.

This emphatic performance set the stage for China where Simoes's miracle almost happened, thanks in large part to Marta. The Auriverde made it to the semifinals with little difficulty, except for a surprisingly resilient Australia, who Brazil beat 3–2 in the quarterfinals. Though Brazil lost 2–0 to defending champion Germany in a well-played final, it was their total domination of the U.S. team in the semifinals by a 4–0 score that was the talk of the tournament, particularly since the Americans had lost only one official game in almost three years. The Stars and Stripes didn't help themselves with internal turmoil and dissent, but the Brazilians exposed the American game—for so long based on strength and power—as woefully behind the times. It was the U.S. team's worst international defeat ever. Marta's performance was little short of spellbinding, particularly her team's third goal late in the second half, which many claim to be the greatest ever scored in a Women's World Cup. In the seventy-ninth minute, with her back to American defender Tina Ellertson, Marta collected a pass from teammate Renata Costa on the left side, lifted the ball in the air with her right foot, then tapped it with the backheel of her left foot to the inside over Ellertson's right shoulder and ran around her to pick up the ball. As she headed towards the goal, she exploded past defender Cat Whitehill, who almost fell in her wake, and blasted the ball into the lower left corner of the goal past goalkeeper Brianna Scurry. Marta won the Golden Ball as tourney MVP and the Golden Boot for top scorer, along with the acclaim of the football world. "Marta is unlike any other player in the world," said her national team coach, Jorge Barcellos. "She's spectacular, phenomenal, a unique talent." Barcellos described Marta's vision to a group of Canadian reporters in Toronto in 2008 as an innate sense, an ability "to see problems and solve them before others have even noticed them." Barcellos also noted her lack of ego: "Marta stands out outside of the field as well as on. She doesn't want to be treated as the best. She wants to be treated as any other team player."

Brazil returned to China for the Beijing Olympics the next summer in 2008 and showed that they had figured out how to best Germany, drawing 0–0 with them in the first round before erupting for four goals in a semifinal rematch, overhauling Brigit Prinz's early strike ten minutes in. Led by Cristiane's five goals (including three in a first round 3–1 win over Nigeria) and three from Marta, Brazil seemed set to win their first world title, but the U.S. defense kept Brazil's forwards in check, and Carli Lloyd's overtime winner gave the United States a measure of revenge for their 4–0 embarrassment the year before. Barcellos soon left to join the new St. Louis Athletica ahead of WPS's debut season in 2009. Eight compatriots would join him in the league, with the most important being Marta.

Despite these phenomenal results on the field (the 2007 Pan American games win, as well as silver medals at the last World Cup and Olympics) the women's game struggles mightily in Brazil for acceptance. Brazil's military government had banned women's soccer until 1979, but the perception continues that it is not an appropriate sport for women, with an underlying sentiment that women who play it are gay. In 1999 Brazilian sports commentator Armando Nogueira explained to the *New York Times* why the national team was receiving little attention during the 1999 Women's World Cup in the United States in which they finished third: "Unfortunately, women's soccer doesn't have a chance in Brazil. The best woman player in Brazil will never be as popular as the worst male player, and the main reason is that women have been idolized as delicate objects of desire, incapable of playing a physical-contact, body-to-body sport."

Eight years on, little had changed; a Brazilian player in a professional set-up in Sao Paolo State said in November 2007, "Because we live in a macho country, the problems women face are sharper when compared to the male universe. . . . Female teams don't have even the basics to train and pursue their main objectives in a satisfactory way." Former national team player Sissi, who played in both American professional leagues and now lives in California, said, "It's all down to chauvinism, since everything is still focused on the men's game." Vanessa de Silva Oliveira, a fourteen-year-old playing in a UNICEF-supported program in Pernambuco State, described the problem succinctly, "The boys want the field to be only for them."

Marta and her teammates used the platform of their Pan Am Games victory and the 2007 World Cup and 2008 Olympic Games tournament successes to plead for more support and infrastructure in the domestic game. Marta said after the 2007 WWC, "We showed to the country what women's soccer can do, what potential it has. We showed the country we have the ability to be on the highest place on the podium, but there's still a lot of work to do. It's imperative that we have a women's league in Brazil. If we had a good structure, I'd come back. I love my country. But while it doesn't happen, I'll keep playing abroad. . . . I can't play in my own country."

Indeed, she had an opportunity to join Santos in late 2007 for their Brazilian Championship run but declined the move. (During the 2009 WPS off-season, Marta, along with compatriot Cristiane of Chicago Red Stars, did play for Santos, leading them to the Copa Brasil and the first South American Copa Libertadores titles. The latter was a women's club competition for champions of the ten CONMEBOL nations, which has been held on the men's side for decades with great success.) Reacting to considerable negative publicity as well as some prompting from FIFA, the Brazilian Football Association announced shortly after the World Cup that they would hold a national women's cup competition, as a forerunner to a future league championship, whereas previously clubs competed only at the state level. Marta was encouraged with the move, saying, "It's a good idea. It would be the first step towards a permanent league with seasons lasting seven or eight months. Players need to be able to keep their fitness up." She addressed girls at home who had hopes of playing the game at the highest level, telling them to not give up their dreams: "Women's football can be a struggle, but us Brazilians [national team members] are here fighting to open up more opportunities and smooth the path [for you]." Her coach, Jorge Barcellos, said that the top men's clubs needed to start women's sides but added, "Culturally in Brazil, [club and state football officials] are not going to stop investing on the men's side to invest on the women's side. That's a big barrier for us."

Domestic League Imports – "What Did I Get Myself Into?"

Over a third of the 2007 Brazilian World Cup team played abroad, in Austria, France, Spain, Sweden, and even Japan. Their trek follows a trail blazed by stars from the 1999 World Cup team that finished third, as Daniela, Katia, Pretinha, and Sissi all joined the WUSA. For those who wanted to advance their professional career and earn some money, the only route available was by going overseas. The Brazilian domestic game is the loser, as the marketability of the teams is reduced without the top players. The perspective of three North Americans who played for Santos, a top women's team in Brazil, in late 2007 reveals a lot about the infrastructure problems, even though it still has the label of a "professional league."

Melissa Lesage is a French Canadian from Montreal who played collegiately from 2000 to 2003 at the University of Toledo in Ohio. She was first team all-conference her senior season and finished number 2 on Toledo's all time scoring list with seventy-one points. She was also an all-conference performer in the classroom, winning academic honors in 2002 and 2003. Lesage delayed finishing her thesis, her last requirement for her master's degree in exercise science, to play top level soccer. She played in the USL's W-League (a summer amateur league) for the Laval (Quebec) Cometes and journeyed to Sweden to play for Bollstanas Sportklubb in Upplands

Vasby. After a short time there, Lesage moved to Brazil and became a key player for Santos in Brazil. She was joined by fellow Canadian Josee Busilacchi (McGill University/Cal State–Los Angeles) and American Katie Ratican (University of California–Berkeley).

Coming from a culture that is accepting of women's soccer, the trio was surprised at the level of discrimination they and their teammates at Santos faced, as well as how bad the support structure was. Their experiences also revealed why they and others like them were willing to accept abject living conditions, a new language, cultural differences, and other obstacles to pursue their sport.

Lesage described her first impressions of Santos:

> The first thing that struck me when I first came to Brazil were the living conditions of my teammates, and that this was the way I, too, was going to live for the next six months. I knew that the conditions would be different from Canada, but I did not think that the differences would be as obvious. In my mind, I was thinking that since Santos was a professional soccer club, one of the best in Brazil, the girls would also be treated as professionals. Unfortunately, women soccer players in Brazil do not live the extravagant life that professional athletes would usually live. In fact, we live in one small house (the size of a house that a family of five in the U.S. would live in) in front of Vila Belmiro [the Santos Stadium].

Things were so bad that the day she arrived in Brazil, Katie Ratican burst into tears, thinking, "What did I get myself into?" and had to be consoled by the coach and his wife. She described what she found at her living quarters:

> When we arrived at the Santos house where the team lives, we walked into the first room in the house, which is probably fifteen by fifteen feet in diameter and contained two sets of bunk beds. . . . I really do not intend to sound narcissistic, but I was rather put-off by the condition of the bed I was given.

The mattress, which was thin to begin with, was brown with dirt, and the cotton cover which was used to cover the foam of the mattress was ripped and falling off. I am not a paranoid person when it comes to germs or dirt, but I was a little scared to let my skin come in contact with the bare mattress.

Lesage found that she had to correct an impression of people both inside and outside of Brazil, including kids, that they were living privileged lives:

Few people know that the twenty professional women's soccer players of Santos are sharing four small rooms, three bathrooms, and sleep on bunk beds (some players don't have beds, therefore they sleep on the floor). Our meals consist of the most basic in common Brazilian food: rice, beans, and meat. There is one small tin of lettuce and tomatoes, sometimes fruits, and two liters of milk daily that is being shared between the whole of the team. The breakfast is a small piece of white French bread with butter. For us foreigners, the food issue was a big adaptation, and we all have had a share of stomach issues.

Ratican shed some light on why their food rations were so minimal: "Santos has a cafeteria where the girls go to pick up the food every meal. It is the same food as the boys who live at the stadium eat, and the only differences are that our food is cold by the time we get it, and there are limited portions for us. I believe that we are not allowed to eat at the stadium because the club does not want any "funny business" by putting the boys and girls together." Ratican was impressed with how well the local girls related to one another in the tight space, readily accepting the housing conditions and minimal food allocations. She said, "The Brazilian girls seem content with their situation. This most likely stems from the fact that many of these girls come from homes in which they live exactly like this, or worse." The imports soon found that the conditions at Santos were typical for women's clubs throughout the country. Lesage said, "This treatment that all the girls are going through is not only happening here in Santos, but in most of the women's clubs. We wash all our clothes by hand, take cold showers, use bikes to travel to practices and games (some girls cannot even afford to buy a bike . . . that is around 60 Reais or $30), practice and play in the old men's uniforms (sometimes we don't have enough for everybody), and earn between 100 Reais and 500 Reais [$50–$250] monthly." Ratican emphasized, "Remember, these are professional soccer players."

In the men's game, professional soccer in Brazil is an avenue to prosperity; it decidedly is not in the women's game. Josee Busilacchi described a twelve-year-old boy in Santos's juvenile team "who gets 15,000 Reais [$8,500] a month, buys a car, and can't even drive. He is making almost four times what the twenty girls get combined [4,000 Reais or $2,300 a month]!" Technically, the women's team is not affiliated with Santos Futebol Clube. They wear the same uniforms made famous by Pele but do not receive any money from the professional organization. Women's soccer backers like Jorge Barcellos argue that all the top Brazilian professional organizations should bring women's teams under their umbrella. The counterargument is that the finances of most men's teams are shaky, and the teams stay afloat primarily by selling their young players onto bigger clubs, mostly in Europe. For women, transfer fees are at their infancy and are not a realistic source of revenue for clubs.

On the playing field, what the North Americans gained was experience with a completely different style of play than they were used to. Lesage explained,

One of the biggest changes for me was the way the girls play. It was a bit hard to feel comfortable with the style of play. I had to say that I was able to adapt easier to the Swedish game that is more physical and organized than the Brazilian game that is more technical and free styled. *The girls do magic with the ball.* They are so technical and master tricks like they master samba. They are even able to control the ball well within the conditions of our fields. We are so used in the U.S. and Canada to playing on perfect fields. Here, one of the fields feels like we are playing in bushes and the other one is right next to a favela [shantytown].

Off the field, the North Americans found that many of their Brazilian teammates came from favelas and had family problems involving drugs and violence. One girl's father died after getting stabbed fifteen times, while another's had passed away from a drug overdose a few years before. Lesage reminisced, "I am amazed to see that, despite the way they are treated in their profession in addition to their own personal struggles, they are able to smile and look so happy most of the time. They thank GOD everyday for giving them health and the gift to be a pro soccer player. . . . My Brazilian teammates are the reason why this is one of the best life experiences I've had. My teammates bring so much joy and love to my Brazilian journey."

In stark contrast to Melissa, Josee, and Katie—college graduates all—their Brazilian teammates had few opportunities outside soccer, and little aspiration beyond kicking a ball. School was not an option for most of them; some of the older girls had not even completed high school, mostly because of the amount of time they devoted to their sport. (Ages ranged between fifteen and twenty-nine, with an average of twenty years for Santos's 2007 roster.) Those who did complete high school and had the desire to pursue higher education often didn't have the money to do so. Lesage felt that it was not their soccer skills that were holding them back:

I can assure you that most of them could easily get a full ride to play soccer for the best schools in [NCAA] Division 1. But I think that few of them would have the educational requirements. For instance, only three of my teammates are able to communicate in English. This year, one of the girls in Santos will leave for a U.S. college because Santos was able to pay for her English classes. The club was only able to give this opportunity to two players. The other eighteen will wait and maybe hope that their chance will happen the following year. When I talked to them about my studies, the countries I have played in and visited, the languages I speak, or the jobs that I have had, they look really amazed that I was able to do all of that, which in our culture is normal. They listen to every word I say with their eyes wide open, and ask questions. I see the curiosity in their eyes, but then at the same time, I don't know if all of them would have the courage or be ready one day to leave Brazil like Marta did for instance. . . . The majority of the girls have never left the Sao Paulo or Rio area.

Lesage found it quite common at home to combine school, studies, and work, but that's not the case at Santos. "In their minds, they don't need to work, because they are *professional soccer players,* and this is considered a job in Brazil despite the minimal salary, if you even want to call it a salary. They don't think about finding another job to be able to put money away. They live in the present, and the little they have allows them to buy the everyday things that they need and send the rest home to help their families." Ratican agreed, explaining that "by living at Santos, these girls are guaranteed a meal and a place to stay. There is no question about whether food will be on the table, whether they will have clothes, or a shower." Planning for the future is something the local players didn't think about. Most come from lower-class backgrounds, and when they can no longer play, they will return home to their families, look for a factory job, or get married. But that's in the future and not their concern; they live for today. As Lesage poignantly added, "Today they are soccer players that play for Santos, the most famous club in Brazil."

Since professional women's soccer is primarily seen as a game for those from disadvantaged backgrounds, it can be a jarring situation when someone from a privileged background joins the team. Lesage explained,

The first day I met my teammates, I could sense the difference in the classes, even within the team. For instance, there is one girl in my team that has a lot of money. She is the only one that is considered in the upper class. You can recognize it just by looking at her clothes, and she is the only one that owns a car and has her own apartment. I did not appreciate seeing that this same girl pays one of her teammates (the one that has one of the lowest salaries) to wash her clothes by hand. I know that for this poor girl, it gives her the opportunity for extra money, but I just think that it should not be happening within a team.

Acutely aware of these social dimensions, the North Americans strove to fit in by staying in the Santos house and eating with the team; they were largely successful in integrating into the unit. However, coming to a culture with so much poverty and huge divisions of class, so different from their milieu at home where social rank is minimized, provided them with salient insights. Lesage noticed that, when living with twenty Brazilian teammates, "I was able to perceive the struggles that my teammates would live [with] and try to overcome everyday. I know that I and my two foreigner friends had more money than most of the girls, but we tried to live like them, at the same level as they live." The North Americans ate the same food, watched the same shows on television, and learned Portuguese. Lesage wanted to be perceived as Brazilian and not a rich North American but realized that "I would never be one of them." She appreciated Canada so much more and had opportunities there that the Brazilians did not.

The North American trio helped Santos to the Sao Paulo State Championship that year but did not return in 2008, as all three focused on jobs and further education while playing amateur ball in the summer in Canada and the United States. Their experiences demonstrate that things are so bad for women's club soccer in Brazil that small upgrades will seem like vast leaps forward. Can the proponents of women's and girls' soccer seize on the positive publicity that Marta and her teammates received at home, particularly from their Pan American Games victory? Will male soccer fans come to women's games to watch top quality soccer, or will they go only for voyeuristic reasons. To grow the game in Brazil, meaningful investments must be made in the players and their infrastructure in order to increase respect for them as athletes. This will make it easier to create a fan base that appreciates the women's game, particularly among the soccer-mad males. As Marta and company have shown, the potential is so vast it's frightening. The next five years will definitely be crucial for the sport in South America's largest country.

Mexico — Leveraging the Anglos

Mexico's passionate support for their men's national team and club sides such as Club America of Mexico City and Chivas of Guadalajara have not translated well to the women's game. The country participated in regional Women's World Cup qualifying matches for the 1991 and 1995 events, but performed poorly (including losing to the Americans by 12–0 and 9–0 scorelines respectively), hindered by inadequate practice time and lack of support from the Mexican Football Federation. So lax was local interest for the women's game that in order to seriously contest qualifiers for the 1999 World Cup, the federation used a team dominated by U.S. collegiate players of Mexican descent. Incredibly, this Mexican National Team did the bulk of their training in southern California. The Mexican Federation realized they had a decent chance to qualify for the 1999 cup, as CONCACAF had an extra spot available, since the powerful Americans were automatic qualifiers as hosts. Former National Team legend Leonardo Cuellar was selected as head coach. Cuellar was captain of their 1978 World Cup team, played over a hundred international games, and competed for clubs in Mexico, the United States, and Spain. He was living in Los Angeles, where he was coaching the men's and women's college teams at Cal State–Los Angeles. Cuellar brought immediate credibility to confront the common view that women shouldn't play this type of sport. Since he had so few players at home to draw from, Cuellar jump-started the developmental process by scouring the United States for top quality college players of Mexican descent, utilizing their superior training. As long as the players had a Mexican-born parent or grandparent, even players born in the United States qualified according to FIFA rules, though the Mexican federation had to petition the Mexican government to allow dual citizens to play for their national teams, receiving approval shortly before the World Cup. The Mexican team had ten Americans on their roster, including forward Monica Gerardo, second on Notre Dame's all-time leading scorer list, along with Cal Poly–San Luis Obispo's Gina Oceguera (defender), San Diego State's Linnear Quinones (goalkeeper), and Kendyl Parker-Michner (midfielder) from the University of Tennessee. Cuellar's justification was "American women are very athletic, very competitive . . . because of the culture; they have the right to imitate what men do. In Mexico, it's almost against our culture to give women that flexibility. The United States has that gift that in the society that we live, the women have [access] to anything."

Another U.S. college find, University of California–Santa Barbara's Laurie Hill, said, "Soccer has always been a part of my life, and now that I play for Mexico it's like a dream. I'm working on my Spanish, because in my house we always spoke English and I hope this will be a positive experience. But at times it's difficult because we don't get much support. We got only $50 for two months, but I hope things will improve." Teammate Andrea Rodebaugh, a graduate of the University of California–Berkeley, felt that qualifying for the World Cup was crucial for the growth of the game in Mexico: "If we don't [qualify], everything will be the same. The Mexican mentality is still that women shouldn't play this type of sport." Coach Cuellar concurred with her sentiment: "Machismo in Mexico is nearly impossible to remove. It's part of the culture. There will always be detractors for women participating in the sport."

After finishing second to Canada in CONCACAF qualifying, they had to play off with Argentina, the CONMEBOL second place team, in a home-and-away two-game series decided by total goals scored. Mexico hosted the first leg and chose high altitude Toluca, outside of Mexico City, as the venue. Four thousand fans witnessed a 3–1 win, with the team securing its spot in the World Cup with a 3–2 victory in Buenos Aires. Their first World Cup was an eye-opening disappointment however, as Mexico was outscored 15–1 in their three matches, losing 7–1 to Brazil, 6–0 to Germany, and 2–0 to Italy. As Mexico exited, Leo Cuellar was both gracious and unapologetic, aware of the positives of what had been accomplished in such a short time: "I'm sure there will be some negative people who look only at the scores. I am very proud of this group. What we have right now is all we can offer."

After that '99 World Cup experience, Cuellar, while still focused on the United States for recruiting and lining up practice matches with college teams, began to develop talent who learned the game in Mexico. Homegrown players were more sophisticated and creative, benefiting from watching top quality men's soccer at home and overseas on television. There were clearly two distinct styles from both sides of the border. Marlene Sandoval, California born and raised who played at Cal State–Fullerton, noticed that "the girls from Mexico develop their touch and notion of the game much better than the girls from the U.S. In Mexico, it's more of a certain style of possession of the ball and having that technical ability." Cuellar's two most notable finds were forward Maribel Dominguez from Mexico City and Iris Mora of Acapulco, the latter of whom went on to play at UCLA and for 2009 W-League champions Pali Blues of Southern California. The Mexican Federation invested in the sport by creating national programs at the U-13, U-15, U-17, and U-19 levels. Cuellar said that it would be common to see a twelve- or thirteen-year-old girl in Mexico playing on the same team as a thirty-eight-year-old woman, but that situation didn't help develop young players.

After finishing third in CONCACAF's qualifying tournament for the 2003 Women's World Cup, Mexico again had to play off with a team from another confederation, this time Japan. Mexico hosted the first leg at the gigantic Azteca Stadium in Mexico City on a Sunday morning in July, allowing people in for free. A shocking 75,000 showed up to root the squad on to a 2–2 tie. (Interestingly, the huge Azteca crowd reminded long-time followers of women's sports that a reported 110,000 packed Azteca for the final of an unofficial women's world cup in 1971. Denmark won 3–0 over the hosts, who had defeated teams from Argentina, England, and Italy. The event was largely discredited in advancing the sport and women athletes in Latin America. In their book *Can Play, Will Play, Women and Football in Britain*, Williams and Woodhouse described the tournament as a commercial venture that capitalized on sexist, showy aspects, while minimizing the sport: "The women involved played into pink goal frames, beauty parlors were installed in dressing rooms, and some teams were encouraged to wear hot pants and blouses in place of the normal football stripes. As a prelude to matches there were rodeos, baseball games and displays by semi-clad majorettes.") A 2–0 defeat in the return leg left the Mexicans out of the 2003 World Cup. Cuellar expressed his concern that his federation's support and funding could dry up after his team's elimination.

To its credit, the Mexican Football Federation continued to back the team and Cuellar; they were richly rewarded less than a year later. Mexico shocked Canada, which had finished fourth in the 2003 World Cup, in the semifinals of the CONCACAF Olympic Qualifying Tournament. Cuellar outmaneuvered the overconfident Canadians, who had won all of their previous ten matches with Mexico, and the 2–1 final score belied Mexico's dominance. In an interview months later, Cuellar said that he prepared his team for the match by ramping up their physical play in practice. Canada expected Mexico to play their usual technical passing game but was surprised when they matched Canada's signature aggressive, battling style and directly attacked the goal. The wily coach felt the match could have a long-term impact on the sport in his country, particularly since it was telecast live nationwide: "What we earned today was another four years of support [from the Mexican federation]. We live in a culture where you have to win to get support. . . . The players deserved this win. They do not get any pennies for this. It has no value financially for them, but emotionally these are tattoos that stay on your heart forever."

Mexico's trip to the Athens Olympics in the summer of 2004 was largely viewed as a success. They finished second in a three-team first-round group, as a narrow 2–0 defeat to Germany along with a 1–1 deadlock with China was enough to see them through to the quarterfinals on goal differential, where they succumbed to powerful Brazil 5–0.

Maribel Dominguez and Gender Inspection

Maribel Dominguez, the leader on the Olympic team, is Mexico's answer to Marta, an idol to girls and women playing football as a hobby in her native land. She is also known by one name—Marigol—on the basis of her goal-scoring exploits; she is Mexico's all-time scoring leader with sixty-eight goals in ninety-two internationals, as of the start of the 2011 World Cup. She grew up in suburban Mexico City and preferred playing soccer with her three brothers to playing with dolls with her five sisters. Her alcoholic father, who worked in a tequila warehouse, did not approve of her avocation: "My father was very old-fashioned, and he didn't like soccer. He didn't even like that my brothers played soccer. When he went to work, I would sneak out of the house to go and practice in the street. When he came home from work, I was already inside the house."

Her father passed away when she was fourteen. She also had to fool the boys on her street. With short hair and a flat chest they called her Mario: "I tricked them for years. . . . They only found out I wasn't a boy when they saw my picture in the paper because I'd got into the sub-national women's team. They went to my house and asked my mother if I was really a girl. They were pretty shocked."

Dominquez had to play with boys, as she didn't find a girls' team to play on until she was in her teens. She explained, "I did have some trouble early on wanting to play with boys. I was looked upon as a tomboy. Truthfully, people didn't like it." In 1997 when she was eighteen, she joined a women's team called Inter. She was forced to have a fully nude inspection of her body by a female Mexican league official to validate her sex, because "she had short hair and played like a man." Dominguez recalled, "I was sitting in the dressing-room one day when a female instructor walked in and told me to take off my trousers to prove that I was a woman. I told her, 'All right, but only if you do the same.' After that, they stopped bothering me."

As she got older Dominguez joined women's teams in different parts of Mexico City, although none was very good. Then, at twenty, she was called up to the national squad and the dream of making a living from football began. Like Marta, she had to leave her home country to further her career. She joined the w-League's Kansas City Mystics as a complete unknown and led the league in scoring with seventeen goals and twelve assists, earning the Most Valuable Player award to boot. Despite the award, she had to battle Japan's Yayoi Kobayashi for the Atlanta Beat's last open spot on the team in 2003. In her first full month, she was selected as the wusa's Player of the Month after notching five goals and two assists in three games.

She credited her initial success to her goal orientation: "If I reach one goal, there's always another to reach for. I began to think like this when I was very young. My first goal was to play soccer. The second was to be a national team selection in Mexico. The third was to play in a foreign league, and the fourth was to play in the United States. Now my goal is to stay here and be one of the best in this league. . . . I have to keep fighting." Nora Herrera, a noted women's football journalist in Mexico said that "Maribel really is very, very good. . . . She has an incredible nose for a goal, she can smell it, and she's fast and courageous, a good header and surprisingly strong too."

After the WUSA's demise, Maribel played for clubs in Spain. In late 2006, she made international headlines when she signed for a team in Mexico—in the men's second division. Celaya, located in the state of Guanajuato, needed a goal scorer as well as some publicity. The only precedent had been attempts by Italian club Perugia to sign Germany's Birgit Prinz and Sweden's Hanna Ljungberg, but these efforts were largely viewed as publicity stunts by a limelight-seeking owner. Among Perugia's signings was longtime Libyan leader Muammar al Qaddafi's son, who played sparingly until he was banned for steroid use. The only holdup in Dominguez's deal was that FIFA had to formally approve the signing. Dominguez was hopeful for FIFA's blessing: "The thing is, that in Mexico we don't have even a decent amateur league for women, so you have to look for other options. . . . I knew that the decision could go either way, but we were expecting a yes." She was aware of the physical challenge of playing in a competitive men's league but approached it realistically: "The hard thing is going to be equaling the physical force of the men, but the technique, the desire, the willpower, those are things I already have." FIFA squashed her plans and the dreams of other women with the same goal when they issued an official statement: "There must be a clear separation between men's and women's football . . . no exceptions." A disappointed Dominguez said, "I just wanted to be given the chance to try. If I failed I would have been the first to say I can't do it, the first to admit it doesn't work. But at least I would have tried." Spurred on by the media frenzy, big business names in Mexico discussed sponsoring a women's league, but as of early 2010, nothing had happened yet. There is hope after Dominguez led Mexico to a shock 2–1 defeat of the United States in the 2011 World Cup Qualifiers in Cancun, forcing the United States into two additional games (against Italy) to qualify through an interregional playoff. The loss was the Americans' first in twenty-four matches with Mexico and their first in twenty World Cup qualification matches dating back to 1991. Dominguez for her part has a long-term plan to open a football school for girls in Mexico after her career is over.

Marta and Maribel Dominguez are important role models in a region where girls and women are not encouraged to play a physical sport that is seen as exclusively a man's domain. Their phenomenal skills and dedication to succeed are impressive, but they also have taken on the role of leading the charge to change the status quo in their respective countries. Both markets desperately need a national league to further the growth of its players and to act as a beacon for youth to attract them to the sport and to keep them involved.

8

Women Athletes

Objects versus Wholesome Role Models

Soccer, like other women's sports, has had to deal with the quandary of the value of selling gender when it comes to marketing. Though having nothing to do with the game itself, the presentation of athletes in sexually suggestive poses has been done under the guise of "creating publicity." Recent incidents in Australia, the United States, and Latin America bring out a variety of attitudes among players, coaches, and management to this issue. At the end of the day, the key question is: does it help the growth of the game, or is it ultimately demeaning to those involved? FIFA, certainly a strong advocate for the women's game, has muddied the waters with a very controversial suggestion for sexier player uniforms by President Sepp Blatter. This contributes to the belittling, lingering perception of the women's game as something inferior to the men's game.

Walking Matilda – in the Nude

Australia's national women's team was a tremendous surprise at the 2007 World Cup in China, making it to the quarterfinals. Cheryl Salisbury's late winning goal against Canada, which sent Australia on to the last eight, was an epic moment for the game Down Under. Unfortunately, when people discussed the Matildas during the tournament, inevitably conversation came around to the twelve players who posed nude for a black-and-white calendar back in 2000. Matthew Hall in the *Sydney Sun Herald* wrote during the 2007 event, "The Matildas? Aren't they those nude chicks?" Australian Women's Soccer Association President Shirley Brown said at the time that it was the only way to increase the profile of the team. "In Australia, women's sport is still considered second rate. No matter how good these girls are as soccer players, that is not enough to get the recognition that they deserve."

Midfielder Alison Forman told the *Sydney Morning Herald* at the time, "It's all about boosting the profile of the team and our sport, and it looks like we're going to achieve that." Though the team members certainly increased their visibility, they had differing opinions on its merits. Forward Katrina Boyd, who posed in one of three full frontal photos said, "I think it's art. If people want to call it porn, that's their problem. No one could make me feel low or sleazy about this. I feel strong and confident with what I have done with my body." Forman controversially posed in one shot with teammate and roommate Sharon Black: "We live together, we train together . . . we thought, why not do the shoot together? It's turned out great, we really love the shot. It's definitely going up on the living room wall." No doubt an interesting conversation piece for visitors. Nineteen-year-old striker Alicia Ferguson said she also was proud to be featured: "The idea was put forward to us and it was our decision whether we wanted to do it or not." Midfielder Lisa Casagrande did not want to participate, explaining, "It's not the way you'd like to promote being female athletes."

If the nude photos weren't enough controversy, there was also a battle over the calendar's proceeds. The twelve players received pennies on the dollar for their efforts, after disagreements over the profit split with the publisher. On the strength of prepublication publicity, the first run of five thousand was increased tenfold for a second run. The calendar retailed for AU$16, and the players divided 64 cents for each one sold. Publishing payouts can be minuscule, but this was pathetic as each player received 5 cents per calendar. Best intentions aside, this effort fell into the category of exploitation.

England National Team Member Alex Smith addressed the infamous calendar in an interview seven years later with British Football Magazine *Four-Four-Two*, responding to the tongue-in-cheek question of whether she would consider posing nude. She nixed the idea, explaining, "Ideally, you want any publicity to be about your football, not because you're a woman who plays football."

At the 2007 World Cup in China, some journalists (including a few women) became obviously excited by the prospect that the Australian women would issue another nude calendar for 2008, a rumor that turned out to be false. It distracted people from an exciting sporting story and demeaned a vibrant group of athletes. Laura Pappano, coauthor of a book about gender in sports and a writer-in-residence at Wellesley College, said after viewing some photos from the 2000 calendar, "When women do hot calendars like that, they are feeding a cultural confusion around what their bodies signify in a public space. If female athletes want their bodies to denote strength, power, and skill, then posing for calendars is a corruption of that." Those promoting the developing sport of women's soccer have felt the need to resort to this kind of publicity "for their sport," but at what price? Does this earn the participants and their sport respect, or is it merely another example of objectifying women? As Pappano asks, "Could you see any female CEO of a corporation posing in the nude? Then why do athletes feel the need to do so?"

Bikinis Mandatory for Practice and *Playboy* Polls

Appropriate responses to risqué photo shoots are not solely an issue Down Under. In Mexico a photojournalist asked national team members to "be a little bit sexier!" What is the proper response? It seems to be that if you want the coverage, silence is the best policy. A promotional calendar for the Cayman Islands' Women's National Team produced by their soccer federation, purporting to show the women training, reveals that the Cayman women's team apparently practices in skimpy bikinis. To show that not all calendars of national teams are tawdry, *Soccer Insider* in Canada produced a calendar in 2003 with game and practice action photos of top players, showing the women simply as soccer players.

At times it is difficult to see who benefits more from these depictions; the clubs or the media. Canadian Josee Busilacchi, who played in Brazil with Santos in 2007, felt that a video that a local television station had produced and which the team had on its website was risqué. The five-minute clip showed a player in her Santos uniform posing seductively, emphasizing her curves, taking her shirt off, lying on a couch, and even posing in the shower, all while Shakira music played in the background. The video was tawdry and at times resembled cheap porn; it could easily have been shot in a brothel instead of the team's residence. There was no footage of her playing the game, sad since she was one of the team's better players. These things are done under the guise of promoting the individual or the team, but this effort in particular turns the player into an object of male lust. The players can be pawns in a decision made by team officials or media representatives to garner more press but that ultimately cheapens the sport and can damage their reputations as well.

In the United States, the high visibility of the national team has presented opportunities for the athletes to participate in feature photo shoots, both with clothes and without. One component of the decision is whether the promotion of women players as sex objects is a distraction from the players' avowed goal to be positive role models to youth. Ultimately, it is the players' choice, and as long as they are compensated for their images and not pressured, that is their right to decide for themselves. However, to do it under the guise of promoting the sport is naïve and self-serving. Pappano said, "As soon as we sell players as cheesecake, we are emphasizing that women have not reached cultural equity." The hot, sexy image is at odds with that of a serious athlete.

So where is the line between a wholesome sex appeal for a woman athlete and exploitation and titillation? David Letterman's "Babes of Summer" label for the U.S. Women's National Team helped bring mainstream attention for their quest for the 1999

World Cup. Oddly, Letterman's support came only following a pre-tourney appearance on his show by Brandi Chastain, after her nude shots in the men's magazine *Gear* (crouched behind a soccer ball, wearing only her soccer shoes.) She later admitted that the *Gear* session was a mistake, particularly since *Gear* kept the rights to the photos and ran a second spread with unflattering photos: "If I had known what kind of magazine it was, I wouldn't have done it. That's my fault. I'm always naïve. I have this belief that people are only going to do right by you. I'm open and honest, but I've learned a couple of things. You have to protect yourself."

Playboy.com polled readers for the sexiest WUSA player that readers would like to see pose nude, as they had done previously with women's golf, tennis, and basketball stars. The winner would have a chance to make upwards of $750,000, an attractive purse in a league where the average salary was under $50,000. Team captain Julie Foudy commented on the poll: "I'm not sure there are any positives, to be honest. It's not our audience. We're after young kids and families. We don't have young kids, I hope, reading *Playboy*. In the short term, people think, 'Oh, it will give us a spike in terms of interest.' But long term it will diminish the game we've made and take away from the focus on athletic achievement." Teammate Tiffeny Milbrett concurred, saying that posing nude is "such a terrible message to send to those young kids. It perpetuates the idea that a woman can only make it in this world if they sell their bodies." Others were more accepting. San Jose defender and later WPS Sky Blue head coach Kelly Lindsey said, "As long as it's done in good taste, and if it brings people to the field, I don't have a problem with it."

Officially, the league agreed with Lindsey. WUSA CEO Lynn Morgan was quoted in the *Atlanta Journal-Constitution* as saying, "If they wanted to do a [center]fold we wouldn't be opposed to something that would show off our players." She meant the poll, but the damage was done, especially since the league had used sexy pictures of Heather Mitts, Mia Hamm, and others in their own publicity handouts. Philadelphia Charge and U.S. National

Team Defender Heather Mitts won the magazine's competition but declined to pose for *Playboy* in the buff, explaining that, "It is not something I would do." *Playboy* asked her again before the 2008 Olympics to pose with swimmer Amanda Beard, who had previously been featured in the magazine. Again Mitts declined, saying, "I just decided it wasn't for me. It's got to be something my dad's OK looking at." Mitts did appear wearing sexy clothes in men's magazines FHM and *Maxim*, and in the *Sports Illustrated* swimsuit edition and on the cover of *Philadelphia Magazine* featuring the most eligible single Philadelphians. Mitts, named ESPN.com "hottest female athlete for 2004," expressed frustration that some reporters want to discuss her dating life or popularity rather than the sport. "It's hard when people want to look past those types of things [soccer, training for the Olympics] and mainly want to talk about the [sex-symbol topics]. . . . I'm a soccer player and that's what I want to be known for." Mexican National Team star and WUSA Boston Breaker Monica Gonzalez felt that photos with clothes on were acceptable. "It's fine to get girls dressed up and dolled up and posing pretty—why not? We're girls. That's what we do."

Another element that underlies the issue of showing players as desirable sex objects for men is that this helps to submerge the stereotype of lesbianism in women's sport. Scholar Pat Griffin discussed homophobia's role in women sports thus: "Homophobia is a powerful political weapon of sexism. The lesbian label is used to define the boundaries of acceptable female behavior in a patriarchal culture. When a woman is called a lesbian, she knows she is out of bounds. . . . Because women's sport has been labeled a lesbian activity, women in sport are particularly sensitive and vulnerable to the use of the lesbian label to intimidate them."

Players have talked about encountering pejorative comments about gays and being asked about the sexual orientation of teammates (or their own). United States National Team defender Kate (Sobrero) Markgraf said that she gets asked frequently by guys how many of her teammates are lesbians. "It makes me so mad! Who cares? Why does that matter? I'm sure there's gay male athletes. No one asks. No one assumes. They assume we're butch, they assume we're lesbian. I wish I knew why this was such a big deal. Maybe it's a way to dismiss the achievement of women. To think that somehow we're not normal. How could we not be normal? I have a huge issue with that. It's none of their business."

As a soccer promoter, I organized a game in 1993 in a midwestern U.S. city between two women's national teams. The event was derided one evening as "dyke fest" by a group of male youth soccer organization board members. I continually had to argue why I brought women's teams rather than men's. My response was it was national team–level soccer, a first for the city, and sex didn't matter. One long-time soccer booster supported me, saying the game was the highest caliber soccer ever seen in the area. The youth soccer organization, though still belittling women's soccer as not appropriate for their young players of either sex to watch, later agreed to buy block tickets for future men's events I promoted but not for any women's games. I refused the offer.

Questions or judgments about orientation know no international boundaries. Santos' Canadian import Josee Busilacchi talked about perceptions of women athletes in Brazil: "I think that there is a stereotype that follows women's soccer [in Brazil], that all women who play ball are lesbians or tomboys. I felt like with many events that happened in the past months, the media and the administration were trying to hide the image by asking the most feminine girls in the team to appear in interviews, to pose for the newspapers in bikinis on the beach with the Santos flag, or with the prettiest girls having a seductive pose." The articles would lead with titles such as:

Meninas da Vila ["Girls who play at Santos FC's Vila Belmiro Stadium] show that beauty and talent can go together.
Futebol is also a girl's thing.
The beauties of Santos FC spend hours in front of the mirror.

A top-caliber player in West Africa was kicked out of her club and national team because officials found out that she was gay.

Though officials admitted that she was not the only one on either squad, she didn't hide her sexual orientation well enough. Essentially banned from playing at home, she continued her soccer career in Europe.

Players participating in "come hither poses," done under the guise of "selling the game" send an indisputable message, primarily to men, of heterosexual women. There appears a strong relationship between "proving the sexuality of women athletes" and posing nude. Promoting a "sexy" team diverts attention away from the "l" word, but it trades one negative portrayal of women for another.

The Future of Football Is Feminine . . . in Hot Pants

Even FIFA has been drawn into the discussion of female imaging, unfortunately in a less than enlightened manner. Sepp Blatter, the president of the sport's governing body said in July 1998 that "the future of football is feminine." It was an important official declaration of FIFA's commitment to the women's game. Six years later, he torpedoed his credibility when he said that women players should wear sexier outfits, helping to sell the game and attract more fans. Blatter said that women should "play in more feminine clothes than the men, like they do in volleyball. They could, for example, have tighter shorts. . . . Beautiful women play football nowadays, excuse me for saying so."

The reaction worldwide to Blatter was blistering. Norwegian player Lise Klaveness pointed out that hot pants were not very practical for soccer and added, "If the crowd only wants to come and watch models, then they should go and buy a copy of *Playboy*." England goalkeeper Pauline Cope responded with annoyance, "He doesn't know what he's talking about," adding that his comments were "typical of a bloke." Two young Canadian National Team stars weighed in with their thoughts. Midfielder Brittany Timko said, "I think women's soccer is already popular and I think that people turn out to watch how we play and not how we look." Forward Kara Lang declared succinctly, "I'd like to see Sepp Blatter wearing hot pants."

Julie Foudy, U.S. National Team captain and past president of the Women's Sports Foundation, chimed in, "[FIFA is] really taking up some issues to try and promote women's soccer. That's why I listen to that comment and it makes me shake my head, because I think that's sad, that that's the mentality when there's so much more that can be said about women's football." The media was equally harsh and irreverent, running headlines such as:

Slip into Something Skimpy: Blatter (*Winnipeg Sun*)
Brief Loss of Blatter Control (*Washington Post*)
Getting Shorts in a Bunch (*Tacoma News Tribune*)

Blatter specifically cited volleyball as his example, trying to dig out of a hole the size of an open pit mine. Beach volleyball's avowed approach to marketing is different from soccer's. The CEO and commissioner of the AVP (Association of Volleyball Professionals) Leonard Armato discussed the increasing popularity of beach volleyball when he said, "We're competing against each other in incredible settings. We have beautiful people wearing bikinis and shorts. It's aesthetically pleasing. . . . We think our athletes are terrific with people and are role models." But the AVP blatantly pushes sexiness, and their audience is young adults; they are not targeting youth athletes, who are soccer's primary base of support.

Just as the furor over Blatter's comments dampened, former UEFA president Lennart Johansson came up with this clanger at the 2005 European Championships: "There are so many companies who could make use of the fact that if you see a girl playing on the ground, sweaty, with the rainy weather and coming out of the dressing-room, lovely-looking, that would sell well." At least he stopped short of suggesting the cameras follow the women into their showers! The English FA president at the time, Geoff Thompson disagreed, feeling that women players should not use their sexuality to sell the game. You have to wonder about football's leaders when they constantly talk in this way, or when you encounter this 2008 headline on the Confederation Africane de

Football website: "E. Guinea and South Africa in Virgin Final." They tried to explain it by saying it was the teams' first time in the African Women's Championship finals, but South Africa had finished second in the event in 1995 and 2000—oops! No one had questioned the wording, or nobody could come up with something better? It wasn't cute; it was demeaning as well as inaccurate.

The issue comes down to whether women's soccer needs more sex appeal or depictions of "femininity" to finally cut into the male-centered sphere of soccer or whether success on the field is sufficient to gain sustainable sponsor, media, and fan interest. The buoyantly defiant Blatter tried to explain his "shorts" comments, causing further damage: "I think that instead of complaining, women players should have applauded what I said." Focusing on the sport alone may take longer, but it is more credible than flash points of attention over decidedly cheapening and polarizing images. Selling sex to grow the sport won't work and merely retards the public's interest in "the beautiful game" as a sport. Wellesley College's Laura Pappano said, "Salacious images, as a fallback for women athletes, objectifies women by focusing on the hotness of their bodies and undercuts their legitimacy as serious athletes." It is disingenuous to excuse these images as "helping the sport" and further harms the aim of gender equity.

Men's vs. Women's Soccer: Different Games or Different Perceptions

Part of what women are fighting is the perception that their sport is something different from the men's and therefore "less important." The most common lament is that the women's game is slower than the men's. Some say that the women's game is not as physical or strong as the men—these people have never seen a Canada–U.S. National Team game, which can make Cage Fighting look tame. For technical skills, women rate as high as men. Some of the most technically precise players in the world have played in Sweden's Top League, the Damallsvenskan. Chicago-based brand strategist Jim Paglia has been involved with soccer for years at many levels and finds it "absurd to compare the two games. After all, women do not complain about men being worse at rhythmic gymnastics or synchronized swimming."

Another adjective that has been frequently ascribed to the women's game since the early 1990s has been "fair play." The men's game excuses instances of players kicking the ball away at free kicks and wasting time as "gamesmanship." U.S. National Team coach and long time Swedish International Pia Sundhage said, "There's a sense of fair play in the women's game, you want to compete but with fair play. It's been like that from the very beginning when I started playing. It's something you take pride in; this is the way the game is played." This laudable aspect, though, can veer into dysfunctional stereotyping of how the women's game should be played in comparison to the men's, rather than an observation of a general trait. There was no better demonstration of this than when clips of a mid-major college women's conference playoff game received millions of views on the Internet and brought undue attention on the physicality of the game, as we will see in the next section.

Elizabeth Lambert and "The Ponytail Tug"

University of New Mexico junior defender Elizabeth Lambert faced a bizarre level of attention for her physical play against Brigham Young in a 2009 Mountain West Conference semifinal playoff game, punctuated by her yanking BYU opponent Kassidy Shumway by her ponytail, leaving Shumway writhing on the ground. Since the game was televised, highlights quickly landed on media site YouTube, with almost 3 million viewings and 5,300 comments over the following few days. Ordinarily, for flagrant play the offender would receive a red card or, in a few grievous situations, a one- or two-game suspension. UNM suspended Lambert indefinitely. In one interview with the *New York Times* the defender sincerely apologized for her actions, saying, "I still deeply regret it and will always regret it and will carry it through the rest of my life not to retaliate. . . . I can't believe I did that."

The general public's reaction to the incident bordered on hysterical. Lambert received threatening e-mails, including one that said she deserved to go to prison. Lambert was taken aback at how the incident was perceived by some as "sexy catfighting" between two women. She was aghast that some men had sent her messages saying, "'Hey, we should meet up some time.' That appalled me," she said. "A lot of people think I have a lot of sexual aggression. I was like, 'Whoa, no, I don't feel that way at all.' That's bizarre and shocking to me." This went far beyond the hype that violent fouls receive in any other sport. North Carolina coach Anson Dorrance said that the only time that women's college soccer makes the news is "when something like this happens."

Lambert felt that the incident received so much attention because it was a women's game. "I definitely feel because I am a female it did bring about a lot more attention than if a male were to do it. It's more expected for men to go out there and be rough. The female, we're still looked at as, 'Oh, we kick the ball around and score a goal.' But it's not. We train very hard to reach the highest level we can get to. The physical aspect has maybe increased over the years. I'm not saying it's for the bad or it's been too overly aggressive. It's a game. Sports are physical."

Terry O'Neill, president of the National Organization for Women, felt that the reaction was over the top (by both the media and the public) and "clearly sexist," adding, "It's obvious there are still some people in this country who just can't accept that women want to play sports, and sometimes sports get rough." Laura Pappano wrote in blogs about the reactions to the YouTube clips, "The image of female athletes as more than skilled players—as good, wholesome people—is a centerpiece of women's sports and a staple of marketing, promotion, and ticket-selling. This has been both a benefit and a limitation that has helped shape women's sports as 'gentler' fare." Pappano felt that this delineation has fed a situation for which male athletes often get a pass for bad behavior, while women are criticized. Carl Cannon, deputy editor of *Politics daily.com* wrote, "It's as though we expect women to play fiercely competitive sports—like men—and yet retain some of the traditional notions of femininity."

Long after the ponytail tug, Lambert was paying heavily, not necessarily for her violent play but due to the intense public reaction. Lambert was portrayed as an out-of-control, Rambo-like monster. Leading up to the incident with Shumway, there was aggressive play on both sides in an amped-up playoff game between league rivals. Game tape shows a BYU player elbowing Lambert in the stomach before she reacted by shoving the opponent in the back in retaliation. Shumway can be seen tugging on the front of Lambert's shorts right before the ponytail pull. The foul should have received a red card and maybe a suspension for an additional game, but no more. Plus, Lambert admitted that she should have been tossed from the game. But a long-term suspension from the team and potentially her sport, no way. That's a grievous injustice. She certainly shouldn't have been the only player red-carded either. The referee needed to be harder with both teams (he showed only one yellow card the entire game), and a source who attended the game said that the physical play ramped up after ten minutes, when it became clear that the referee was making no attempt to punish the fouling. The coaches also must accept some responsibility for not controlling their teams. New Mexico coach Kit Vela admitted she had not seen the incident with Shumway or she would have pulled Lambert from the game immediately. Since the coaching staff should always monitor and manage the team's style of play, why did the University of New Mexico not suspend Vela and her staff as well?

Lambert, an exceptional student, maintained stellar grades during the incident but was suspended from spring soccer and prohibited from working out with any team members. She was seeing a psychologist—at the university's direction—and working with youth teams. Not practicing all spring certainly doesn't help a player maintain Division I–level standards. The following season, New Mexico went 12–3–5, won their conference regular season title, and qualified for the NCAA tournament, where they lost to eventual champion Notre Dame, 3–0. During her senior season, Lambert played a total of ninety-eight minutes—the equivalent of a little over one full game—when in 2009 she played in all twenty-one games and led her teammates in minutes played. Despite assurances from the University of New Mexico Media Relations representatives and coaching staff that they had "put the Elizabeth Lambert situation behind them," one still had the feeling that she was made a scapegoat by the university, on top of the harsh and dehumanizing criticism she has endured from the general public.

The unfortunate side of the Elizabeth Lambert incident is that female athletes are still perceived by many as having to perform less aggressively or tactically differently from their male counterparts. If women break the norm, they are fiercely questioned and labeled as deviant. As the Lambert drama shows, general perceptions of women athletes can still have an impact on decisions, particularly since this fire was lit largely by nonsoccer aficionados. As all women's sports expand at the high school, college, professional, and Olympic level, with more opportunities to watch games in person and on television, the hope is that more people learn to enjoy women athletes perform their craft, in the exact same way as they do with men's sports.

Playing with the Boys

At youth level, it's common to see girls and boys playing on teams together until around age ten or eleven. Women's national teams frequently play training games against boys U-16 through U-18 teams. Even WPS players in the off-season try to find good amateur men's teams or just work out with college and professional male athletes, to keep their skills sharp and maintain good fitness. FIFA prevented Maribel Dominguez's attempt to play with a Mexican Second Division side, but in the next ten or fifteen years, will we see a top-level women's player in a men's professional league? I think it's possible, though right now the few instances of top players performing in male amateur leagues have been purely to stay in shape, and there has been some resentment.

Lorrie Fair, who won a World Cup title with the United States in 1999, wanted to play on a semiprofessional male team in California before joining Chelsea's top level women's team in England. Some opposing teams objected to playing against a girl. The league told her team there were rules against it, but conveniently they weren't written down. Fair wasn't trying to make a statement or cause turmoil; she wanted a high level of play before going abroad. She explained, "When you're female and you're playing amongst men, they're bigger and faster so you have to think quicker and your touch has to be better. It's a great training environment. I've always believed girls should play with boys." The NCAA, though, is less enthused and in 2009 was investigating whether to prohibit men participating in women's practices in all sports, arguing that it takes practice time away from nonstarters. Soccer coaches want to be able to make that decision on the own, and many find that experienced male athletes increase the competitiveness of practices.

Australian National Team starting goalkeeper Melissa Barbieri took a route similar to Fair's before the Australian W-League began in late 2008. In order to stay in top game shape, she combined national team camps and *futsal* league games with playing outdoors for a Victoria State men's league side (just below the professional A-League). She signed for Richmond FC after a trial period in early 2007, but she didn't want her stay to be viewed as a circus act. "It's really a huge honor for me, and it's a massive highlight in my career, but I know I'll have to earn my stripes," Barbieri (twenty-eight at the time) said. "Rest assured, this is no marketing gimmick. I'm here to prove myself." Victoria Football Federation (FFV) media and communications officer Mark Van Aken said the organization was initially surprised by the proposition but moved quickly to make it a reality, "It came out of the blue to us, but we're very happy to be able to assist Melissa, especially ahead of the World Cup. We sought advice from lawyers and from medical experts, and once we received the green light, we were happy for it to go ahead." He said that the fact that Melissa was a goalkeeper made it an easier situation than for one of the ten field positions. Van Aken said, "Obviously the game is quite different in the outfield, and it really would have to be an exceptional case for us to look at it. Being a goalkeeper has definitely helped [Barbieri's] cause."

In May of 2008, after an exciting 5–4 loss to the United States (her fifty-fifth appearance for the Matildas) Barbieri said of her time in the men's league: "It's awesome. It really does get my game experience up, and the men do play the same sort of game as international standards, that pace, but it's not over what I can cope with. The game is very quick and it gets me up to that international standard level." At the time, her team was in second place (but finished the season in fifth) and Barbieri was playing consistently, when she wasn't touring with the Matildas.

Despite her success with the men's team, Barbieri saw her future in the w-League, for which she played with Melbourne Victory in 2008–10. She felt that it was important that the national league players join the new entity so that "we have enough national players keeping it alive and keeping it productive so people come to the games and watch." Melissa Barbieri, though a pioneer with her involvement with men's leagues, is wholly invested in the growth of the women's game and remains one of the most positive personalities in the global game today.

Unfortunately, women soccer players still face gender stereotyping as they pursue their sport, even in countries like the United States and Australia, where women are equal in many activities. Just as women still strive for equality at work, where even in the United States women still make about 25 percent less than their male counterparts for the same position, women athletes strive to be taken as seriously as men. Prescripts of how women should play continue to pigeonhole and limit the athletes. Cheesecake photo spreads perpetuate the idea of "sexy heterosexual athletes," holding back the advancement of cultural equity and the day when people will evaluate women players solely on their play on the field.

THREE

Building Leagues and National Team Programs

9

Ancestral Roots

Leveraging the Diaspora to Build the Game Abroad

For women, playing abroad is a recent trend, begun largely after the WUSA's demise in 2003. (A few players from the 1991 U.S. National Team including Michelle Akers, Kristin Lilly, and Mia Hamm, played in Sweden in the mid-nineties, while Brandi Chastain played in Japan and Canadian Charmaine Hooper played in Italy, Norway, and Japan.) U.S.- and Canadian-raised men have been trying out with European soccer sides for the past few decades in increasing numbers; they earn more abroad and generally find a higher level of league play then they would domestically. Sometimes a player must try out for a number of teams before landing a contract. Unlike for men, women's trips overseas are less for the money, as they would generally do better by using their degrees for jobs or further education. Women make contacts with the clubs through foreign-based friends who played there, or through networks developed by their club and college coaches, and occasionally through a few specialist agents. They come on short trials (normally a few days to a few weeks) or short-term contracts (from a few months to an entire season) with their expenses covered. They hope to make a positive impression so they can either be offered a more lucrative contract or be spotted by a more affluent team. By nature this path is unstable, but those who pursue it talk about the positives while minimizing the negatives, explaining that after college is the best time to travel and move on short notice. Playing overseas allows them to play high-quality soccer, experience the personal growth of living in another culture, add well-recognized club names to their soccer resumes, and keep their options open for professional playing opportunities either in the WPS at home or in another country.

Using Heritage for Opportunities Abroad

A prime example of playing overseas to be noticed at home was native Californian Anna Picarelli, who leveraged her Italian ancestral roots to keep her soccer career alive. She began playing the sport in the Los Angeles area when she was five and was switched into goal at age fourteen when the starting keeper was hurt. Though she wasn't thrilled with the change at first, she kept with it and starred for four years at Pepperdine University in Malibu, California, graduating in 2006.

Despite leading Pepperdine to two NCAA Sweet 16 playoff rounds in four years, Picarelli always fought a perception that her short stature (five-foot-four) was a liability, as most coaches look for keepers who are at least five-foot-nine. Tim Ward, Pepperdine's head coach, reflected on the effect Picarelli had on his program: "We had some great victories because of her." Though her smaller size scared away other coaches during the recruiting phase, he saw that she was skilled at her position. "What was cool about Anna is that a lot of people passed on her during the recruiting process because she's small for a goalkeeper, and I had a chance to see her play enough to know that despite her size, she played huge. She's one of the best athletes we ever had in our program. Her quickness, her jumping ability and her spring were just outstanding. Her reflexes were laser sharp."

After finishing college, she was called up to a United States U-21 camp but was told by the head coach, Jillian Ellis, that she was too short to ever make it at the full national team level. Ellis explained that Picarelli would be a "tactical disadvantage" when facing teams like Germany and Norway, with tall powerful strikers. Coach Ward

4. Italy's Anna Picarelli punches clear from Abby Wambach in the United States' 2–0 victory in the 2008 Peace Queen Cup. (Anna Picarelli.)

chuckled when remembering that tryout, explaining, "She's really good at dealing with crosses but visually she doesn't have that presence, but when you see her play and see her fly, she's out of this world."

Picarelli decided to try her luck in Italy, where her father was born. After some phone contacts with his assistance as interpreter, she flew to Verona during a vacation at the 2006 Mens's World Cup in Germany and was signed by Serie A side Bardolino after only an hour tryout. Even though she only played Italian Cup games her first season, Bardolino won the title when she saved three of five penalty kicks in the tiebreaker. She was a part of three Serie A title winners during her time at Bardolino. She came to National Team Head Coach Pietro Ghedin's attention after a stirring 3–3 tie in the UEFA Women's Champions League versus Arsenal in 2007.

She won her first cap in January 2008 and soon worked her way up to starter.

Her game improved in Italy where, compared to the United States, the physical aspect was less important than footwork and technical ability. Picarelli said, "Playing in Italy made me learn to use my feet. . . . [T]he focus on your touch, even for a goalkeeper, is just as important as being able to make a save. In three years, I've come a long way from distributing with my feet."

In August 2009 Picarelli was the revelation at the European Women's Championships held in Finland. Only tewnty-four, Picarelli first led Italy to a shock 2–1 opening match win over England and then shutout Russia 2–0 during the group stage. Italy exited the tournament in the quarterfinals after a narrow 2–1 loss to Germany, the defending World and European Champions. It came as a surprise to many that Picarelli was an American.

One challenge for American women playing abroad is that they can encounter far different perceptions of what are acceptable sports for women to play. Picarelli found that Italy was, "a decent fifteen years behind the U.S." She described some of the reactions her team received: "Many people don't even acknowledge women's soccer in Italy. Many times when traveling with my team, people would ask what we were. We would respond 'a soccer team.' And then the questions would start . . . 'How many of you are on the field at a time'? We'd respond '11,' then they would go on . . . 'But the field is smaller right?' 'No' . . . 'The ball is lighter?' . . . 'No.' 'The goals are smaller?' . . . 'No.' 'You only play 35 minute halves?' . . . 'No.' It is very hard for people to grasp that we play just like the men."

In Italy, girls and boys play on the same teams until age fourteen because few clubs had dedicated female youth teams, but beyond that age there are limited options. Picarelli feels that more opportunities for younger girls to play with other girls will assist the growth of the game, "You can notice the influence of men's soccer in the women's game, whereas in the United States the two are very different, each with its own image. Italy as a whole is still a very macho country. Women are breaking down stereotypes every day, but even in a country as advanced as it is, it is hard for Italians to break away from the traditional views of women."

Anna Picarelli is a successful role model for a North American college graduate who wants to continue her soccer career professionally but doesn't have youth national team experience on her resume that many coaches in America value. Her advice to others following in her footsteps is to "just have the courage to do it." The language, cultural, and playing aspects in training and games were radically different adjustments, but that's why she has gained so much from the experience: "I've learned a lot, having played in a different soccer environment for three years, and I think every American can learn a thing or two overseas."

As an established player for the top team in Italy, Anna could easily stay for years in Italy but wanted to come back to the United States. Her fiancé was based in Los Angeles, and she wanted to be closer to her family. On the soccer side, she talked passionately about the WPS: "There isn't any other league that plays at the same level, the same speed, and the same skill. My goal from graduation was to go overseas and prepare for the return of the league. Now that I feel more prepared, I hope to get my foot in the door." In 2010 Anna Picarelli played with WPSL runner-up Ajax of southern California, along with a short stint in Sweden with Kristianstads DEF while commuting to Europe for Italy's National Team games. Italy just missed out on a World Cup spot after losing a final playoff round to the United States, by a 0–2 aggregate score.

From Goshen to Kalush

Aivi Luik was another American college graduate who played overseas for the cultural experience and to help make her national team (Australia). Luik played at the University of Nevada–Reno and was a key midfielder/defender for FC Indiana's championship teams in the WPSL in 2005 and 2007. She played with FC Naftokhimik of Kalush, Ukraine, after FCI's 2008 season for their first UEFA Cup games. She was joined by current and former FC Indiana players:

Veronica Phewa (South Africa), Rorro Hernandez (Spain), and Anjuli Ladrón de Guevara (Mexico). On the field the imports helped the Ukrainians win their four-team first-round UEFA Cup group, with Luik scoring the game-winner in all three matches, versus Poland's AZS Wroclaw (1–0), PAOK FC of Thessaloniki, Greece (1–0), and Estonia's FC Levadia Tallinn (2–1).

Despite the on-field success, Luik did not find the training competitive, even with sessions twice per day. She explained, "They never worked on their fitness together. We had to do this on our own. The Ukrainian style of play was much less physical and the imports had to temper their game, as a normal play in the United States would be whistled for foul play." She found that the coaching was below what she was used to in Australia and the United States. Even when Coach Valeriy Sushko drew on the board to overcome the language barrier, she never understood what he was trying to get across. She also found the fields they played and trained on were horribly bumpy, with pockets of overgrown grass and poor drainage.

Yet Luik talks glowingly of what she learned by diving into a different culture. She loved the Ukrainian people and was particularly inspired by a teammate who had been orphaned as a young girl. With a goal to join Australia for the 2011 World Cup in Germany, Luik would not return to the Ukraine, because she needed a more challenging soccer environment. After FC Indiana's 2009 season, she played with Brisbane Roar in Australia's W-League, trained with the national side, and won the 2010 Asian Cup with the Matildas.

Boston Breaker forward Tiffany Weimer played in a "second tier league" in Finland in late 2008 to prepare for the launch of WPS. She explained, "I went [overseas] to play ninety minutes every weekend. In the fall, there is nothing here except college soccer. . . . In Finland we [Åland United] were in the middle of the pack. We got to play the top three to four teams, but the rest weren't good. The level of practice in Finland wasn't as high as I would have liked. Some good [Finnish] players have gone to Sweden." If she ever returns to play overseas, she would target a higher level league: Australia, Germany, and Sweden intrigued her.

Besides the individual migration of players abroad, a few national teams have been actively recruiting their diaspora in North America to create a core group of experienced players who can help build the sport in the country of their parents or grandparents.

2004 Greek Olympic Games Team – Building with Diaspora

Outside of Scandinavia and the traditional "top five" markets of England, France, Germany, Italy, and Spain, many European countries are in the early stages of building programs for girls and women. Drawing from the diaspora has helped them jump-start the game and even compete for major European and World Cup tournaments. Mexico used the same approach for the 1999 World Cup, stocking half their roster with Americans of Mexican descent. Greece applied a similar model, using eight American college players and graduates with Greek ancestry to support ten from home to build a competitive team for the 2004 Olympics, for which they were seeded directly into the finals as host nation. Walker Loseno, whose great grandparents were born in Greece, was a junior forward at Gonzaga University in Spokane, Washington. While surfing the Internet, Loseno found Greece was looking for players. A week later she flew to Greece to try out, made the team, and then practiced with their national team over the next two years, while her family worked to validate her lineage to her great-grandparents from Plomari, the ouzo capital on the island of Lesvos. Loseno finally picked up her Greek passport in New York on the way to the Olympics. Defender Sofia Smith of Houston played at Cornell and was in her third year of law school when she took a leave of absence to play for the team. Goalkeeper Maria Yatrakis, who grew up in Brooklyn and played at the University of Connecticut, coached in college before later continuing her playing career in Sweden. Midfielder Tanya Kalivas was raised in New Jersey, graduated in 2001 from Princeton, and qualified via her Corfu-born father. Unlike Kalivas, who had visited Greece on numerous occasions during her youth, Yale University defender Eleni Benson had spent only three weeks there with her family when she was in eighth grade.

Kalivas, in an interview in 2008, provided some interesting insights into the experience. In early 2003 she had read in a San Francisco Greek American newspaper that Greece's women's national team was looking for players of Greek heritage, so she found the coach's e-mail address through Google and contacted her. Kalivas paid her own way to Europe for a tryout, and then the team reimbursed her (mostly) from that point on. To Kalivas, who had spent considerable time in Greece, including summers as a kid as well as researching her college thesis, the opportunity was more than just about the soccer: "Being in the Olympic Games was great, but it was more than that. It was also about reconnecting with being Greek and having an opportunity to live there. I had family there; my grandfather was still alive. With my teammates, we all became very close; we were so different and came from different upbringings, but we shared a common heritage." Eleni Benson added, "Our families were Greek, we felt Greek." She said that many people in Greece "were thrilled that we were there, coming back to our roots."

Despite that common heritage, there was a lot of tension with the home-based players when the Americans were first trying out. Kalivas explained, "Once it was clear that half of the team was American, things settled down. It was a stipulation that we weren't on the team unless we were [capable] of playing in the starting eleven. They wouldn't bring in an American to sit on the bench, and deprive a [native] player in that way." Loseno said just before the Olympics that "they caught on pretty quickly that we were just making their team better. Ultimately, that's all they cared about." Kalivas said that part of the difficulty stemmed from different perspectives since their American upbringing was much different than that of the native Greeks who didn't go to college. Kalivas said, "All they did was play soccer. A lot of Greece is very traditional;

you live in your village until you get married, and sometimes even then you stay there. A lot of us Americans had college and were going to have careers. We had life differences to overcome."

Cultural differences came across on the field as well. The Americans brought an advanced understanding of tactics and sophisticated training, while the home-based players had creative ball skills from their years of informal street soccer games. Benson explained that even differing approaches to practice sessions caused problems initially: "We came in with a very American attitude, to train as hard as you can—fitness, fitness, fitness. The Greeks emphasized skill and rest. Plus the American attitude is if something is wrong fix it, complain about it, and take control. In Greece you are not supposed to complain and confront the coach. It was frustrating; we didn't feel like we were getting the training that we needed to compete at the Olympics." Kalivas remembered that it took time to resolve the conflict: "As we got closer to the Olympics, we [ex-pats] were able to convince them that it was okay to play hard in practice. Before that, they [native Greeks] would get really mad. People would coast in practice. Our [American] approach was 'It's not about hurting someone; it's about playing 100 percent.'" That perhaps entered into Greek National Team head coach Xanthi Konstandinidou's thinking when she insisted that the Americans return to the United States every month; even as the Olympic Games were approaching, despite the long transatlantic flights. Kalivas surmised that "she was afraid we would be influenced by Greek ways; that the Greek lifestyle would contaminate us in a sense, and we would get lazy. It was a paranoid way to run a team." Emphasizing the disparate foundations of her team, before the Olympics started Coach Konstandinidou asked the Americans to "play with your American heads and Greek hearts," mixing their knowledge with their passion for their ancestral homeland.

Kalivas made it clear that playing for Greece was a sacrifice: "It wasn't a magical experience. It was realistic, I learned how hard women's lives are in countries where soccer is not supported. We didn't have money for rent at times. We would go three or four months at a time without a check. [The federation was paying all the players 500 Euros, about $600, a month but couldn't find any sponsors to help the women's team.] It makes me appreciate my life in the U.S. so much more."

The Americans saw themselves as pioneers much like Mia Hamm, Joy Fawcett, and Brandi Chastain—who were also their opening game opponents—had been at home for many years. The "new Greeks" had taken on a major task: to popularize the game in a country where few played and fewer accepted it. They embraced the opportunity to help change perceptions about the sport they loved, perceptions that were very different from their experiences in the United States. "When I tell people I play soccer, I get laughed at," Kalivas said in 2004. "It actually inspires anger. I've had a couple people say, 'What are you talking about? Women are supposed to stay home. Soccer is only for men.'" Loseno was told by a taxi driver during a heated discussion about women's role in Greek society that "women's feet are not made for soccer." One of their Greek-born teammates had to sneak out of her home to play soccer as a kid. Coach Konstandinidou said, "Our goal is for this team to really open the road so that women's soccer in Greece becomes accepted. That's the problem, that it is not socially accepted. Soccer in Greece is a man's sport."

When the team tried to hold a soccer clinic for girls, only eight girls showed up and were far outnumbered by boys. Kalivas and one teammate thought about staying in Greece after the Olympics, taking jobs, playing in the domestic league, and developing camps, even bringing in coaches from the United States. Kalivas explained that this became a nonstarter after they did one clinic, because the federation wanted to control everything: "Our coach held us back from doing anything outside our strict structure. It became clear it was a one-time deal. . . . I never got paid for our last month of playing—none of us did."

At the Athens Olympics, Greece's first game versus the United States brought 15,757 to the stadium in Heraklion for their 0–3 loss. This was fifteen times more than the record crowd to see the team, which typically played in front of a hundred people. It was also five thousand more than the gold medal match in Piraeus between the Americans and Brazil. More telling were some of the attendance figures without the Greek team, such as the 1,418 who saw the U.S.–Japan quarterfinal in Thessaloniki or the 1,511 in Patras for the Sweden–Brazil semifinal. Greece lost their second match by a 0–1 score to Australia in front of 8,857, again in Heraklion, before falling to a tremendous Brazil side 0–7 in front of 7,214 in Patras. Though the team did not score a goal in the tournament, the FA's goal of presenting a credible side was largely achieved in a challenging group.

Though playing in the Olympic Games was a special experience for Kalivas, she feels strongly that something more could have been made from the effort to improve the national team. Greece could have used the Olympics as a first step to something greater for women's soccer, but Kalivas termed it "a missed opportunity." She explained, with frustration apparent in her voice, "We built some support and media attention for women's soccer. . . . It baffles me to this day. Partly it was because of money, but my intuition is that Greece was concerned with image and having a presentable team during that time of the Olympics. After the Games, they just didn't care any more what happened. I think some of it was laziness, not putting in effort to push money towards women's soccer."

The team went into mothballs, not playing a competitive game for fourteen months after the loss to Brazil. The World Cup qualification campaign started in the fall of 2005, but the Americans weren't called in. Goalkeeper Maria Yatrakis even offered to pay her own way back to play, but the federation told her no. Greece bombed out of their group, losing all eight of their home and away matches to Norway, Italy, Ukraine, and Serbia-Montenegro, scoring only two goals while letting in twenty-eight. The progress made for the Olympic Games was completely undone. Despite the Greek FA's unwillingness to build upon the Olympic team's efforts, Kalivas did feel the Americans made a positive impact for the sport in the country: "I like to think we changed attitudes. We did do a lot of media interviews. The games were televised. I went back to Corfu [her father's village] for a couple of weeks after the games; they knew me there and watched my games. A couple of parents came up to me and said, 'My daughter plays soccer too, and she loves it.'" Eleni Benson said in 2008, "At least young girls saw that Greece had a women's soccer team. We tried to tell young girls that they could play too."

The native Greeks went back to playing in a league well below the quality of the amateur w-League and wpsl in North America, with little pay. Greece still lacks the developmental structures to grow the sport at the youth level. For the Americans, they gained a tremendous amount from the experience, learning more about their ancestral home and its people. Eleni Benson said, "All in all, the whole experience with the Greece team was exhilarating." Kalivas is more measured in her assessment, calling it "probably the best thing I've ever done, and yet, it's been the most difficult." She was disappointed that the team became a one-off event, rather than leading to sustainable growth of the sport. Greece committed to the short-term plan but bailed when it came to long-term support. Five years after their Olympic experience, Benson was in medical school in Texas and Kalivas had finished law school at Fordham. Both still followed the sport but only played sporadically around their busy schedules.

Portugal's Active Pursuit of Diaspora

Other countries are more committed to the long-term growth of their national teams and structures to develop young women players, and North American–trained imports are crucial to that plan. Among those countries that are most aggressively pursuing imports are Portugal. In 2004 the Portuguese Federation signed a cooperative agreement with the North American amateur league, the w-League, to identify American and Canadian girls and women of Portuguese heritage. The program was designed to "aid other nations in strengthening their women's national team programs, utilizing the deep pool of talent available in North America." Eighteen-year-old Canadian striker Alex Valerio of the Ottawa Fury was invited by Portugal's Women's National Team head coach Monica Jorge to try out for the U-19 team in early 2008. Unlike Greece, where the ex-pats largely contacted the federation, Portugal's National Team coach actively scouted and recruited their diaspora. Invited players had to pay for their trip to Europe for a weeklong tryout. If the head coach brought them in for future camps and games, the federation paid all expenses.

Maria Joao Xavier played for Portuguese women's teams from 1991 to 2003, winning five championships for two different teams, Gatoes FC and 1 Dezembro-Sintra. She won seventy-six caps for the Portuguese National Team, scoring four goals from her defensive midfield position. After retiring, she worked in administration on the club side and with the Algarve Cup, an annual spring international invitational competition for national teams. Having played all of her soccer at home, she talked about integrating foreign players into her national team. Xavier was open to the diaspora idea: "In my opinion all the players should have the same opportunities to play for the national team. This includes the players from other countries; however, with one condition. They have to be better than the others playing in Portugal. If they can't bring more quality, skill, and ability, I think the effort made by the Portuguese FA is not worth it, since the national team is still not developing." In that situation, Xavier believes that improving the infrastructure for the home-based players would be a better tactic. Xavier described conditions at the club level: "It's very hard to be a soccer player in Portugal. Mostly teams don't have appropriate conditions for practice, like the women teams have to share the field with youth male teams, or women teams are the last ones beginning their practices. This is a natural consequence, since all the players [have] other occupations. Some of them are studying, but most work until 6:00 p.m. or later. We can't live just playing soccer in Portugal."

Xavier found that most of the imports were good players and helped to improve the national team setup because they played in more competitive leagues and had better training, particularly in speed and strength elements. They challenged the Portuguese players in practice, which increased the locals' abilities, while the ex-pats learned more technical skills and a different approach to the game. They also expanded the very small pool of players in the country. Alex Valerio told the author in late July 2008, before a Fury playoff game that "we're told that only 1,700 females are registered in total to play soccer in Portugal. Some club teams in Ontario have more than that!"

Xavier also felt that sending home-based players, who were very good on the technical skills side, overseas benefited the individual and the entire league when they returned. She recalled, "In 2002 we had three players in China [Sonia Silva, Carla Couto, and Edite Fernandes], and Fernandes was considered the best player in the Chinese league. It was amazing when they returned to the Portuguese league. They were better players, since they had the chance to improve their skills playing at a higher level. They could share their experience with the younger players." Others have gone to play in Denmark, Iceland, and Spain.

The six-team first division (playing twenty games a year) has had the same champion, 1st Dezembro-Sintra, since 2002 and supplies at least ten players to the national teams, including the U-19 team. Players want to play at this club because they have such a strong side, but their success comes at the expense of the other five teams in the league. This is a common problem throughout Europe: a few teams dominate, and the rest are of a much lower quality. Players could be distributed via a draft among the league teams, but this is really only feasible when one entity owns all the franchises (like in the WUSA) or when the federation sets up and runs the league. Otherwise, the independent clubs, trying to build viable entities, will resist a "dictatorial" approach to player distribution. The hope is that, as more youth adopt the game, they will join senior teams. An eighteen-team second division (divided into three regions of the country) feeds the top tier, but additional divisions (third, fourth, and fifth tiers like on the men's side) are needed to be able to expand the first division to ten to twelve teams, like in northern

European countries. Since 2009–10, the first division has had ten teams.

Xavier feels the league needs more support, calling it the "underprivileged parent of all soccer in Portugal." She does not feel that it is necessary to turn the women's league into a fully professional enterprise, however. She said, "Personally I don't agree [with the idea], but the players should have some compensation from the Portuguese FA or at least have other conditions. Not long ago, some players lost their jobs because they were absent from work when representing the national team. . . . The women have the same right to play soccer, so why are we still not having the same support as the men's teams? I think this "battle" has just begun."

Kim Brandao, a Rutgers graduate and former W-League champion in New Jersey, has played for Portugal for a number of years. She felt that the federation has been supportive of the women's program, but "we need more money to fund the game, more media input, and a semiprofessional league. This will gain more interest/ respect from the people in Portugal."

In the next five to ten years, Brandao, who admittedly has ambitious goals, hopes to see "stadiums belonging to the women's game, women's club pitches rivaling those in the U.S., and a team to challenge the best in the world. . . . I believe in the potential that Portugal has, seeing it is already a nation that loves soccer."

Ireland — Modeling the Men's Success

The Republic of Ireland is another country using diaspora to improve its national team program, but the challenge there is not convincing people that women can play football, fighting against cultural barriers like in Greece or Portugal. In the Emerald Isle, the challenge is generating interest in soccer against another strong competitive football game that women have played for years: Gaelic football. Played with a round ball (slightly heavier and smaller than a soccer ball), the game is played with fifteen players on each side, who try to kick or punch a round ball into a goal or between uprights. Gaelic games have a tradition in Ireland dating back to the late 1800s and were important in establishing a communal sense of Irish uniqueness, particularly during the struggles with Britain over home rule and then independence. A British Army invasion in 1920 at Croke Park, the national Gaelic sports stadium, reportedly in retaliation for assassinations of British agents earlier that day, resulted in fourteen deaths and further linked Gaelic sports to Irish nationalist feelings. Until two decades ago, soccer was very much a minor sport, in part due to its perception as "the garrison game" brought to Ireland by British troops. For women today, the choice between playing Gaelic football or soccer is not political but comes down to availability of teams, what their friends are playing, and future opportunities.

The Ladies Gaelic Athletic Association has been holding a National Football Championship since the mid-1970s. Paul Swift, a member of the Ulster Provincial Council for the LGAA, explained that before the Gaelic Football women's championships began, until age fourteen both sexes played together on teams, and while older females weren't banned from playing, teams for women weren't organized, because women weren't seen "as fit for the tough sport." When women began to play Gaelic football, negative opinions changed quickly, since the athletes had grown up with the game. The rules were modified slightly for the women's game; for example, deliberate shouldering, which is allowed on the men's side, is prohibited. According to Michael Forde, a member of the LGAA Public Relations committee, "Girls who become involved in Gaelic football have stepped onto a path that will open doors for them, in college, work, at home, or abroad, and the friends they make at an early age will stay with them as they progress through life."

The LGAA has 130,000 players involved in the sport; eight times the 16,000 girls and women who play soccer. Forde found that, even in 2009, women's soccer was not very well developed, particularly outside of the larger cities. He cites the example of his own home, County Wicklow, in which there was not a women's soccer league: "Girls can play soccer and Gaelic football with boys' teams up to the age of fourteen, so if there is no ladies soccer in the area, they will go on to play ladies Gaelic football." A major domestic women's Gaelic football final can attract twenty thousand people, whereas a soccer international draws a few thousand.

Ireland's national soccer team has used the diaspora's quality and experience for a specific goal, qualifying for a first European or World Cup tournament, believing this will help to popularize the game at home. Besides actively recruiting in the United States, Ireland's Women's National Team spent two months in America's Midwest in the summer of 2009, preparing for their yearlong World Cup 2011 qualifying group, which started in September of 2009. Head Coach Noel King based his squad in Lafayette, Indiana, at the invitation of former W-League and WPSL power FC Indiana. In exhibition games, Ireland defeated their hosts (2–1), the WPS's Chicago Red Stars (1–0), the WPSL's Chicago United Breeze (6–0), and the University of Louisville (3–0). Their only defeat came against the Irish—of the University of Notre Dame (0–1). Coach King explained his rationale for the extended training camp abroad: "If we're going to try to be successful at that [qualifying for a European or World Cup tournament for the first time], while all the teams ahead of us are full-time training, they are all at camps, they all are highly organized and well funded; we have to try to reach their levels of fitness as well. So that's the reason behind coming out to America, to build strength, fitness, and condition while also working on our tactical play and playing against better opponents. That's the theory behind it."

Another benefit of the American training camp is that the United States has become a crucial recruiting ground for players of Irish descent. Ireland has a unique history with the concept on the men's side. For two decades, they utilized players born in England or Scotland who could join the team because their parents or grandparents were born in Ireland. After decades in the doldrums, since 1988 the Republic has played in three Men's World Cups and two European championships, galvanizing the country behind the sport. King was personally involved in that effort of creating a team built on second- and third-generation Irish players and sees that model as appropriate for his female squad: "If we could do something similar [on the women's side] by recruiting players and making the team stronger, making it qualify for the European or World finals where it would get public recognition and live television coverage, I believe that it would give the women's game the jump start that it needs. . . . It is the right policy at this time."

On their extended trip to the United States, King and his staff found two players who made the team for the first World Cup tests, forward Fiona O'Sullivan, who played at the University of San Francisco, and ex–University of Illinois midfielder Shannon McDonnell. King's focus was to find a few top quality players rather than trying to recruit half of his team abroad for cost and developmental reasons. King is committed to drawing most of his team from Republic-based players in order to build the game at home, where the women lack a national league, which King describes as "the biggest problem we face." Currently, the only national competition for women is an annual cup competition. These regional leagues and structures have, according to King, "haphazard standards, so it's very difficult for an Irish-based player to maintain their fitness to play at the highest level week in, week out. It's just not possible."

The Football Association of Ireland has tried to extend more college scholarships for players to stay in Ireland, whereas in the past the FAI has encouraged women to attend school in America. King explains that "there's been a tradition where girls would go to the States in college. We tried to stop that in the past couple of years as part of the development plan where we would implement scholarships of our own, but it was only a piecemeal effort to try to keep some of the girls at home, but without a national league it's very difficult to encourage girls to stay." Identifying career paths to college and beyond are vital, because Gaelic football stresses these opportunities to their players. King does not see Gaelic football as hurting soccer; fundamentally, both are round ball–kicking games, and boys and girls now grow up playing both sports. King does acknowledge that the two codes do compete for top players: "Gaelic football is quite strong with women athletes, and lots of those players would be searched out and pursued by the Gaelic game, where we would also be chasing them in the soccer game. There is an acceptance of girls playing sport in Ireland; there's no question about that, but the awareness of soccer for girls is only starting to grow, and we're a far stretch behind the Gaelic at this stage."

The Football Association of Ireland has made great progress in growing soccer from the national team on down to the youth level, particularly given that in the early 1990s they actually disbanded their national teams program for women after an embarrassing 10–0 loss to Sweden. A World Cup or European Championship finals berth should further drive more girls and women to the sport. Though Ireland finished third in their difficult 2011 World Cup qualifying group behind Switzerland and Russia, their U-17 team qualified for Ireland's first ever World Cup in Trinidad and made the quarterfinals, where they narrowly lost to Japan (1–2). Success for Ireland on an international stage will be an interesting challenge for Gaelic football, which, though played on a limited basis in North America and Australia, is still very much a domestic game.

For countries developing the women's game, though the long-term goal is to build the game at home, an experienced diaspora can be a key part of that process. They add a level of sophistication, tactical knowledge, and understanding of how to promote the game in America that translates well to countries building the sport, particularly in Europe. The new players bring a discipline that many times is lacking with the home-based players, since many even at the national team level do not play in regular leagues but only informally. Usually the motivation (and the additional funding it takes to shuttle the new players from their home bases) comes from trying to qualify for a major tournament like a World Cup, Olympics, or regional championship, but it must be simply the start of a longer term investment, as in Ireland or Portugal. Like utilizing battery cables to start a stalled automobile, the vehicle must be inspected and improved quickly or the charge will have a "one-time" impact. A few of the imported players may play for their new nation for many years, but without investing in youth programs (particularly in schools) and developing leagues for girls and women, the sport will forever be seen as an unimportant avenue for girls, and their parents, to devote significant time to.

10

National Leagues around the World

At the 2007 Women's World Cup, FIFA President Sepp Blatter declared a critical need for many countries to establish national women's leagues. Though most begin as amateur loops, as they mature into semiprofessional organizations, top players can earn some money from the game and decrease their workloads. In many European countries, the youth division has been a focus of growth efforts, and these have resulted in a solid increase in numbers. Now these young players need a top level league to aspire to, or they could give up the game. These leagues also act as the primary provider for future national team squads.

Sweden and the Damallsvenskan

In northern Europe, when UEFA encouraged their members to start supporting the game in the 1970s, Denmark, Germany, Italy, Norway, and Sweden stepped forward and built structures to support the sport over the next couple of decades, more than ten years ahead of the North Americans. Sweden, Norway, and Germany in particular developed a strong base of young female players. Their efforts have brought World or European titles at the national team level, and all three countries have high quality national leagues. Germany probably came the furthest: women players had been banned from forming a national league in 1955, with the FA explaining at the time, "The attractiveness of women, their bodies, and souls will suffer irreparable damage and the public display of their bodies will offend morality and decency." The ban was lifted in 1970, but the FA established different rules from the men, such as a lighter ball and sixty-minute games. Heike Ullrich, the head of women's soccer for the German Football Association, said in 2007 that hosting the Women's World Cup in 2011 was important because "we've reached the minds of the German people. We've overcome the argument that football was just for boys. We are over that."

The Scandinavians made huge strides for girls' and women's soccer because of their historically egalitarian cultures and liberal attitudes toward equal rights. Women have worked full-time jobs for years in Scandinavia and have long had access to sporting activities. Sweden in particular warrants more scrutiny, with a league (known in Swedish as the Damallsvenskan) that began in 1973 and has long been viewed as the top women's league in Europe, both in quality of play and attention from sponsors, the media, and fans. Thanks in part to the National Team's exciting run to the 2003 World Cup final, where they lost in overtime to Germany (while 44 percent of the country watched live on TV4, the channel's highest rating ever and one of the ten most watched events in the history of Swedish television) there is strong awareness in the country for the teams and individual players such as Victoria Svensson, Hanna Ljungberg, and Charlotta Schelin. Sweden's Damallsvenskan is a very popular destination for world-class players. Goalkeeper Nadine Angerer, a star from Germany's triumphant squad at the 2007 World Cup, joined Djurgarden of Stockholm, while Australian scoring sensation Lisa DeVanna signed with cross-town rivals AIK for the 2008 season. Brazilian superstar Marta played for Umeå for many years. Ten of the Finnish National Team squad selected for a friendly versus Iceland in May of 2008 played with Swedish clubs at the time.

One downside to the Damallsvenskan is in terms of attendance, which drives revenues and ultimately salary payments to players. The league average gate was between 800 and 1,100 over the past eight years, and though it seems low, it still exceeds the average for the German league (811 per game for twelve teams in 2008–9, up from 581 for 2005–6) and more than quadruple that of Norway's league (227 per game for twelve teams in 2007). Umeå's team of stars brought in strong gates, generally double the league average, until Marta left for WPS after the 2008 season. Attendance declined 30 percent, from 1,925 in 2008 to 1,336 in 2009. Newcomer Piteå was the top drawer that year at 1,820 but far below the WPS 2009 average of 4,493. Sweden's men's sides, very much seen as minor compared to those in England, Germany, Spain, and Italy, still draw 9,000 to 10,000 a game (see table 12 in the appendix).

The average salary in the Damallsvenskan was SEK55,000 (U.S.$9,100) a year in 2008. This is about the same as the men's average *monthly* wage in the Swedish first division, Allsvenskan. International forward Jessica Landström joined Linköpings FC in 2008 for about SEK20,000 a month ($3,400), six times her 2007 salary of SEK3,000 a month ($500) at Hammarby. Most players can't survive without another job. World Cups and Olympic Games capture lots of attention, but women's soccer still does not pull in financially viable crowds for weekly leagues even in the best conditions, including a top league and a supportive culture for women in sport. Without larger gates and other funding, a team's fortunes depend primarily on sponsorship revenues. Stattena qualified for the Damallsvenskan in 2009 and saw its annual turnover rise almost fourfold, from SEK700,000 ($85,000) to SEK2,500,000 ($300,000), losing their top-notch coach Thomas Persson as a result, but not because he wanted to leave. Their club chairman Michael Freitag explained, "We decided to keep the expenses for the coach position and use the money on players instead." A low finish can drive sponsors away, resulting in tighter budgets, with player salaries among the first items pared back. It also affects parity on the field, and every year only four clubs at the most are seen as serious championship contenders among the twelve top division teams.

The next few years will be crucial to the Damallsvenskan, as another half dozen top players have defected to WPS for the 2010 season. Sweden has a number of good young players, but until the clubs can demand realistic transfer fees or pay professional salaries, overseas clubs will continue to recruit them. Without increasing attendance and building a fan base among young adult men and women, the league's clubs will struggle annually to retain players, coaches, and sponsors. Sweden's attendance has seen a downward trend over the past few years, while Germany's average has generally increased by about a hundred a game each year. Further downturns in crowds and budgets could see Germany become the top-drawing league on the continent, particularly with the anticipated boost in attention from hosting the 2011 Women's World Cup.

Russia's Potential

Russia is not a top contender when you think of challengers to Germany's World Cup and European title reign. However, one well-respected women's coach feels that Russia is ideally poised to become a world power within the next five to seven years. Russia has a large population base, top quality infrastructure, and financial muscle, thanks to vast oil and energy reserves. Those resources allow Russian professional teams to import playing and coaching talent from around the world. In late 2009, Shek Borkowski, a top semiprofessional coach in the United States, was recruited as head coach of the two-time reigning league champions and UEFA Champions League runner-ups Zvezda-2005. Based in Perm, a city of 1 million about seven hundred miles east of Moscow in the Ural Mountains, Borkowski found many differences between professional women's teams in Russia and the United States.

Borkowski, a native of Poland who played at the University of Akron, started FC Indiana in tiny Goshen (population thirty thousand) and led it to two WPSL league crowns, two U.S. Open Cup titles, and a W-League second-place finish in five years. FC Indiana sent nine former players to WPS in 2009. Borkowski always ran FC Indiana like a professional European club, which made it appealing to him to run a fully professional side like Zvezda-2005.

Annual budgets for the seven teams in the Russian Top Division range from about $1 million to $9 million. The top few teams all have budgets that are much higher than WPS's per team $1.5–$2 million estimate. It's tough to compare the two leagues, as Russia's entire organizational approach is radically different. To survive, WPS teams are concerned with controlling budgets, growing marketing dollars, and boosting gate receipts while minimizing expenses. Russian teams don't bother much with these issues; teams don't even have marketing officers. Their budgets are used primarily for coaches' and players' salaries. Admission to games is free, and sponsorship money is negligible. Teams don't pay rent for their municipal facilities, a few of which are new developments with multiple grass, turf, and indoor fields plus hotels, dormitories, and restaurants. Typically, the team's home region provides about half of the yearly budget, with the rest coming from a local benefactor, usually a business owner or industrialist. The state governments relish the chance to garner prestige with national officials in Moscow and internationally by winning Russian and European titles. The number 1 driver of larger budgets is success. In North America, winning titles frequently increases costs (in unbudgeted playoff trips, excessive player salary demands, and other hidden expenses) and can result in belt-tightening the following year. As one W-League team owner said to me, "I want to be competitive, but winning costs me way too much." In Russia, individual owners bask in the accolades that come from making a civic contribution to the area they draw their employees from.

The seven teams in the top division comprise primarily players and coaches from Russia and former Soviet Republics. Players sign twelve-month contracts (or longer) and typically play for ten months, including training camps in places like Turkey and South Africa. Players can clear $35,000 a year and not have to pay for food or housing, comparable with WPS's average gross pay per season.

Borkowski found quite a high standard of play in the Russian league. Players were very technical and understood tactics but were not as physical as North Americans. Borkowski said, "The United States and Germany play a very physical style of soccer; that is new to the Russians."

Borkowski felt that Russian women's soccer officials were too focused on domestic and European club success. As the head coach at a leading club, he hoped to influence local Russian players, through his training regimen and different approaches to playing styles, to have a greater impact on the global game. Borkowski used his international contacts that he leveraged in Indiana, bringing in fifteen imports from Africa, Europe, and North America to try out during his first training camp in early 2010. Russian league rules allow four non-Russians on the field at any one time, but there is no ceiling on how many a team can sign for its roster. Zvezda-2005 had a $4 million annual budget to work with. Borkowski's team flew free on a regional airline, because Perm is so far from the other league cities. Zvezda-2005 trained from 11 a.m. to 12:30 p.m. and then ate lunch in the club's cafeteria afterward. Borkowski described the food as "superb," with caviar, beef, fish, and fruit typical fare. Players can even take food home with them.

Borkowski saw some major differences between the psychology of players in Russia and North America. In Russia, soccer is simply a job. They come to train and return home to their other interests. North Americans expect social bonding with their squads, spending a lot of time with their teammates off the field, in large part because that's what they experienced in college. Like on Noah's Ark, Borkowski believed imported pairs from a country did better than stand-alones, because Russia, though a fantastic country, is quite different from their homelands.

Borkowski was able to focus on coaching and player development at Zvezda-2005, freed of fundraising, sponsor development, and other organizational issues he had with FC Indiana. He and Rashid Rakhimov, the coach of the local men's Premier team Amkar Perm, visited area schools and met with youth teams to implement a standard playing curriculum. Young players first joined school teams, then moved up to interscholastic and city teams within the region. Parents have considerable influence on youth teams in North America, but not in Russia. Promising twelve-year-olds are drafted into Zvezda-2005; the team has its pick of the best players from the Perm-Krai region of almost 3 million residents. Zvezda-2005's reserve team plays in the twenty-seven-team Russian second division and comprises sixteen- to nineteen-year-olds. A future avenue for growth is to add to the seven top tier teams, perhaps in tandem with some of the sixteen men's Premier league and twenty-two first division sides. Earlier editions of the national women's soccer league, begun in 1992, have had ten, twelve, and even fifteen teams. Expansion teams must be formed tactically, with strong government and owner commitment so that the new sides are able to compete within a few years.

When a top American women's coach who has been linked to national team jobs joins a club team in Russia, leaving his family behind in Indiana, it had to be for extraordinary reasons. Borkowski felt that he could contribute to Russian teams' growth in international competitions and bring back some of the uniquely Russian approaches to the soccer experience, particularly in how they treat players. Borkowski said, "Overall, from a football [soccer] perspective it's a great set up." Borkowski ran into some severe owner interference issues, however, and returned to Indiana during the summer of 2010, but other European club teams were interested in his services.

A New National League in Australia

Women have been playing Down Under since the early 1970s; the first national championship was held in 1974, the same year the Australian Women's Soccer Association was formed. In 2007 Australia's National Team, better known as the Matildas, were a revelation at the China World Cup, a result of their youth soccer structures and strong numbers. Led by their gregarious and jovial head coach Tom Sermanni and a bright and engaging group of players, they were scintillating to watch. They swept through the first round undefeated and clinched a quarterfinal spot for the first time thanks to Cheryl Salisbury's heart-stopping goal late in injury time to tie Canada (voted by the Australian public as 2007's favorite sporting moment), putting the Maple Leafs out of the tournament. Sermanni termed the game "the longest day at the office," while goalkeeper Melissa Barbieri labeled the last minute dramatics as part of their culture: "That's what we do. We're Australian; we fought to the bitter end." In a stirring quarterfinal, they overcame a 2–0 deficit against Brazil, tying the game before a late Samba team goal put them out of the tournament. Forward Sarah Walsh told the author after that loss in Tianjin, "People recognize us that we can play good football. We did our country proud."

There was one area that Australia needed to address, and that was the lack of a senior league. Alicia Ferguson had been playing for the national team for ten years, since age fifteen, winning sixty-six international caps, and commented after China, "Our domestic situation certainly needs sorted [out], because at the moment our league set-up is pretty nonexistent, and we end up playing against boys teams more often than not. I just hope that this competition [2007 Women's World Cup], and this [national] team can provide the impetus we need to get things up and running in that respect."

Most of the Matildas worked part-time jobs or were unemployed. The twenty-one members of the World Cup squad received just over AUS$5,000 each in bonuses for reaching the World Cup quarterfinal. Twenty-three-year-old Lisa DeVanna, the team's leading scorer in China with four goals, and a member of FIFA's All Tournament team, returned after the World Cup to Perth and her regular job of pumping gas at a service station. She soon was spirited away by AIK of the Swedish Damallsvenskan and eventually signed with WPS' Washington Freedom in 2009.

Coach Sermanni was afraid the sport would slide backward unless a league started very soon, building on the basic structure of the country's academy programs: "There are national leagues for women in netball, basketball, hockey, and water polo, yet football, where the numbers are booming, doesn't have one. There is such a wide gulf between the academy programs and the national team.

And when a player drops out of the national squad, they simply don't have anywhere to play. We desperately need the league to start up again, even if it's not got all the bells and whistles. I would be happy with just a single round of matches to get the ball rolling."

To their credit, Football Association officials leveraged the attention from the World Cup run to hastily launch its second attempt at a national women's league, the w-League, the following year. (Australia's first national league, the Women's National Soccer League, folded in 2004 after nine seasons. The WNSL's format involved six to seven teams who played one another twice during a two- to-three month season. Most of the teams were formed from state-based elite academies, such as in Queensland and New South Wales.) The Australian Government granted operational funding for the w-League through Football Federation Australia. Additional contributions came from state soccer associations and title sponsor Westfield Group, a shopping mall developer. The players received no salaries, just expenses. Football Australia leveraged their four-year-old men's professional A-League sides for marketing support, except for Canberra United, which was a women's only team, replacing the Wellington, New Zealand–based men's side. Daniel Lato, press secretary with Queensland (now Brisbane) Roar, explained that "only one or two of the A-League clubs are profitable, so to integrate women's teams operationally and fiscally now was not economically viable." The lone exception was Adelaide United, which fully folded the women into its organization. Bonita Mersaides, the former head of corporate and public affairs for Football Australia, explained that their long-term goal was to create a super club scenario with franchise-owned youth, men, and women senior sides. The players felt that using the men's team names helped them establish credibility with fans as a national league. Running largely separate operations avoided the situation of dependent offshoots of top men's clubs; A-League sides are subject to massive budget cuts and can even face dissolution, as the yearly fortunes of teams in the five-year-old league can change dramatically.

The w-League kicked off in October of 2008 with eight teams, each playing ten regular season games, with four teams qualifying for one-game semifinals. The Queensland (now Brisbane) Roar defeated Sydney FC on penalty kicks after a 1–1 draw, while Canberra United downed Newcastle Jets 1–0. The winners contested the Grand Final, with the Roar adding the overall title to its regular season crown after a 2–0 win over Canberra before 4,500 fans in Brisbane (see table 13 in the appendix). Australian coaches and players were pleased with the first season, particularly since just six months before, officials weren't sure if they had enough time to start. Jeff Hopkins, the head coach of w-League Champions Queensland (now Brisbane) Roar, reflected on the league's value: "The inaugural w-League has proven to be a great success in many areas; most importantly, it has given the best Australian women footballers the opportunity to play in a highly competitive league, regular week-to-week games, and [strive] for starting places." Sermanni said the national team will be a direct beneficiary of the league environment:

I think the w-League is a huge asset to women's football. Coming towards the end of this tournament, I'll be making some difficult decisions in relation to the formation of the national squad and for some players; this is critical for their future as part of the national team. I think what we're supposed to see in this competition is someone who perhaps hasn't been on the radar before, as well as see how the younger players match up to the more established players in the competition. In regards to recruiting new players, these are the sort of things I'll be looking for.

An example of how the league has helped young players develop is Roar's starting goalkeeper, sixteen-year-old Casey Dumont. Dumont is also the U-20 national team backstop and third on the full national team's depth chart.

w-League Goalkeeper of the Year for 2008 Melissa Barbieri said,

"I think given the circumstances the year was a tremendous success. It was put together quite quickly and for the competition to be as even as it was obviously bodes well for the future."

A few imports who had played for their national teams or been called into their training camps joined for the inaugural w-League season, including:

Canada—Brittany Timko (Melbourne Victory)
New Zealand—Rebecca Tegg (Melbourne Victory), Marlies Oostdam (Melbourne Victory) and Rebecca Smith (Newcastle Jets)
Singapore—Shiya Lim (Perth Glory)
Sweden—Sanna Frostevall (Newcastle Jets)

Perth Glory's Lisa DeVanna said after the first season that she would like to see more foreign players in the future. Hopkins agreed, feeling the imports will "lift the bar of quality players." DeVanna also felt that the league should run longer, affording a full home and away schedule.

One of the first-year imports, Canadian international midfielder Brittany Timko—a nominee for w-League player of the year for Melbourne—felt that the venues were good; the league was well organized and was headed in the right direction. She found the quality equal to North American's amateur w-League, and good for the first year. Coming from Vancouver, where the Whitecaps had averaged three to four thousand a game during her time there, Timko felt that Australia's w-League attendances were noticeably low (about five hundred a game) and that more joint marketing efforts of w-League games held the same weekend as A-League fixtures would build the fan base, but overall she felt that the league had a lot of positives during the first year to build upon.

Bonita Mersiades, formerly of Football Australia, felt that a plus for the league was arranging a weekly nationally televised game on free television. She said that no new franchises would be added for a few years because "we think it is more important to consolidate

5. Queensland (now Brisbane) Roar celebrate their Grand Final win in Australia's w-League inaugural campaign in 2008–9. (Courtesy Daniel Lato, Queensland Roar.)

with the existing eight teams rather than expand in a climate of economic tightening. We also have to ensure there are enough quality players to participate in the w-League." Hopkins felt more sponsors should help to increase funds for promotions and operations.

In year 2 of the w-League, Sydney won the league, and Brisbane Roar and Canberra repeated as playoff participants, with the Central Coast Mariners replacing the Newcastle Jets, who finished last in 2009 with just two ties in ten games. Sydney beat Canberra 3–0 in one semifinal, and Brisbane knocked out Central Coast by a single goal. Sydney added the grand final title to the regular season crown, dethroning the inaugural champions Roar 3–2 (see table 14 in the appendix).

More imports came to the w-League in 2009, boosted by five

6. Queensland (now Brisbane) Roar coach Jeff Hopkins and team captain Kate McShea address the media. (Daniel Lato, Queensland Roar.)

loan players from the WPS. Kendall Fletcher, Jill Loyden, and Lydia Vandenbergh all boosted the Central Coast Mariners' fortunes, while Julianne Sitch and Alex Singer joined Melbourne and Perth, respectively. Other imports included:

Canada – Katie Thorlakson (Melbourne Victory)
Denmark – Cathrin Paaske and Julie Rydahl (both Sydney FC)
New Zealand—Marlies Oostdam (Melbourne Victory)
Taiwan—Tseng Shu O and Lin Chiung Ying (Canberra United)

Jill Loyden, on loan from the WPS's St. Louis Athletica, won goalkeeper of the year for Central Coast, while teammate Michelle Heyman topped the league goalscorer's table with eleven. Loyden found the experience beneficial, particularly since, as backup to U.S.

National Team veteran Hope Solo, she rarely played in St. Louis. She found the w-League focused on young (seventeen- to twenty-one-year-old) future national team prospects, which in Australia was typically the age range at which players dropped the sport, forced to enter the work force or advanced schooling. She and her two American teammates had to provide a lot of teaching, including organizing practices and even talks on how to be a professional. In some ways, she found the game lagged American soccer by a good ten to fifteen years. Everything was so new for both the coaches and players, but she saw huge potential in the league. She liked the fact that more games were held before their partner men's A-League games in year 2. The doubleheaders created a more intense atmosphere and more publicity for the league.

Australia has shown that a national league can be started quickly, providing a model to countries such as Brazil that have struggled to launch a premier level women's league. The w-League leveraged existing professional men's teams for marketing purposes while running largely independently funded operations. The federal and local governments provided significant grants at the start, not unlike in Russia. With controlled growth, Australia's w-League should develop into a strong entity, assisting with the continued improvement of the Australian National Teams and the expansion of the sport in Southeast Asia and Oceania.

Strong national leagues benefit a country's national teams program and give young players a home platform to aspire to. Australia added a unique wrinkle to the key decision for countries starting a national league: whether to fully integrate into an existing men's organization or stay fully independent. Their hybrid model, using common names and marketing organizations with the men's teams but keeping separate budgets, has worked in the short term—particularly for a rapid launch. In addition, it allows future flexibility to either keep the present model, more fully integrate with the men's A-League franchises, or create a completely separate identity.

11

Overcoming a Fifty-Year Ban in England

England holds the enviable titles as the historical birthplace of soccer and the great exporter of the game throughout the world. In
the late 1800s and early 1900s, British military troops, engineers,
and other ex-pats took the game far and wide, including to Brazil,
India, South Africa, and the United States. Many times the locals
quickly adapted the sport after watching the British play amongst
themselves. In other cases the visitors actively introduced the sport
to the locals, providing equipment and teaching them the rules,
in a fashion not unlike religious missionaries. It's not surprising
then to find that England was also an early adapter and propo-
nent of the women's game. The first recorded women's football
match took place in North London in March 1895, when British
Ladies Football Club organized a game with a northern schoolgirl's
team, who beat their rivals from the south 7–1 before ten thousand
people. The sport had a Camelot period in the 1920s led by the
Dick, Kerr Ladies of Preston, a World War I–era works team that
drew thousands to exhibitions and donated hundreds of thousands
of British pounds to various charities. Their success threatened
the custodians of the men's professional game so much, however,
that in 1921 the English Football Association (FA) banned the
women from using fields and stadiums controlled by FA-affiliated
clubs (men's teams), an edict that was not rescinded until 1971,
half a century later. The English women's game has still not fully

recovered from the setback, and this explains why they trail other European countries at the national team and league level, despite the fact that the largest continental countries didn't actively support the women's sport until the 1970s or even 1980s. Women in England still face discrimination in terms of media coverage, facilities, coaching, and respect; meanwhile, efforts to turn a moribund national league into a semiprofessional outfit were seemingly always "a year away." Understanding the history will fully explain why England lags behind; all the more striking when compared with the Netherlands, where a three-year-old national league is thriving under traditional male professional set-ups.

England's Current Struggles

England had been a minor player at the national team level until the 2007–9 period. The Three Lions had only qualified for the World Cup twice: in 1995, when they made the quarterfinals after a pair of 3–2 wins (over Canada and Nigeria), and in 2007, when they again made the quarterfinals via a much more difficult first-round grouping.

Putting a damper on England's success at the 2007 China World Cup was that, despite untoward publicity at home, the players received only £40 (U.S.$80) a day while they were away. The FA or team sponsors didn't compensate them for lost wages in the process. St. Louis Athletica/Atlanta Beat striker Eniola Aluko and her teammates received £1,400 ($2,800) for five weeks of World Cup preparation and play. She explained that players had to take time off without pay for China and didn't have any more leave time, so their training suffered. Aluko said, "We are all grateful that we went to the World Cup but realistically we can't sustain the level of progress because of employment issues. Our fitness levels that were tested at the last camp [for the 2009 European Championship qualifiers] were significantly lower than they were at the World Cup in China."

The English Football Federation is one of the richest in the world. Women's soccer doesn't draw anywhere close to what men's league and internationals do, but the number of female players at the youth level are significant and bring additional registration fees and fuel a future fan base. It's perplexing that a football association that is flush with money can't allocate some salary and bonus payments for their female players. However, the history of the FA's relationship with women's soccer shows that the players' battle for compensation for lost wages and other issues will not be easily won. At its root is a conflict that is close to ninety years old, from a time that was viewed as the golden age of women's soccer in the country, symbolized by one team, Dick, Kerr Ladies.

When the English Women's Premier League teams typically attract gates of a few hundred and the national team attendance record is 14,107 for a World Cup qualifier versus Germany in 2002 (outside of three larger crowds for European Championship matches that England hosted in 2005), it is mind-boggling that in the 1920s, women's soccer was routinely drawing crowds in the ten to twenty thousand range. The sport blossomed during the World War I years as women took factory jobs to replace the men who went into the armed forces. Women factory workers started recreational teams, the most famous of which was the Dick, Kerr Ladies, which was named after its two Scottish founders, W. B. Dick and John Kerr, who manufactured trams and munitions during the war. Based in Preston in the Northeast, Dick, Kerr actually began after a challenge between men's and women workers at the plant in October of 1917, the result of which was unknown. The women then scheduled exhibitions against other women teams, with the gate receipts going to charities. Their first game was played at Preston's main football stadium (Deepdale) on Christmas Day 1917 versus Arundel Coulthard Foundry, with Dick, Kerr triumphing 4–0 in front of ten thousand people. Six hundred pounds were donated for wounded soldiers at a local hospital. Dick, Kerr Ladies continued to play matches for charity, usually on behalf of veterans or children. Dick, Kerr's popularity grew, despite some complaints that females were not built for a rough game; a few hysterically claimed that playing the game could cause sterility. In 1919 Dick,

Kerr tied Newcastle United Ladies at St. James Park in Newcastle in front of thirty-five thousand fans. In 1920 twenty-five thousand came to Deepdale to see Dick, Kerr play a touring women's team from France.

On November 20, 1920, at Leicester, women played the first ever night football game under lights, using anti-aircraft search-lights on the field with approval of Secretary of State for War Winston Churchill. The crowd of 22,000 yielded £600 for the un-employed ex-servicemen's distress fund. The largest crowd ever to attend a women's football match at club level came to Goodison Park in Liverpool on December 26, 1920. Fifty-three thousand were jammed inside with at least another 10,000 outside for Dick, Kerr against St. Helen Ladies. Dick, Kerr won 4–0 while raising £3,115 for charity. Two weeks later, they brought 35,000 to Old Trafford, home of Manchester United. As the crowds grew, so did their schedule, causing the players to give up more and more of their weekends. The girls didn't complain; they were dedicated to their game and the cause of helping needy charities. That same year, nine of their side played for England in their 22–0 win over Scotland, the first women's international. In 1921 Dick, Kerr played sixty-five games for charity all over the British Isles, with a total recorded gate in excess of 850,000. Forty of the games attracted at least 10,000 while eight exceeded 25,000 for an overall average of 13,315.

Dick, Kerr's success boomeranged on them after the Great War ended, with repercussions that still affect the game to the present day. The men's game, largely dormant during the conflict, began once again. Dick, Kerr, previously popular for their bright play and volunteer efforts, now faced hostility from the administrators of the sport, who saw them as a viable threat to the men's version. Dick, Kerr had attracted larger gates at times than the men's team typically would in the same stadium. Their success threatened the men's professional game so much that the administrators worked to kill it off, or at least severely limit its impact. They attacked Dick, Kerr Ladies again on the medical side but did the most damage on the money equation. Dick, Kerr had to defend themselves against charges that not all their gate receipts went to charity. Gail Newshaw, who authored *In a League of Their Own!*, a thorough history of the team, does raise some doubts about team manager Albert Frankland, who may have personally benefited from his long association with the team, but the women played only for expenses and reimbursed lost salaries. Frankland argued that Dick, Kerr had raised fifty thousand pounds for charity through 1921, but ultimately the women players were the ones hurt by the allegations. On December 5, 1921, the English Football Association passed the following resolution:

> Complaints having been made as to football being played by women, the council feel impelled to express their strong opinion that the game of football is quite unsuitable for females and ought not to be encouraged. Complaints have also been made as to the conditions under which some of these matches have been arranged and played, and the appropriation of receipts to other than charitable objects. The council are further of the opinion that an excessive proportion of the receipts are absorbed in expenses and an inadequate percentage devoted to charitable objects. For these reasons the council request clubs belonging to the [English Football] association to refuse the use of their grounds for such matches.

The Magna Carta this was not. Dick, Kerr's captain Alice Kell said, "We play for the love of the game and we are determined to carry on. It is impossible for working girls to afford to leave work to play matches all over the country and be the losers. I see no reason why we shouldn't be recompensed for loss of time at work. No one ever receives more than ten shillings per day."

Newsham wrote that the players were convinced that the FA instituted the ban because they drew bigger crowds than the men. The FA's draconian ruling forced women's teams to play on rugby grounds and in other facilities. Dick, Kerr more easily fought the physical controversy, inviting twenty members of the medical community to one of their games. The *Lancashire Daily Post* reported no negative reactions from the doctors, who felt soccer was physically the same for women as playing tennis or field hockey.

Interestingly, Dick, Kerr Ladies chose the next year for an extended tour abroad, to get away from the oppressive FA ban, even though the ruling body opposed that too. They sailed to North America for their only visit. The Canadian Soccer Association's forerunner, the Dominion Football Association, prevented Dick, Kerr from playing any games in the country, with strong encouragement from the English ruling body, Newsham hypothesized. The more independent-minded former colonies allowed the team to play, drawing crowds ranging from four to ten thousand, similar to those of a touring men's team from Scotland earlier in the year. The unique twist was that Dick, Kerr played nine U.S.-based men's teams, since there were no women's teams at the time. On the field, Dick, Kerr's 3–3–3 record was outstanding, given that they played mostly men's professional teams that regularly participated in the U.S. Open Cup for amateur and professional clubs, the highest level of annual competition in the country. Opponents Patterson Silk Sox were the defending U.S. Open Cup (national) champions, and J & P Coats won the 1922–23 American Soccer League title when the league, with a number of British imports, rivaled the standard of play in England and Scotland. For the game in Fall River, Massachusetts—a hotbed for the sport—the *Fall River Evening Herald* called the match, "One of the biggest things in soccer ever to have visited the United States." The ASL's per game attendance averaged four thousand, so Dick, Kerr was a solid draw for fans (see table 15 in the appendix).

Newsham wrote that the newspapers reported Dick, Kerr Ladies showing great stamina, clever combination play, and considerable speed. The individual performances of several players compared favorably with the skills of the professional male players. Their games in the United States not only helped promote the sport, struggling against the more popular gridiron football and baseball, but also were a precursor to the future success that the women's game would have in the country. Their results against professional men and crowds in the States must have scared FA officials at home about the damage they could do to the profitable men's games if they played against men at home. The FA needn't have worried; despite their successful tour, Dick, Kerr never played men's teams again, determining that their game was best played against women. The FA's protective approach to the all-important revenue the men's game generated resulted in continued efforts to repress the women's game for many years to come.

In 1926 the squad's manager Alfred Frankland fell out with the Dick, Kerr foundry owners, and the team changed its name to the Preston Ladies, though they were frequently referred to by their old moniker. Most of the players landed jobs with a local psychiatric hospital that enabled them to continue their athletic careers. The FA's ban shunted them to more obscure locations, and their gates averaged about five thousand during the 1930s. In the summer of 1937 they were matched with Edinburgh Ladies, the Scottish women champions, in Blackpool. Preston Ladies won 5–1, to claim an unofficial title of world champions. At a dinner held in their honor, Captain Cobb, Member of Parliament for Preston, said he had heard of this wonderful football team who beat all their rivals, but had imagined that ladies who played such a vigorous game would be "pretty tough guys." The audience laughed, and he continued to say that he was glad to have that impression changed because he now realized that women could play a "man's" game without losing any of their feminity. The team's efforts to change attitudes, particularly with men, were an important part of their mission.

Still, the players faced obstructions and discrimination. The Welsh FA banned a women's charity match from taking place in Wales in 1938, with their secretary Ted Robbins declaring, "It's a man's game and women don't look well playing it." In 1947 the English FA banned a referee for overseeing a women's game. The disgraced official, an ex-RAF corporal, wrote, "All these girls are doing is what in war times would have been classed as a man's job. Where would the country be now if the powers that be had said, 'That is a man's job and girls must not do it—they might bring the country into disrepute'?"

The 1950s presented a different struggle as Dick, Kerr had to advertise for players for the first time, while the men's game grew exponentially. In 1951 only twenty-six women's teams existed in the entire country. The end was clearly near for the club during the 1960s. In 1962 the Welsh FA was at it again, banning two games between Dick, Kerr and Oldham Ladies in Rhyl. The secretary of the Welsh FA said, "Our rule book prohibits ladies football on any ground affiliated to the association. We think that football is a man's game and that there is no place for lady players." The English FA banned a game at a British Legion ground at Newton that was used by a minor Lancashire Combination League that was completely amateur. The FA ban had effectively stilted any growth or development of girls' or women's soccer. Attracting players from a tiny base was the ultimate death knell for Dick, Kerr. They scheduled fewer games each year, with sixteen in 1963, followed by twelve games in 1964 and only three in 1965. On August 21, 1965, two years short of their fiftieth anniversary, they played their final game, a 4–0 win against Handy Angles. On the field, Dick, Kerr/Preston Ladies played 828 matches, winning 758, drawing 46 with only 24 losses, and scored over 3,500 goals. Off the field, the team had 160 civic receptions in their honor and raised around £175,000 for charity.

The State of the Game after Dick, Kerr

It was sad that Dick, Kerr was not around a few years later, in 1969, when a women's football association was formed, followed by the FA rescinding their ban on women playing on men's fields in 1971, fifty years after they had instituted it. The Women's Football Association operated until 1993, helping to advance the game with very little support and income, when the English FA took over responsibility for women's football. At the youth level the game was expanding nicely, with approximately 1 million girls playing the sport in schools at the turn of the century. At the top tier however, it was badly organized and undercommitted. Despite the vast resources of the richest and best-supported men's professional league in the world, the English Premier League, the women's equivalent was strictly amateur and very much off the radar.

One professional men's side tried to change the status quo in the women's game. Fulham FC started the first fully professional women's team in the world in April of 2000, a year before the eight WUSA teams started. Fulham was one of the most ambitious clubs in English soccer, owned by Harrod's entrepreneur Mohamed Al Fayed. Al Fayed saw potential after the unprecedented crowds and media attention in the United States for the 1999 Women's World Cup. Al Fayed expected other teams to follow his example with Fulham Ladies, particularly those affiliated to top men's sides like Chelsea and Arsenal, but no one else did. He took Fulham Ladies back to amateur status in 2003 when it was clear that talk of a fully professional women's league for the 2003–4 season would not become reality because of a lack of capital. Al Fayed blamed the setback on the failure of English soccer authorities to develop the women's game: "The mediocre advances in women's football during this period have made it impossible for me to continue at a professional level. I have invested millions of pounds into Fulham FC [the men's side], and the priority for me is to focus on the club's core business of Premier League football."

An outsider who looks at the lineup of the thirty-six teams of the English Women's Premier League and second tier Northern and Southern Divisions in 2008–9 would be impressed by the cavalcade of the names of storied men's professional sides: Arsenal, Aston Villa, Chelsea, Everton, Leeds United, Manchester City, Newcastle United, Nottingham Forest, and Sheffield Wednesday. Even lower-division professional sides such as Brighton and Hove Albion, Colchester United, and Tranmere Rovers field women's sides. Beyond the nomenclature however, one finds that just because professional clubs sponsor women's soccer doesn't mean it's taken very seriously. The women's program is strictly an amateur endeavor, with less support and resources than some boy's teams. In the years after Fulham's decision to revert to an amateur approach, there were a constant stream of teams cut loose by their men's sides—including Manchester United, Sunderland, Charlton, and Cardiff City. Birmingham City couldn't invest £75,000 ($150,000) for their women annually, when they spent ten times that in transfer fees for average men's players. Leeds United stopped their support of the women's side in 2006 and even prohibited them from using their practice facilities. The Leeds women's team gallantly forged on, signing a long-term sponsorship with Leeds Metropolitan University, but were sued by their former benefactor for continuing to use the men's logo and team colors. Again citing financial viability issues, pioneers Fulham completely eliminated its funding for the women's team three years after going back to an amateur setup, blaming the decision on poor attendance and a lack of media attention. The club, now known as WFC Fulham, has survived as an independent organization but spent a year in the second division after losing Al Fayed's support.

The lack of backing by the clubs follows to the stands; league attendances typically average between one and two hundred people a game, according to FA officials in 2008. As England and Arsenal forward Lianne Sanderson (who scored five goals in twenty-one games for the Philadelphia Independence in 2010) said, it was demoralizing to return to the tiny Premier League crowds to play "in front of one man and his dog again," after playing in front of tens of thousands of fans at the 2007 World Cup in China. Suggestions have been floated to increase the competitiveness of the league, including moving the women's season to the summer from the winter, cutting the number of teams in the Premier League from twelve to eight, or limiting the number of internationals that can play on any one team. Often these became smokescreens and tangential items; the underlying issue was the commitment level from the FA and team administrators. If they made the women's game more important and devoted more resources to it, then the public would respond as well.

Arsenal is an example of a team that is making an effort to grow the women's side. Their women's team was UEFA Cup (European) Champions in 2007, and have won eight of the last nine league titles since 2000–2001 and eleven of seventeen since the FA took charge of women's football in 1993. In 2007 the Lady Gunners won an unprecedented League, FA Cup, League Cup, and UEFA Cup quadruple. The squad is coached by Arsenal's men's team kit man (essentially the equipment manager) Vic Akers, who has been doing it on a volunteer basis since the team was founded two decades before. When he began with the women, Akers recalled, "They said I must be crazy. At the time there was little support for women's football; I had to change people's views, and for that we needed role models. . . . The girls are [now] seen as athletes and the game is more accepted. All the girls ever wanted was for their own game to be respected, and I think we've achieved that."

English goalkeeper Rachel Brown is an articulate advocate of the sport. Like a growing number of Europeans, she played college soccer in the United States, in her case, at the University of Pittsburgh. She was named Goalkeeper of the Year for the Eastern Conference every year and also holds the university record for the least goals conceded in a season. As a fifteen-year-old, she was with Liverpool when they contested the 1996 FA Women's Cup Final. Brown's dramatic save from Germany's Kerstin Garefrekes just minutes from the final whistle preserved a 1–1 tie that was crucial to her team advancing to the quarterfinals of the 2007 World Cup.

In an interview after England's first-round win versus Argentina in China, she discussed what she thought her team's World Cup success would transpire to at home: "The domestic game needs a lot of looking at, and I believe the FA knows about that and is addressing that at a different stage. . . . The [Women's Premier League] I think will be addressed and be restructured in the next few years, and hopefully we'll continue to bring through younger players to the national team program. Hopefully the knock-on effect will work, since we've done so well in it [the 2007 Women's World Cup] so far and has had a really positive effect back home."

Brown felt that the top-level league really needed the support of the FA now that the youth and national programs were in good shape:

> I think the youth program has been very well structured. The infrastructure is in place and seems to be quite successful. We have Centers of Excellence [elite training facilities] from U-10 all the way up to U-16, and we have international youth setups now which start at U-15, which we've not had until recently, so these are all strides that the FA has made to improve the quality. Now that the grass roots has taken place, more girls are playing than ever have been. Developing elite players at grass roots level, that's been successful, and at senior international level, we've improved so much over the years. Only thing between is the domestic game, which is now the next thing to be addressed because that does need to improve.

Many of the top British players go to play college in the United States, like Rachel Brown did, and they do so because it's a vast improvement over what they find at home. Jodie Taylor played for Tranmere Rovers, one of the professional men's sides to sponsor a women's team, before joining Oregon State University. In comparing her team in England to her college experience, she said, "We [Tranmere] were a young team playing in the women's league. I played with them for seven years. Only a few teams are funded. We didn't get any money or anything like that. . . . In the States, it's a lot bigger and more accepted. In England, the women's game is not given as much respect."

Arsenal should be commended for their support of the women's program, and the team has been hugely successful at the domestic level as well as internationally. Assistant Coach Emma Hayes was appointed the first head coach of Women's Professional Soccer's

Chicago Red Stars. However, the year-to-year funding scenario that many Premier League sides find themselves facing is detrimental to the sport in the long term and hinders their ability to compete with Arsenal. England National Team manager Hope Powell felt that "Arsenal's dominance is not conducive to international progression. . . . The [Premier League] games, week in, week out, aren't very competitive, which makes it very difficult for the girls to sustain the level of play needed at international level. It isn't the best thing for the game overall. . . . If we want to move forward we are going to have to change the structure of the league."

An FA public relations official justified the current status of the English women's league in late 2007 when he said, "The point to make here is that the men's game has had a one hundred year start on women's football and we hope in the not-too-distant future that the women's league will be a completely different product." This is ironic, because it could have been so different if the FA had supported the game's growth nine decades before. The spokesperson also said that the FA was struggling to determine "how we can make that product [the women's game] more attractive to sponsors, broadcasters, and people who want to come in and watch the game." As far as compensation for players, he said, "Clearly we hope that the finances we might generate filter through to the players." Though surely unintended, the FA official's unfortunate phrasing, "filter through to the players," reinforces the feelings that the women's game will always struggle in the Mother Country because the players are the last priority after sponsors, television, stadiums, and so forth. The FA official ended his soliloquy, defending the FA by saying, "Women's football has made a breakthrough [at the 2007 WWC] but clearly there's a long way to go and we know that, which is why we're working incredibly hard to try and change that status quo." The status quo unfortunately is due to almost ninety years of neglect, ninety years of impediments thrown up for elite women athletes, and ninety years of rock-bottom financing. Despite some progress, there is still much work to be done to build the game to a level of respect that it has in North America.

Finally, there is the promising sign that perhaps things are improving on the league side. The FA is starting a new semiprofessional league in the summer of 2011 with eight teams from the current top two divisions, which will continue to play in the winter. The new FA WSL (Women's Super League) will include Arsenal Ladies, Birmingham City Ladies, Bristol Academy Women's FC, Chelsea Ladies, Doncaster Rovers Belles, Everton, Lincoln Ladies, and Liverpool Ladies. The Football Association is investing nearly U.S.$5 million in the project, including $110,000 initial grants to each team. Each club can pay no more than four players an annual salary of $31,000, similar to the pay structure of the WPS. In addition, international players receive $25,000 a year from the FA to support their training efforts. Clubs are expected to have annual expenses of $250,000. The hope is that the FA and the teams will build better facilities, create better sponsorship plans, develop career opportunities for women players, and keep more top players from emigrating to the WPS. ESPN in the U.K. will broadcast games during the first season.

The key decision for officials in the women's game, which applies not just in England but in other countries struggling to advance their top leagues, is whether it is better to align with the men's teams or plot an independent path. Clearly, the women's programs are low priority to English men's sides, and funding is at risk every year, particularly when the men's side can be relegated to a lower league, which results in much lower gate, television, and sponsorship income. In 2008 about half of the Women's Premier League sides had partial or full funding from men's professional sides. Some of the women's teams now are actually separate organizations but take the name of their more notable men's club (Charlton Athletic WFC, Doncaster Rovers Belles, Cardiff City, Birmingham City LFC), while others are completely independent and solely dedicated to women's soccer. One example is Newquay Ladies FC, a female-only organization with nine age group teams and eighteen qualified coaches. Other independent clubs receive their funding from county associations or sponsors. This does not have to be an all-

or-nothing decision. Arsenal seems to be coexisting well within its more famous men's side, but independent organizations can thrive as well. Whichever model is adopted, the foundation and support structure must be able to support long-term development for the women, including dependable budgets, equal use of facilities, and marketing. Given the long, difficult history between the men's professional game and women's soccer, it would seem wise to be extra cautious when working with men's organizations; perhaps a path leading to full independence seems to be a more secure route for the women's game to take in England.

Future U.K. Development Options: The Netherlands Experience

As England considers other models to improve their top women's teams, one northern European country provides a stark juxtaposition of how men's professional sides can work with a top-level women's league. In the Netherlands, the Eredivisie Vrouwen, or Women's Premier League, was started for the 2007–8 season by six leading men's clubs: ADO Den Haag, AZ Alkmaar, SC Heerenveen, FC Twente Enschede, FC Utrecht, and Willem II Tilburg. Royal Netherlands Football Association media officer Tonny Dijkhuizen explained that players did not receive salaries but were reimbursed for their expenses and lost income from work. Though technically an amateur loop, the women benefit from the professional structure of the parent organizations. Dijkhuizen said, "It's a step to a more professional attitude towards women's soccer, because of the connections to the clubs." Attendance varies depending on the venue, but some games have drawn crowds in the five- to ten-thousand range at a club's stadium, while other fixtures are played on fields at the training complex.

Dijkhuizen attributes the Netherlands' first qualification for the Women's European Championships in Finland in 2009, in which they made the semifinals, to the Women's Premier League. The league is considering bids for two more teams for the 2010–11 season, again coming from professional men's sides. The league's future growth is hinged on the burgeoning number of girls and women players. During a half dozen years, the number of registered females rose 38 percent, from 70,000 in 2003 to 112,000 in 2009. Soccer will soon surpass field hockey as the most popular team sport for girls and women in the country, and the federation's stated goal is to have 200,000 registered female players by 2014. The FA has launched grass-roots programs such as "Girlfriend Days," when a player can bring a friend to learn about the club and about soccer. They also have a schools program whereby licensed trainers from nearby amateur clubs run activities for children during and after school.

The paramount ingredient to grow the women's game within men's organizations is having a long-term commitment, so that club officials do not view women's teams as an expense line item or a burden that can be curtailed when things get difficult in other departments of the club. This model has worked successfully in Canada and Australia. Other groups may decide they want independent finances for women so they have control and are not dependent on men's teams. Whatever the model, the litmus test is whether the club's or league's structure advances females' ability to play, coach, market, and administer their game. One can only imagine what England can achieve with their resources if they mirrored the Netherlands approach and commitment to grow soccer for girls and women.

12

Canada's Youthful Road to Success

Canada, utilizing a strong youth base, quickly went from international bottom feeder to top ten power within a few years. Their
success can, in many ways, act as an effective development model to
other countries trying to build competitive national team programs,
even more so than the neighboring Americans' "big bang" effect
of Women's World Cup 1999. The fact that Canada's Women's
National Team program has attracted more funding and support
than the men's side is a unique aspect of the Canadian story. It all
began with Canada's faith in the power of youth.

The Early Years

The Canadian Soccer Association (CSA) has done an excellent job
in growing youth soccer in the country. There are approximately
nine hundred thousand youth and adult players, with women and
girls making up more than a third of that figure, the highest percentage of any nation in the world, according to FIFA's 2006 Big
Count survey. Significantly, soccer's numbers eclipsed the national
pastime of hockey a few years ago, in no small part thanks to the
female players. Canada began its Women's National Team program
in 1986, a year after the United States, with two games against the
Americans in Minnesota, but for many years the team would only
get together shortly ahead of games and then disband immediately
afterward. Still, they were the second team in the weak CONCACAF

region behind the Americans and qualified for the 1995 and 1999 World Cups. In their two World Cup appearances, they had four losses and two ties in six games, never coming close to making the quarterfinals. After Canada limped out of the 1999 World Cup with one point despite playing in a weak group, forward Charmaine Hooper was blistering in her criticism of her federation's support, "I hope this is a wakeup call for the CSA. I'm hoping this program doesn't take ten steps back, or take two or three years off before we come back. Because we're just going to go through the same thing in the next World Cup." To be fair, the CSA had been challenged financially for both men's and women's soccer ever since their lone Men's World Cup appearance in 1986. By missing the quarterfinals in 1999, the Canadian women's team lost out on a spot in the 2000 Olympic Games in Sydney, Australia, and more funding from government sources.

Even Pellerud's Arrival

To the CSA's credit they made the commitment to improve the women's program. By the end of 1999, they had brought in Norwegian Even Pellerud as head coach and technical director. As head coach of Norway's National Women's Team from 1989 to 1996, Pellerud posted a record of seventy-five wins, seventen ties, and twelve losses. Under his leadership, Norway won the World Cup title in 1995, finished runner-up in 1991, and captured a bronze medal at the 1996 Olympic Games to go with a European title in 1993. Former Norwegian star Linda Medalin called Pellerud "the best coach I have ever had." Pellerud made it clear in early discussions with the CSA what he needed to make Canada competitive on the field, including at least twelve matches a year (playing against the most challenging teams) and a minimum of ninety days together with the team. Kevan Pipe, former Canadian Soccer Association CEO, said about Pellerud a few years after his hiring, "I can attest to his feedback with the players. He's a tremendous motivator and he gives tremendous information back to his players after every single project."

7. Canadian Women's National Team coaching staff (*from left*): Even Pellerud, Bob Bolitho, and Ian Bridge. (CanadaSoccer.com.)

Pellerud brought instant credibility as a top-class coach dedicated to the women's game along with huge changes to the moribund program. Pellerud combined superior coaching techniques with a considerable increase in CSA investment and commitment, building around a wonderful generation of youth players to propel Canada to the world elite within four years.

The Power of Youth and the Miracle of Canada

For Canada's international games, Pellerud brought a number of prospects in the fifteen- to seventen-year-old range, while increasing the number of games and camps for youth select teams. Canada's focus on its youth paid off just a few years into his tenure. FIFA awarded the first U-19 World Cup in 2002 to the CSA, which chose to hold the games in British Colombia and Alberta. This was originally thought to be just another end-of-summer youth tournament in a year chock full of them, with only parents and friends in the stands. Expectations were low, but the two-week-long event became a unifying story nationally. Canada won five games to make their first ever world championship game in soccer at any level, men's or women's. The final was held in Edmonton's Commonwealth Stadium before a sold-out crowd of 47,784 while another 900,000 watched on television, the largest audience ever on Cable Sports Network TSN. The rapture displayed by Edmonton's fans was particularly shocking since the city had hosted a disastrous men's national team exhibition tournament in 1999 with small crowds, the losses from which forced the CSA to severely cut back its spending that year. TSN announcer Gerry Dotson, opening the broadcast of the FIFA tournament final while the camera panned over the packed stadium exclaimed, "This thing has transcended sport across the country. It is more than just a game today; this is an event culturally, socially, of course a sporting event. It also is a watershed mark perhaps in the sport of soccer in this country. Things will never be the same, I dare say." FIFA president Sepp Blatter succinctly labeled the tournament the Miracle of Canada. Though Canada lost to the United States 1–0 in overtime, it couldn't suppress the magic the team had created. Forward Candace Chapman said, "[To win the championship] would have just been icing on the cake. We might have lost the tournament but we won the heart of the nation. I think that says it all." The exciting young Canadian team drove an explosion in media coverage and fan interest, mirroring in some ways what the U.S. team did in 1999 at the senior World

Cup. What makes the Canadian story even more extraordinary is that the team comprised players between the ages of fifteen and eighteen; most were still in high school.

Years later, after announcing his retirement in 2008, Pellerud reflected on his tenure in Canada in a telephone interview with this author and admitted that he had not come to Canada with a set plan to focus on youth development. Pellerud explained, "I coach what I see. The current base that I inherited, I didn't see the talent or commitment [I needed] so I was really forced to look to younger players. I started youth teams and put together a national coaching staff to develop them. The FIFA U-19 2002 tournament reinforced the process and linked well together. But I was really forced into it. We had a good base of the 1983–1984 age group that is now the core group of the current national team. They have matured well."

The U-19 tournament provided a platform for teenagers Sasha Andrews, Tanya Dennis, Kara Lang, Diane Matheson, Christine Sinclair, and Brittany Timko to slot into the full national team. A year later they would experience even more success. Canada's full national team stormed to the World Cup semifinals behind the magnificent play of their third-string goalkeeper, Tanya Swiatek, and those 2002 U-19 stars. Losing a 1–0 lead over Sweden in the last few minutes prevented them from reaching the final with Germany, but a fourth place finish overall was a stunning achievement, particularly since they had never won a World Cup game in two previous appearances.

Maintaining Elite Status

Canada's young national team hiccupped the year after their fourth-place World Cup finish, failing to make the 2004 Olympics after losing surprisingly to Mexico in a semifinal for a CONCACAF berth. They recovered well and went to China for both the 2007 World Cup and 2008 Olympics. Canada's players have been prime targets for American college teams, and many have been stars. Diane Matheson played at Princeton and said, "In order to go far in soccer, I needed to come here [to the United States]." Others who played at U.S. colleges and universities include Sinclair at the University of Portland; Aysha Jamani, Andrews, and Timko at Nebraska (coached by former Canadian Women's National Team assistant coach John Walker); Mel Booth at Florida; Erin McLeod at Penn State; Chapman and Katie Thorlakson at Notre Dame; and Amy Vermeulen at Wisconsin. Kara Lang, star of the 2003 World Cup, was an All American at UCLA and led her team to three final four appearances by her junior season.

Pellerud also helped improve the financial side for his players during their long residency periods (held before the 2006 Gold Cup, 2007 World Cup and 2008 Olympic Qualifying and Games). Since the W-League and WPSL include college-tied amateurs, full-time players could only receive housing assistance; Pellerud helped secure a twenty thousand dollar training wage for each of his players during residency camp in 2007. This came from the Greg Kerfoot Foundation, begun by the owner of the Vancouver Whitecaps, the men's A-League and women's W-League franchise, which was in addition to the funding players already received from the Sport Canada Athlete Assistance Program. Kerfoot also housed the players in an apartment complex he owned. Coach Pellerud said, "This residency camp will provide us the best opportunity ever to attend a World Cup Final with an optimum level of preparations. For the first time, the team can, in principle, be run like a club team. This program allows us to set up daily, weekly, and monthly schedules and technical programs that include fitness, tactics, skills, and psychology."

In total for 2007, the national women's program worked from a budget of $700,000, of which the CSA contributed around 20 percent ($155,000.) The rest came from the Canadian Olympic Committee, Sport Canada, and Kerfoot. Unfortunately, aside from practice games against boys' teams, the Canadians had to travel far and wide to prepare for the World Cup, journeying to Brazil, China, Japan, and New Zealand. The CSA couldn't afford to stage a home game for the women, as then CSA president Colin Linford explained that the federation would "go bankrupt if they held a game in Canada." The Canadians were disappointed with their results in the World Cup, missing out on the quarterfinals due to Australia's last-second goal in their final group game, which put the Matildas through at the Maple Leafs' expense.

Canada relied on the residency program for a few years, following the lead of the Americans who have held them at various times for over a decade. Turning the national team into a full-time club-type of environment can certainly help a team prepare effectively for a tournament, particularly without a full-time league, but there are drawbacks. Canadian assistant coach Ian Bridge commented on the advantages and disadvantages of the residency program in an interview while he was scouting a Mexican National Team game in Tempe, Arizona, in February 2008:

> Obviously the advantages are the access, having the players around all the time, the amount of work they can do, the control we have over what they do, a day-to-day thing almost like a club team; I think the off-the-field stuff is very key, the team lives together and gets to know one another very well, it's a great group to work with every day. I think the downside, and we've discussed this lately, sometimes we don't get enough competitive games. With most national teams, their players return to their clubs. They are starters and then they come to the national team camp; they train and go back to their clubs. With us we have that missing piece of club play where they are getting the week-in, week-out, meaningful league games. We play good competitive games against boy teams and we play between eight and twelve international games each year. But that daily practice and weekly league play that almost any other country has is the missing piece. We've been finding that's the biggest challenge to keep the players match ready and match fit, where other countries are already on that level because they have a league.

Even a FIFA top ten nation like Canada shows the importance of regular national league play for elite players and developing new talent. In 2009, a number of their national teamers, including Chapman, McLeod, and Sinclair, joined WPS teams.

The CONCACAF regional qualifying was next on tap in 2008. Even Pellerud's squad battled Mexico away in Ciudad Juarez in front of a near-sellout crowd of twenty-two thousand and furious winds with gusts of up to fifty miles per hour. Canada rode out the adverse conditions after a first-half goal by Melissa Tancredi for a glorious first-ever Olympic berth for Canadian women's soccer. It was another important step in the growth of a national team program that was almost literally left for dead just nine years before. Pellerud later told the author that the crowning point on his eight years in Canada was "qualifying for the first time for the Olympics; the biggest moment."

For the Maple Leafs the Americans are a natural benchmark as their most frequent opponent. Before Pellerud arrived, the Maple Leafs were far off the pace of their southern neighbors, winning only once in twenty matches from 1986 through 1999. In the twenty-two games since the turn of the new century (as of June 2008), they won two games and tied four times, but have been very competitive when it mattered, losing the 2002 Gold Cup in overtime, the 2003 World Cup third-place match 3–1 after a halftime draw, and the 2006 Gold Cup title controversially on a penalty in injury time; all three games were played in Los Angeles. In the finals of the 2008 Regional Olympic Qualifying Competition in Ciudad Juarez, Canada lost the title to the Americans on penalty kicks. The United States, with a far larger base of players to draw from, knows that Canada provides a tough foe, or as U.S. forward Abby Wambach said ahead of the 2006 Gold Cup Final, "We have a target on our back [for Canada]. It's always a grudge match."

Pellerud's goal in the Olympics was to make the quarterfinals, and he felt comfortable that his team had adequate preparation. The team still did a lot of traveling for meaningful games, including Australia, Cyprus, New Zealand, Singapore, and South Korea, but the CSA managed to provide a home game in Toronto at BMO Field. Canada tied Brazil 1–1 before an enthusiastic crowd of 13,500, which Christine Sinclair called, "a perfect atmosphere for soccer." Importantly, the large gate emphasized the continued popularity of the team at home, or as Pellerud said afterward, "They haven't forgotten us as they came back. The women's game in Canada is very popular."

At their first Olympics, the Maple Leafs achieved their goal to do better than in 2007. After a first round win over Argentina 2–1 and a 1–1 draw with the host nation China, the Canadians knew they had made the quarterfinals before their final group game with Sweden, which they lost 2–1. The defeat placed them as one of two third-place qualifiers, and they met a group winner, which in this case was a familiar foe . . . the United States. Canada had another heartbreaking defeat against their neighbors, losing 2–1 on a goal just minutes from the end of extra time, to drop to 3–37–4 all time against the Americans.

When he announced his retirement from his national team job a few months before the Olympics, effective when his contract ended at the end of 2008, Coach Pellerud expressed confidence in the future of the program, as long as the CSA continued to support women's soccer: "We need better plans for the women's program. We need defined national team program goals and more clear action plans. We need stronger leadership from the top. We need a league structure and better leagues [at all age levels]. . . . A Canadian team in WPS would be helpful. . . . We have succeeded in spite of not having these." Pellerud felt particularly pleased with the fact that soccer was now the number 1 sport for girls and women in Canada: "Females have an amazing interest in the sport. Canada's women's [soccer] status is higher than the men's.

His players and team officials were disheartened to see him go. Kara Lang said, "It's undeniable the difference he's made and the effect he's had on the program. . . . He made everybody buy into the philosophy. That's probably the biggest thing, the kind of respect he demanded of people." Christine Sinclair added, "Ever since I've been on the national team, he's been the national coach. We would never have made it to finishing fourth at the Women's World Cup or made it to these Olympics without him. He took us to new heights." Team manager Les Meszaros said, "Even has reshaped the landscape for women's soccer in Canada, guiding the program from one which had no direction to one where we have youth teams and our full team qualifying for World Cups and major tournaments on a regular basis. It's going to be an incredible challenge for the CSA to maintain his professionalism and continue to foster this program. His professionalism, honesty, and attention to detail is best recognized when you see the respect he has amongst the coaching fraternity around the world." Pellerud later took a job in Trinidad and Tobago ahead of the 2010 FIFA U-17 World Cup they would host.

Though the CSA is continually cash strapped, their stunning success in a short period of time is a good model for federations throughout South America, Asia, and Africa to follow. Their emphasis on young players yielded almost immediate success and had the added benefit of building a unique groundswell of support for these women across the country. The Miracle of Canada can be duplicated in other countries; even without the presence of Even Pellerud, the man this author once labeled the pied piper of women's soccer.

Conclusion

"The Future of Football Is Feminine"

Girls' and women's soccer has experienced incredible growth around the world over the past couple of decades. In more and more countries, soccer is now seen as a normal and appropriate female activity, particularly at the youth level. At the adult level, there are still difficulties to overcome in some countries with regard to perceptions, support, and funding, but in Australia, Canada, Germany, Sweden, and the United States, the players have received significant attention and support for major events. So what does the future hold and what will the sport look like for the next generation?

What women ultimately want with soccer (or any activity) is to be treated with respect in the same way that men are. They don't want to be evaluated differently because of their sex, with qualifications asserting that they are weaker, less adept, or something less than the men who play the game. They want people to discuss their games as they discuss men's games—discussing great players, certain players they like or dislike—rather than whether they should even play the game, how they should play it, or what they should wear.

FIFA deserves tremendous accolades for their dedicated and consistent efforts to expand opportunities for girls and women to play the sport. During the 2007 Women's World Cup in China, FIFA held a seminar among leaders to discuss key issues for the sport. FIFA's future objectives for the sport included:

Developing partnerships with governments' sports, health and education departments.
Establishing development plans and the funding initiatives to support them.
Building support structures (including publicity) and growing them with resources (commitment, financial, people.)
Continuing grass-roots development programs, not only in schools but in clubs and communities for girls and women.
Furthering the expansion of national and regional tournaments.
Continuing to create opportunities for women in leadership roles, including administration, coaching, referees, and executive levels.

A final goal is particularly salient for future growth: "Taking the initiative to dismantle cultural or social barriers to women's and girls' readiness to participate in the sport of football, and to take whatever actions are necessary to promote the acceptance of football as a sport for women and girls." Women's Professional Soccer chief operating officer and former FIFA director of development Mary Harvey felt that this was the sport's key challenge. Harvey explained, "Getting people to view soccer as a socially acceptable activity for girls; everything stems from that. Whether it is religious reasons, cultural reasons, or what have you; the challenge is to convince parents, administrators, the public, clerics, that it's a socially acceptable activity for girls and women to be doing. That is the core of everything." Spanish coach Marta Tejedor has been working in Chile with their national teams program for the past few years and voiced a similar theme to Harvey's: "We have to make society see women's football as something perfectly normal, which would automatically lead to women taking up the game in numbers."

The efforts that people take to allow girls and women the chance to play are all important, no matter how small they seem. Whether it is soccer moms in Kansas driving girls for hours to a tournament in Iowa, coaches leading organized after-school programs in the Netherlands, a women's coach scouting rural villages in Burkina Faso for players, a business owner sponsoring teams and leagues so they can meet their budget in Papua New Guinea, or managers of senior teams in Norway holding open tryouts, these are all happening in greater numbers than ever before. They all contribute to the ultimate goal: universal acceptance that it is proper, acceptable, and beneficial for girls and women to play soccer. FIFA's statistics cite the number of females who play the game globally at 26 million; for every ten players, only one is female compared to nine males. However, as Mary Harvey points out, one of every five new players being registered around the world is female. Between 2000 and 2006, the number of registered female players grew by 54 percent. Harvey explained that beyond the total numbers, "the acceleration rate, that's what you really look at because that's where it's heading." FIFA, at the macro level, has driven this growth surge with "U-20 and U-17 World Cups every twenty-four months, as well as expanding the number of participants at the Olympics and Women's World Cup." FIFA facilitates the grass-roots efforts through youth programs and training coaches specifically for girls and women.

The growth has been stunning; in less than twenty years since the start of the first World Cup in 1991, it has become the most popular team sport played by women in the world. The U.S. National Team returned to New York with the 1991 World Championship trophy, and no one knew who they were or what they had done. Eight years later, they became cultural icons, and the number 1 sports story of the summer of 1999. In 2002 a group of teenagers drew almost fifty thousand people in Edmonton, Canada, and fascinated a country in the first FIFA youth tournament for female players. A few months earlier, five thousand would have been an unrealistically silly goal. Marta was earning a reported five hundred thousand dollars a year salary in 2009 at the age of twenty-three, when three years before she made a tenth of that, and six years before that she was playing in the streets of her rural Brazilian hometown. The United States has had two pro leagues since 2001, amazing since the first U.S. national senior amateur league didn't start until the mid-1990s. Harvey explained, "When you overlay some upcoming big events, the 2011 Women's World Cup in Germany with twenty-thousand-seat stadiums (that could be entirely sold out in advance) or the 2012 Olympics in London, it will just continue to drive more women to the sport."

One reason that national leagues around the world are so important is that they provide the highest level of sustained visibility for the sport (boosted by the cyclical FIFA or regional tournaments of a few weeks at a time every few years). Television is also essential, not as much for the revenue—which is still lower than men's leagues—but to build awareness. For the 2007 World Cup, over two hundred countries and territories televised games, up from 144 in 2003 and more than double the 67 for U.S. WWC '99. More television, more leagues, more youth programs, and more players increase familiarity, which drives the quest for legitimacy and acceptance. The more avenues that people see girls and women playing, the more that they talk about it. They'll stop staring in shock when they see females play. It will become more common, and women who play will be more mainstream and less marginalized. Opinions will become less staunchly held, and then acceptance is next. A seven-year-old in Iran who asks her parents to let her play can point to watching the national team play in the Gulf Cup on television, or even better, to the fact that her friend Tasneem from school plays. All the World Cups, national leagues, and FIFA programs support the grass roots. It's when the parents encourage their daughters to play (at any age) that the sport has won, then the available programs, fields, and coaches facilitate her play. Social acceptance is the necessary condition for soccer's growth, and that is accomplished at an individual level. There are still countries around the world where soccer is still struggling, but the sport is advancing.

Looking ahead for the next generation, I hope that more women's organizations control their own budgets, but are able to work in tandem with men's teams for occasional doubleheaders, special events, and marketing. This will be for the "good of the game." Then maybe men's team promoters and administrators will view women's supporters as a market to access and grow in tandem, rather than a threat to their resources.

A challenge that cuts across all countries, not so much a federation issue as a local team/league level concern, is field availability, quality, and time of access for women. Ideally, in ten to twenty years, women's clubs will have some dedicated stadiums and training grounds in more and more countries. Currently, girls in Latin America and Africa play on fields cows wouldn't want to be seen on, or have to wait until boys have finished practicing.

I hope that we see more players (and not just professionals) transferring to overseas clubs. Besides the life experience of living in another culture, imports exchange ideas on playing styles, training, marketing, and club management. Also, particularly for countries struggling with antiquated views of women's roles, diaspora and other imports act as role models for young players and portray a different social order for their parents. A superstar will eventually eclipse Marta (though she is still only twenty-five, so she's got a long way yet to go), and this athlete will come from Iran, India, Bolivia, or some other country currently lagging in support for the game.

There is marked improvement in attitudes toward the game in Latin America. Particularly in Mexico, things have improved substantially in the last few years, but perceptions and funding still lag. We are all hoping that Brazil becomes one of the leading women's soccer nations at all levels, just as they have for years on the men's side. They have so much to offer in terms of skills, creativity, and passion.

I hope that a vibrant Women's Professional Soccer (WPS) reaches its teenage years with sixteen teams in the United States and Canada and will consider plans for a second division . . . with a team in

Mexico. Ideally, half of the clubs will control their own five- to ten-thousand-seat stadiums while the rest rent facilities from colleges and minor league baseball teams. In its commitment to the global development of the game, the league should have attracted players from over fifty countries and every region of the world. A team comprising players from four East African countries may even play in a strong market like Rochester, New York. Prospective funding sources could come from the respective federations and local sponsors. Though young players and their parents will remain a strong base of support for WPS teams, we should see them attract a substantial number of young adult viewers, and the number of adult women (many former players) who watch will grow every year.

Will women's soccer ever be at a level of a Barcelona–Real Madrid derby, or Manchester United playing AC Milan in a European Champions League tie? It's important to dream, because we wouldn't be at this point without big ideas, but the goal is not to hurt, replicate, or supplant the men's game; that is unrealistic. What women want is gender equity and fairness so the sport can reach its potential around the world. Women's soccer has brought passion and energy to the sport and has much more to offer. The future looks very bright indeed.

Afterword

2011 Women's World Cup

The 2011 Women's World Cup in Germany in late June and early July made new inroads for women's soccer into the consciousness of mainstream society, both in North America and throughout the rest of the world. Host Germany, the two-time defending champions, presented a well-organized event with solid attendance figures, despite losing at the quarterfinal stage to Japan. Utilizing primarily smaller stadiums (25,000–30,000) for most games, Germany broke away from the model of previous tournaments in which the majority of games were held as doubleheaders. Publicity in Germany was high, with over a half-dozen magazines dedicated to the tournament, while others ran prominent reviews. Panini Stickers, the European equivalent of Topps Baseball Cards, produced a women's set for the first time, with over three hundred players from the sixteen teams. The stickers themselves (sold in packages of five) were extremely popular, and the sticker books sold out. Granted, a small thing but evidence of further mainline acceptance of the game.

There were two very salient aspects of the sixth edition of the FIFA World Championships. The first was the emergence of fluent, flowing play from two of the semifinalists—France and Japan—who had never made it that far before, while the United States team moved away from its traditional hurly-burly style to more of a ball possession game under their Swedish coach, Pia Sundhage. The improvement on the field established a sense of parity for the first time among all sixteen participants, without any of the 11–0 or 7–2 blowout results we saw just four years ago. The highest margin of victory was four goals, from France's 4–0 win over Canada and Japan's 4–0 defeat of Mexico, both during the first stage.

The second positive was the reaction in the United States, sparked by the team's mesmerizing quarterfinal win against Brazil, which spurred enthusiasm that had not been seen since 1999. The Americans took an early lead through a Brazilian own-goal by defender Daiane, but powerhouse Brazil kept attacking and had the chance to deadlock the match when Marta was taken down in the box, some thought overdramatically, by defender Rachel Buehler. Referee Jacqui Melksham of Australia sent off the distraught Buehler with a straight red card in the sixty-eighth minute and awarded a penalty kick. Hope Solo saved Cristiane's attempt, but the referee ordered a retake, which Marta took and scored to tie up the game. The crowd in Dresden felt that the Americans were wronged and supported the Red, White, and Blue from that point forward. Marta scored again a few minutes into the thirty minute overtime period and left the United States chasing the game. In the dying seconds of injury time, midfielder Megan Rapinoe launched a long cross from the wing, for which Brazilian goalkeeper Andreia came out late, completely missing the ball, leaving forward Abby Wambach with an uncontested header that she buried in the net to tie up the game. The three minutes of injury time—a rare occurrence—were given by the referee to counteract the bizarre behavior of Erika, who seemingly just fell down in her own penalty area with a few minutes remaining. While she simulated an injury, it took some time to take her off the field, where she immediately jumped off the stretcher like a healthy foal, eager to return to the game. If she hadn't engaged in that silly time-wasting maneuver, Brazil would have won and Wambach's dramatic goal would not have gone down in soccer annals as one of the most memorable U.S. goals ever—men's or women's. The United States made all their penalty kicks while Solo saved Daiane's kick, and Brazil—one of the favorites to win the World Cup—was stunningly out. Poetically, the United States' incredible comeback over Brazil took place twelve years to the day of the famous 1999 U.S.–China final in Los Angeles.

The Americans then came from behind to defeat France 3–1 in one semifinal while Japan shutdown Sweden 2–0 in the other match. France was one of the revelations of the tournament, playing insightful, creative soccer along the way, and was acknowledged by many as the far better side against the Americans, who fought back with a determined performance. France's twenty-five-year-old midfielder Louise Necib was acclaimed as a certifiable superstar. Necib was close to joining the WPSL's FC Indiana in 2007, when the French Federation vetoed the deal, wanting Necib to stay at home at their national training center in Clairefontaine.

Japan, on the other hand, just simply shocked everyone with their performances. They destroyed a good Mexico side 4–0 in the first round in an exquisite example of on-the-ground ball possession and creative passing. Japan had qualified for every Women's World Cup but had only made the quarterfinals once, always seemingly in the shadow of first China, then North Korea, and lately Australia. No more: the team has a nice mix of veteran talent along with youth coming up from their U-17 2010 FIFA World Cup runner-up side. A sentimental favorite after the country had endured a devastating earthquake, tsunami, and nuclear plant meltdown a few months before that tragically cost the lives of more than twenty thousand people, they would thank the crowd after each game with a banner that read: "To Our Friends around the World—Thank You for Your Support."

The Americans, now positioned as a team of destiny after its pulsating win over Brazil and comeback win over France, now faced the Cinderella side from Asia for a chance for a third world title, their first since 1999. The United States had defeated Japan by identical 2–0 scores in two friendlies in mid-May in Columbus,

Ohio, and Cary, North Carolina, and though Japan played fluently, they never looked capable of defeating their opponents. After an hour, Western New York Flash rookie Alex Morgan gave the United States the lead, but Japan scored late to bring on overtime. The United States took the lead early in overtime through the indefatigable Wambach but Japan's Homare Sawa, a veteran of WUSA and WPS, scored off of a corner kick with a few minutes remaining. Penalty kicks again; this time the United States folded, with Shannon Boxx and Tobin Heath having their shots saved and Carly Lloyd blasting her attempt over the bar. Wambach's goal and Solo's save of Yuki Nagasato's kick were not enough, and Japan was champion.

The reaction in the United States was quite impressive; people appreciated the team's heart and persistence, and when they returned home, they received as much attention and acclaim as if they had won. The focus on this World Cup was not on the cultural aspect as with the 1999 heroes; it was their exciting style of play that people commented on and stating how much they enjoyed it, without the qualifying comment "not bad . . . for a women's game." Soccer fans tuned in and compared their games to the U.S. men's 2010 World Cup team, which scored a last second tying goal against Algeria to qualify for the round of sixteen, where they lost to Ghana in overtime. The 2011 Women's World Cup final attracted over 13 million viewers (7.4 ratings points) and more than doubled the previous record for a soccer game on an ESPN network, which was 6.2 million (4.0 ratings) for the men's dramatic World Cup win over Algeria in 2010.

Veteran women's sports journalist Christine Brennan wrote a few days before the final, "Win or lose Sunday, this team proves that the progress of women's sports has taken us to a place where success isn't always measured by deeper truths and the bigger picture, but by the ability to produce awe-inspiring athletic results." After the final she wrote, "There was no shame in this, in losing to Japan. The positives about this game for the U.S. team and the worldwide game they represent so well will eventually bubble to the surface and there are many. It was a much more entertaining game that the o–o final at the Rose Bowl in 1999, and not just because there was actual scoring. The speed and skill of the women's game have improved tremendously. . . . No one has to explain themselves for loving women's soccer as they did in 1999." Brennan believed that people will remember this game, and the excitement will entice more girls to play the game around the world.

Lawrie Mifflin, who has covered soccer for many years, admitted that in years past she found the quality of play at the Women's World Cup "dreadful." She applauded the heroes of 1999 for motivating millions of girls to play competitive sports, but she watched them, "only on charitable terms, the way you would buy a candy bar to support your local school team." She did not see much improvement in the quality of play in 2003 and 2007, but this time, she admitted: "Today, it's so different. The skillful passing of the French team; the "wow" quotient of Brazil's Marta; the slick ball control and darting movement off the ball of Japan's Aya Miyama; Hope Solo's defiant goalkeeping and the leaping power of Abby Wambach heading into the net—these are just a few highlights of a very impressive tournament. As good as the best men's teams? No. Worth watching? Absolutely."

For once, American professional soccer, always dreaming of a World Cup bump, saw it. The weekend after the final saw an average of 8,141 for four games in WPS, compared with the first half of the season with the six team league floundering at 2,792 per game (well below the 2009 total of 4,684 and 2010's average of 3,601). Abby Wambach always draws large crowds in Rochester, but this time, a few days after the final in Germany, Sahlen stadium was packed with 15,404, an all-time WPS record, and Wambach didn't even play. Can this last? Probably not, since the last weekend in July's average dropped off to an average of 3,064 for WPS's next four games. More than the WWC afterglow attracting more fans to games, WPS's best hope is that more potential team owners become excited about the sport and join for 2012 or 2013, since they currently have only six franchises, a bare minimum to play. WPS has one owner (magicJack's Dan Borislow) who many wish would take his team and go away . . . to Cuba. Borislow purchased the Washington Freedom franchise in late 2010, rebranded it as magic-Jack after his telecommunications company, and shipped the team to West Palm Beach Florida, where they play in a thousand-seat college stadium that is light years away from professional standards. Borislow saved the league from extinction, but WPS brought on a contentious character that has caused them heartache and stress at every turn. Borislow fired his original coach and tried to steer the team himself but was forbidden from coaching after the players union got wind of some abuse of his squad, to which he responded in an email: "I believe it was a player or players who were let go [involved in the grievance]. You can ask the players with character and heart if they think it's true or you can believe a player who does not belong in the league who was only there because the league decided to have amateurs play while the [national team] was away." After the World Cup Final, Bosislow named Wambach as head coach for the rest of the season. At magicJack, Wambach is surrounded with world-class talent like Hope Solo, U.S. captain Christie Rampone, Canadian international Sophie Schmidt, and Australia's Lisa DeVanna. Her leadership should help the team maintain its playoff spot and be a threat for the title, but magicJack is an embarrassment to the league, and many view Borislow as an unreasonable, out-of-control owner. The key question for the league is can they replace him for 2012 and retain the other teams?

There were a few negative stories to emerge from the 2011 Women's World Cup. Nigeria head coach Eucharia Uche, one of six women head coaches at the tournament, undid that positive when she asserted that Nigeria's team, thanks to her vigilance and "divine intervention," was free of lesbians, which she felt was a "dirty issue" and "spiritually, morally very wrong." She attempted to explain her approach: "Yes, lesbianism used to be a big problem in the team, but since I took over as the chief coach of Falcons, I think the problem has been dealt with. Lucky, some of the girls played with me and they know my dos and don'ts. They know that

I cannot tolerate such a nasty practice. In fact, lesbianism does not currently exist in [the] Falcons' camp and nobody discusses it." Uche also brought in Pentecostal ministers to pray with her players, who regularly read the Bible. Uche's team was eliminated after the first round despite defeating Canada in its last game, and FIFA was investigating her comments, which go against their equality mandate, so she may have to change her approach on this issue in order to work within soccer. This incident shows that there still are some struggles for women athletes to overcome.

Germany 2011 was an important step in the advancement of the women's game of soccer, showing the game as a top-class athletic event, largely devoid of social justification issues. More girls and women, after watching the high level of soccer on display for three weeks, will adopt the game, even in countries where playing has not been encouraged by societal norms, thanks in large part to FIFA televising the event throughout every corner of the globe. The fact that a non-European and non-American nation won is an important signpost to girls and women in developing nations, in Asia, and in other regions. The key for continued growth is to create smaller steps forward at the country level—based on youth, leagues, and further national team results, and not depend on the four-year cycle of the Women's World Cup.

Appendix of Tables

TABLE I. Number of NCAA Institutions Fielding Soccer Teams

	Division I		Total of Divisions I, II, III	
	Men	Women	Men	Women
1981–82	182	22	521	80
1989–90	190	75	547	294
1993–94	194	131	609	446
1997–98	190	233	682	724
2007–08	197	307	770	951

TABLE 2. WUSA Founding Players

Michelle Akers	Midfielder	Retired in 2001
Brandi Chastain	Defender	Bay Area CyberRays
Tracy Ducar	Goalkeeper	Boston Breakers
Lorrie Fair	Midfielder	Philadelphia Charge
Joy Fawcett	Defender	San Diego Spirit
Danielle Fotopoulos	Forward	Carolina Courage
Julie Foudy	Midfielder	San Diego Spirit
Mia Hamm	Forward	Washington Freedom
Kristine Lilly	Midfielder	Boston Breakers
Shannon MacMillian	Forward	San Diego Spirit
Tiffeny Milbrett	Forward	New York Power
Carla Overbeck	Defender	Carolina Courage
Cindy Parlow	Forward	Atlanta Beat
Christie Pearce	Defender	New York Power
Tiffany Roberts	Defender	Carolina Courage
Briana Scurry	Goalkeeper	Atlanta Beat
Kate Sobrero	Defender	Boston Breakers
Tisha Venturini-Hoch	Midfielder	Bay Area CyberRays
Saskia Webber	Goalkeeper	New York Power
Sara Whalen	Midfielder	New York Power

TABLE 3. WUSA International Player Distribution

Ann Kristin Aarones	Norway	Forward	New York Power
Kristin Bengtsson	Sweden	Defender	San Diego Spirit
Gro Espeseth	Norway	Defender	New York Power
Doris Firschen	Germany	Defender	Philadelphia Charge
Charmaine Hooper	Canada	Forward	Atlanta Beat
Ulrika Karlsson	Sweden	Goalkeeper	San Diego Spirit
Katia	Brazil	Forward	Bay Area CyberRays
Maren Meinert	Germany	Midfielder	Boston Breakers
Bente Nordby	Norway	Goalkeeper	Carolina Courage
Pretinha	Brazil	Forward	Washington Freedom
Hege Risse	Norway	Midfielder	Carolina Courage
Roseli	Brazil	Forward	Washington Freedom
Homare Sawa	Japan	Midfielder	Atlanta Beat
Sissi	Brazil	Midfielder	Bay Area CyberRays
Kelly Smith	England	Forward	Philadelphia Charge
Betina Wiegmann	Germany	Midfielder	Boston Breakers

TABLE 4. Final 2001 Women's United Soccer Association Standings

Team	GP	W	D	L	GF	GA	PTS
Atlanta Beat	21	10	7	4	31	21	37
Bay Area CyberRays	21	11	4	6	27	23	37
New York Power	21	9	5	7	30	25	32
Philadelphia Charge	21	9	4	8	35	28	31
San Diego Spirit	21	7	7	7	29	28	28
Boston Breakers	21	8	3	10	29	35	27
Washington Freedom	21	6	3	12	26	35	21
Carolina Courage	21	6	3	12	28	40	21

Semifinals: Bay Area def. New York, 3–2; Atlanta def. Philadelphia, 3–2

Founders' Cup: Bay Area def. Atlanta 3–3 (4–2 PK)

TABLE 5. Final 2002 Women's United Soccer Association Standings

Team	GP	W	L	D	GF	GA	PTS
Carolina Courage	21	12	5	4	40	30	40
Philadelphia Charge	21	11	4	6	36	22	39
Washington Freedom	21	11	5	5	40	29	38
Atlanta Beat	21	11	9	1	34	29	34
San Jose CyberRays	21	8	8	5	34	30	29
Boston Breakers	21	6	8	7	36	35	25
San Diego Spirit	21	5	11	5	28	42	20
New York Power	21	3	17	1	31	62	10

Semifinals: Washington def. Philadelphia 1–0; Carolina def. Atlanta 2–1

Founder's Cup: Carolina def. Washington 3–2

TABLE 6. Final 2003 Women's United Soccer Association Standings

Team	GP	W	L	D	GF	GA	PTS
Boston Breakers	21	10	4	7	33	29	37
Atlanta Beat	21	9	4	8	34	19	35
San Diego Spirit	21	8	6	7	27	26	31
Washington Freedom	21	9	8	4	40	31	31
New York Power	21	7	9	5	33	43	26
San Jose CyberRays	21	7	10	4	23	30	25
Carolina Courage	1	7	10	4	31	33	25
Philadelphia Charge	21	5	11	5	30	40	20

Semifinals: Washington def. Boston 0–0 (3–1 PK); Atlanta def. San Diego, 2–1
Founder's Cup: Washington def. Atlanta 2–1 (OT)

TABLE 7. WUSA Attendance Figures Year by Year

	Regular Season		Playoffs		Total	
	Games	Avg.	Games	Avg.	Games	Avg.
2001	84	8,116	3	13,657	87	8,307
2002	84	7,126	3	9,150	87	7,114
2003	84	6,667	3	8,099	87	6,716
Total	252	7,303	9	10,302	261	7,406

TABLE 8. Final 2009 WPS Regular Season Standings

Team	GP	W	L	T	PTS	GF	GA	+/-
Los Angeles Sol z	20	12	3	5	41	27	10	17
St. Louis Athletica y	20	10	6	4	34	19	15	4
Washington Freedom y	20	8	7	5	29	32	32	0
Sky Blue FC (NJ) y	20	7	8	5	26	19	20	−1
Boston Breakers	20	7	9	4	25	18	20	−2
Chicago Red Stars	20	5	10	5	20	18	25	−7
FC Gold Pride (Bay Area)	20	4	10	6	18	17	28	−11

NOTES: z = clinched WPS regular season title; y = clinched playoff berth.

Semifinals: Sky Blue FC def. Washington Freedom 2–1; Sky Blue FC def. St. Louis Athletica 1–0

Final: Sky Blue FC def. Los Angeles Sol 1–0

TABLE 9. Final 2010 WPS Regular Season Standings

Team	GP	W	L	T	PTS	GF	GA	+/-
FC Gold Pride (Bay Area)^z	24	16	3	5	53	46	19	27
Boston Breakers^y	24	10	8	6	36	36	28	8
Philadelphia Independence^y	24	10	10	4	34	37	36	1
Washington Freedom^y	24	8	9	7	31	33	33	0
Sky Blue FC (NJ)	24	7	10	7	28	20	31	–11
Chicago Red Stars	24	7	11	6	27	21	27	–6
Atlanta Beat	24	5	13	6	21	20	40	–20

NOTES: z = clinched WPS regular season title; y = clinched playoff berth.

Semifinals: Philadelphia def. Washington 1–0 (OT); Philadelphia def. Boston 2–1 (OT)

Final: FC Gold Pride def. Philadelphia 4–0

TABLE 10. Vancouver Whitecaps Attendance Figures versus Top European Teams

	2008–9	2007–8	2006–7	2005–6
Vancouver Whitecaps	3,481	2,801	3,941	3,697
Umeå (Sweden)	1,925	2,078	1,685	3,271
1FFC Frankfurt (Germany)	1,638	2,045	1,286	867
FCR 2001 Duisburg (Germany)	1,215	1,357	920	981

NOTE: Linköping averaged 1,983, with a high of 9,413 for Umeå game in an 8,000-seat stadium in 2008–9, eclipsing the Swedish club record of 8,900 held by Umeå in 2004.

TABLE 11. Male and Female Players in FIFA's Regional Confederations

	Males	Females
AFC (Asia)	80,075,000	5,102,000 (6.3%)
CAF (Africa)	44,940,000	1,361,000 (3.0%)
CONCACAF	33,071,000	10,038,000 (30.3%)
CONMEBOL	24,703,000	3,074,000 (12.4%)
OFC (Oceania)	486,000	56,000 (11.5%)
UEFA (Europe)	55,283,000	6,364,000 (11.5%)
TOTAL	238,558,000	25,995,000 (10.89%)

CONCACAF = North America/Central America/Caribbean

CONMEBOL = South America

Source: FIFA Big Count 2006

TABLE 12. Swedish Damallsvenskan Average Annual Attendance

2009	824
2008	892
2007	976
2006	814
2005	1,110
2004	1,127
2003	922
2002	703
2001	468
2000	339

TABLE 13. 2008 Australian W-League Final Standings

	GP	W	T	L	GF	GA	PTS
Queensland Roar	10	8	1	1	27	7	25
Newcastle Jets	10	5	2	3	17	12	17
Canberra United	10	4	4	2	14	10	16
Sydney FC	10	4	2	4	15	14	14
Melbourne Victory	10	4	0	6	13	13	12
Central Coast Mariners	10	4	0	6	15	20	12
Perth Glory	10	3	2	5	14	24	11
Adelaide United	10	2	1	7	13	28	7

Semifinals: Queensland Roar def. Sydney FC 1–1 (PKs 5–4); Canberra United def. Newcastle Jets 1–0

Final: Queensland Roar def. Canberra United 2–0

Source: www.A-league.com.au

TABLE 14. 2009 Australian W-League Final Standings

	GP	W	T	L	GF	GA	PTS
Sydney FC	10	7	2	1	25	10	23
Central Coast Mariners	10	7	1	2	24	7	22
Brisbane Roar	10	6	3	1	24	7	21
Canberra United	10	4	2	4	17	12	14
Melbourne Victory	10	4	2	4	9	10	14
Perth Glory	10	4	1	5	11	22	13
Adelaide United	10	0	3	7	7	31	3
Newcastle Jets	10	0	2	8	7	25	2

Semifinals: Sydney FC def. Canberra United 3–0; Brisbane Roar def. Central Coast Mariners 1–0

Final: Sydney FC def. Brisbane Roar 3–2

TABLE 15. Dick, Kerr Ladies 1922 American Tour Results

September 24: Dick, Kerr Ladies 3 vs. Silk Sox FC (Paterson (NJ)   6 L
Attendance: 5,000

September 30: Dick, Kerr Ladies 4 vs. J&P Coats FC (Pawtucket RI)   4 T
Attendance: 8,500

October 1: Dick, Kerr Ladies 5 vs. Centro-Hispano FC (NYC)   7 L
Attendance: 7,000

October 8: Dick, Kerr Ladies 4 vs. Stars FC (Washington DC)   4 T
Attendance: NA

October 12: Dick, Kerr Ladies 5 vs. All-Stars (New Bedford MA)   4 W
Attendance: 6,000

October 14: Dick, Kerr Ladies 8 vs. New York FC (NYC)   4 W
Attendance: NA

October 15: Dick, Kerr Ladies 2 vs. Marksmen FC (Fall River MA)   2 T
Attendance: 4,000

October 22: Dick, Kerr Ladies 4 vs. Baltimore FC   3 W
Attendance: NA

November 4: Dick, Kerr Ladies 4 vs. All Stars (Philadelphia)   5 L
Attendance: NA

Selected Bibliography

1. Title IX, Soccer Moms, and Pioneering Players

U.S. Soccer's Annual Media Guides from 1990 to the present were great resources for statistics on the early Women's World Cup tournaments and the number of youth players. The NCAA website tracks the number of men's and women's collegiate programs. *Soccer America*'s writers offered tremendous perspective on the beginnings of the women's game, particularly Bryan Alvarez (August 22, 2005), Scott French (May 24, June 14, and June 21, 1999), Bob Griendling (November 6, 2000), Mike Woitalla (February 10, 2003), and a general news article of March 24, 2003. FIFA's website has official reports and statistics on past Women's World Cups. I also interviewed Lori Walker for this chapter. Other sources include:

Crothers, Tim. *The Man Watching: A Biography of Anson Dorrance.* Ann Arbor MI: Sports Media Group, 2006.

DiCicco, Tony, Colleen Hacker, and Charles Salzberg. *Catch Them Being Good.* New York: Penguin, 2003.

FIFA *Women's World Cup '95 Sweden Official Program.*

Haner, Jim. *Soccerhead.* New York: North Point, 2006.

Litterer, Dave. *Women's Soccer History in the USA: An Overview.* U.S. Soccer Archives, February 9, 2005.

Pennington, Bill. "The Scholarship Divide: Expectations Lose to Reality of Sports Scholarships." *New York Times*, March 10, 2008.

Pettus, Elise. "Soccer—From the Suburbs to the Sports Arenas." In *Nike Is a Goddess: The History of Women in Sports,* edited by Lissa Smith, 245–66. New York: Atlantic Monthly, 1998.

2. U.S. National Team, 1996–1999

Soccer America was an excellent chronological resource for the 1996–99 period, particularly articles by Lynn Berling-Manuel (August 2, and August 30, 1999), Marianne Bhonsley (February 8, February 15, and June 21, 1999), Dean Caparaz (March 29, July 5, July 19, July 26, August 16, and August 30, 1999), Lindsey Dolich (September 2003), Scott French (March 1, June 9, June 21, July 5, July 19, July 26, and August 2, 1999; and November 26, 2001), David Hershey (July 24, 2000), Paul Kennedy (July 26, 1999, and May 24, 2004), Bob Luder (October 25, 1999), Ridge Mahoney (March 1, 1999, and June 21, 2000), Jim Murphy (August 2, 1999), Mike Woitalla (July 10, 2000, and August 16, 2004), and general news articles from November 16, 1998, thru December 27, 1999, and January 31, 2000. USA *Today* stories by Christine Brennan (December 2, 1999), Peter Brewington (July 12, 1999), Jill Lieber (July 12, 1999), and David Moore (July 12, 1999) provided perceptive insights on the 1999 Women's World Cup. I interviewed Marilyn Childress and Dr. Bob Contigulia for this chapter. Other sources included:

FIFA *Women's World Cup '99 USA Official Program*

Hong, Fan, and J. A. Mangan. *Soccer, Women, Sexual Liberation.* London: Frank Cass, 2004.

Longman, Jere. *The Girls of Summer: The U.S. Women's Soccer Team and How It Changed the World.* New York: Harper Collins, 2000.

Markovits, Andrei, and Steven Hellerman. *Offside: Soccer and American Exceptionalism.* Princeton: Princeton University Press, 2001.

Wangerin, David. *Soccer in a Football World: The Story of America's Forgotten Game.* London: WSC, 2006.

3. Professional Women's Soccer and the WUSA

Soccer America provides a historical record on the development and operations of WUSA and its quest for U.S. Soccer sanctioning, particularly articles by Lynn Berling-Manuel (September 17, 2001, and October 6, 2003), Marianne Bhonslay (July 12, 1999), Dean Caparaz (January 17, February 7, February 14, April 24, June 12, and December 25, 2000; and July 23, 2001), Terry Conway (November 1, 1999), Scott French (October 4, 1999; February 28, April 17, April 24, May 1, and May 8, 2000; January 22 and September 17, 2001; February 18, May 27, and September 9, 2002; March 3, April 14, June 23, October 6, and November 10, 2003; January 26, March 29, June 14, and July 26, 2004), David Hershey (April 16, 2001), Paul Kennedy (January 18, 1999, and February 7, 2000), Will Kuhns (April 16, and April 30, 2001; and October 6, 2003), Ridge Mahoney (June 21, and August 28, 2000), Mike Woitalla (October 6, 2003), and general news articles (September 27, October 4, and October 25, 1999; February 14, May 15, and June 5, 2000; May 19, May 26, and June 23, 2003; July 5, 2004; and February 14, 2005). *Soccer America*'s WUSA/Women's Soccer Insider Online Newsletters, edited by Scott French, of 2003 and 2004 reported closely on the the league and its players. I also utilized the WUSA League and Team Media Guides from the 2001, 2002, and 2003 seasons and conducted interviews with Nancy Augustyniak-Goffi, Dr. Bob Contiguilia, Mark Krikorian, and Jennifer Rottenberg. Other sources included:

FIFA *Women's World Cup USA 2003 Media Guide.*

French, Scott. "John Hendricks Q&A: We're Able to Invest with Confidence." *Sports Illustrated*, January 21, 2000, 20–21.

Jones, Katharine. "WUSA: What Went Wrong?" *Four Four Two* (February 2004): 87.

Litterer, Dave. "The American Soccer History Archives 2001–2003." U.S. Soccer Archives Online.

Samuelson, Maisy. "Women's Soccer: What Happens to a Dream Deferred?" *Stanford Daily*, October 16, 2003.

Stars of the WUSA. *Girl's Guide to Soccer Life.* Nashville TN: Cool Springs, 2003.

"U.S. Women's Soccer League to Begin Next Spring." AugustaChronicleOnline, September 12, 1997, http://www.chronicle.augusta.com.

4. Women's Professional Soccer

Women's Professional Soccer's website is a tremendous source of news, which I used along with their press releases and media guides from the individual teams. The websites for United Soccer League's W-League and Women's Premier Soccer League were useful for tracking players entering WPS. Jeff Kassouf's *The Equalizer* (equalizersoccer.com) consistently breaks stories on WPS happenings, particularly the restructuring difficulties after the 2009 season. Womensworldfootball.com was a good source of information before it ceased operations. For this chapter, I conducted interviews with Tonya Antonucci, Shek Borkowski,

Kiersten Dallstream, Mary Harvey, Emma Hayes, Tobin Heath, Karina LeBlanc, Jill Loyden, Kristen Luckenbill, Analisa Marquez, Nikki Marshall, Heather Mitts, Albertin Montoya, Charlie Naimo, Gareth O'Sullivan, Christie Rampone, Joe Sahlen, Christie Shaner, Christine Sinclair, Gary Weaver, Tiffany Weimer, and Kacey White. Other sources included:

Berling-Manuel, Lynn. "Short Passes." *Soccer America,* December 20–27, 2004, 49.

Canales, Andrea. "WPS Rebuilt It, Now Will They Come?" Sports Illustrated.com, April 6, 2009.

Dure, Beau. "Freedom Await Women's Soccer League Rebirth." USA *Today,* July 12, 2007, 10C.

———. "Pro League Linking Launch to World Cup, Venues to MLS." USA *Today,* July 12, 2007, 10C.

Eisenmenger, L. E. "Boston Breakers GM Andy Crossley Speaks on WPS Challenges in 2011, Including World Cup." Examiner.com, November 1, 2010.

FitzGerald, Tom. "Women's Soccer League Opens with High Hopes." *San Francisco Chronicle*, March 24, 2009.

French, Scott. "WUSA Six Degress of Separation Anxiety." *Soccer America*, January 26, 2004, 44–50.

Goff, Steve. "CONCACAF Champions League Draw, DC United Honors, WPS Update, Americans Abroad." WashingtonPostBlog, November 1, 2010.

———. "Washington Freedom Officials Respond to Report That the WPS Club Is Going to Fold Soon, WPS Update, Americans Abroad." *Washington Post Blog*, November 1, 2010.

Gooch, Charles. "Can a U.S. Women's Soccer League Ever Thrive?" *Kansas City Star*, November 1, 2010.

Gray, Ashley. "It Was a Wrench to Leave Arsenal But I Couldn't Pass Up the American Dream, Says England Striker Kelly 'Zidane' Smith." Dailymail.com, March 30, 2009.

Grainey, Timothy. "Women's Professional Soccer Intends to Launch in 2008, Says League Chief Tonya Antonucci." *World Football Pages,* December 2006.

Gregory, Sean. "Is Women's Pro Soccer Really Coming Back Now?" Time.com, March 29, 2009.

Howell, John. "WPS in Crisis Again as Two More Franchises at Risk of Folding." Bleacherreport.com, November 1, 2010.

"Marta Heads Billing for Inaugural WPS Season." ESPNsoccernet.com, March 24, 2009.

"Meet the Red Stars: Natalie Spilger." Womensprosoccer.com, March 9, 2009.

O'Sullivan, Kate. "Can a Savvy Finance Strategy Propel Women's Professional Soccer to Post-Olympic Glory?" CFO *Magazine*, July 15, 2008.

Paglia, Jim. "Is Women's Pro Soccer Doomed Again?" *Soccer America's Soccer Business Insider*, October 17, 2007.

———. "Why I'm Not Likely to Own a Women's Pro Team." *Soccer America's Soccer Business Insider*, October 31, 2007.

"Pichon's Lament—French Star Misses WUSA." *Soccer America*, February 14–21, 2005, 19.

Read, Hillary. "Welsh Set to Arrive in Los Angeles with a World of Experience." Womensprosoccer.com, February 14, 2009.

Smith, Beverley. "NWHL Commissions Feasibility Study." *Toronto Globe and Mail*, July 11, 2007, 58.

Sokolove, Michael. "Kicking Off." *New York Times*, April 5, 2009.

Turnbull, John. "Playing against Boys: Professional League in Waiting, Competitive Instincts Still Burn for U.S. Women." Theglobalgame. com, August 24, 2007.

Van Riper, Tom. "For Women's Pro Soccer, a Different Goal." Forbes. com, July 9, 2008.

"Women: Investors Commit to Launch of New Major League." *Soccer America's Soccer Business Insider*, February 28, 2007.

Women's Professional Soccer 2009 Championship/All-Star Game Official Program.

Women's Professional Soccer 2010 All-Star Game Official Program.

"Women's Professional Soccer League to Launch in 2009." WPS *Press Release*, September 4, 2007.

Yanda, Steve. "Back Yard Is Where the Heart Is: The Washington Freedom Practices behind a Family's House in Boyds While Waiting—and Hoping—for the Rebirth of Women's Pro Soccer." *Washington Post*, July 3, 2007.

Ziegler, Mark. "Women's Pro Soccer Revival Delayed." *San Diego Union Tribune*, August 17, 2007.

Ziegler, Robert. "New Women's Pro Soccer League Looking to Earn Support among U.S. Fans." *Top Drawer Soccer*, July 22, 2007.

5. The State of the Game in the Middle East

FIFA *Magazine* has done some very good articles on women's soccer in this region, including those by Hennies Ranier (December 2002 and January 2006) and Thorsten Schmitz (March 2004), and a general note in May 2004. Other sources of information were the FIFA, AFC, and CAF websites, as well as the websites for individual country federations. Interviews were conducted with Dr. Sahar El-Hawary, Deena Rahman, and Monika Staab. Other sources included:

Afshar, Afshin. "Iranian Women and Football." WorldCupBlog.Com, March 12, 2006.

"Coverings: Donning the Hijab for a Full 90." Theglobalgame.com, October 7, 2005.

Darinoush, Majid. "Predicted Rollback Hasn't Yet Happened, Say Women Activists." www.commondreams.org, June 28, 2006.

"FIFA Big Count 2006: 270 Million People Active in Football." FIFA.com, May 31, 2007.

"In Islamic World, Head Scarves Not Always Compulsory Football Equipment." Theglobalgame.com, March 11, 2007.

"International Sports Initiative Fall 2006." U.S. Soccer and U.S. State Department. *U.S. Soccer Publication*, 2006.

"Iran Bars Women from Attending Soccer Matches." Associated Press, May 8, 2006.

"Iranian Law Gives Advantages to Men." *Arizona Republic*, April 29, 2007, A25.

Mahoney, Ridge. "Sepp Blatter: The Bar Has Been Set Very High." *Soccer America*, March 1, 1999, 12.

Mekay, Emad. "Egyptians Break Barriers." *Soccer America*, October 26, 1998, 31.

"Offside Trap: Iranian Women, in Panahi's Film, Move Beyond a Boundary." Theglobalgame.com, March 28, 2007.

Steiner, Susie. "Why Is Sharia Law in the News?" *Guardian Unlimited*, August 20, 2002.

"Women Dominate as Iran Hosts Com-Unity." FIFA.com, May 10, 2006.

6. Challenges and Successes in Africa

FIFA's and CAF's website provided historical and statistical background on regional competitions. On African players in Scandinavia, for 2007–9 I used the excellent English language website *Damallsvenskan*

Newsblog, which unfortunately is now defunct. FIFA *Magazine*/FIFA *World Magazine* was always helpful, particularly articles in March 2007 and May 2009. Interviews were conducted with Ann Chiejine, Anton Maksimov, Veronica Phewa, and Ben Popoola. Other sources included:

"Adokiye Versus the NFF." Supersport.com, November 10, 2010.

Akalonu, Eddie. "Nigeria: Falcons, NFA War over Match Bonus." *Lagos Vanguard*, September 16, 2007.

"AWC Inadequacies Pose Challenges for CAF." NigerianObserverNews .com, December 2008.

"Cheats Prosper: FIFA Is Turning a Blind Eye to African Countries Who Are 'Buying' Their Own National Teams." *World Soccer*, April 2009, 45.

Doyle, Jennifer. "Testing the Gender Boundaries: Caster Semenya, Maribel Dominguez and Nokoi Matlou." www.pitchinvasion.net, August 21, 2009.

"Flourishing League Kicks Off Again." BBC Sport.com, March 17, 2001.

French, Scott. "Nigerian Connection—Super Falcons' Hopes in U.S.-Based Coaches' Hands." *Soccer America*, October 21, 2002, 32.

"I Won't Play for Nigeria Again—Maureen Mmadu." All Nigeria Soccer .com, March 5, 2010.

Klein, Jeff. "How a Nigerian Pay Dispute Could Help the U.S. Women." *New York Times*, September 17, 2007.

"NFA Denies Issuing Transfer Certificates to Bayelsa Queens' Players." TheTidenews.com, August 4, 2007.

Okpara, Christian. "Sacked Super Falcons Stars Face Deportation from Sweden." *The Guardian (Nigeria)*, November 2006.

"Program Launched in 2006 Combines Efforts of U.S. State Department and U.S. Soccer; Morocco One of Six Countries Visited by U.S. Soccer Players and Coaches." U.S. Soccer.com, April 7, 2008.

Saner, Emine. "The Gender Trap." *The Guardian*, July 30, 2008.

"She-Kobs Back after 2 Years on the Bench." *The East African*, June 5, 2000.

"Thirty-Two Nations Feature in Mock 'World Cup.'" *People's Daily (China)*, January 6, 2008.

Turnbull, John. "Women's Soccer Haze; Even with World Cup Rush, Sex Always Gets Headlines." Theglobalgame.com, June 3, 2006.

"Where the Falcons Got It Wrong in Malabo." Ngrguardiannews.com, November 29, 2009.

7. Latin America

FIFA *Magazine* was very useful for background stories, particularly Rainer Hennies's articles of September and October 2004. For Mexico's use of American-born players, *Soccer America* had substantial information including articles by Scott French (March 1, 1999, May 19, 2003, and March 29, 2004), Amparo Simon (June 21, 1999), and general articles on October 26, 1998, and February 14, 2005. For Marta's career in Sweden and efforts to fight off WPS overtures, the now-defunct *DamallsvenskanNewsblog* (2007–9) had extensive coverage and links to Swedish-language news articles. FC Santos's website was valuable for the section regarding the North Americans playing in Brazil. I also used country-specific football federation websites, as well as those of FIFA and CONCACAF. Interviews were conducted with Jorge Barcellos, Josee Busilacchi, Leonardo Cuellar, Melissa Lesage, Marta, Katie Ratican, Lydia Vandenberg, and Tiffany Weimer. Other sources included:

Bachelor, Blane. "Mexico's Dominguez Overcomes Long Odds." *USA Today*, August 4, 2003.

"Dominguez the Toast of Mexico." Theglobalgame.com, March 5, 2004.

Graciano, Diego. "This Book Is Dedicated to Other Martas, Barefoot and Dirty." Theglobalgame.com, September 8, 2008.

Grey, Ashley. "I Have the Skill to Play in the Men's Game—People Say I'm Like Ronaldinho, Says World No. 1 Woman Marta." Dailymail.com, March 30, 2009.

Jones, Grahame. "Marta Has Come a Long Way, Takes on New Challenge in U.S." *Los Angeles Times*, Feb 25, 2009.

Klein, Jeff. "The Brazilian Women Demand More Support." *New York Times*, October 2, 2007.

"Mexican Women's Soccer Team Get Its Footing." *Los Angeles Times*, February 22, 2008.

Read, Hillary. "Marta Set to Star in WPS with Flair. Womensprosoccer.com, March 25, 2009.

Tuckman, Jo. "It's a Man's Game." *The Guardian*, January 5, 2005.

Turnbull, John. "Born in 'Invisible Town,' Marta Gains Life in Visible Ink." Theglobalgame.com, September 15, 2008.

———. "Do Other Martas Exist? in 'Machista' Brazilian Culture, One Cannot Be Sure." Theglobalgame.com, September 12, 2007.

———. "The Negotiation Was Long and Difficult, Says Farah of Creating Marta's L.A. Story." Theglobalgame.com, January 10, 2009.

———. "Northern Latitudes Helped Make Marta a Player of Sol Importance." Theglobalgame.com, January 12, 2009.

"Woman Signs for Mexico Men's Team." Theglobalgame.com, December 16, 2004.

Ziegler, Mark. "U.S. Women Joined by Mexico in Nailing Down Trip to Olympics." *San Diego Union-Tribune*, March 4, 2004.

8. Women Athletes

Soccer America provided useful articles by Dean Caparaz (December 20, 1999), as well as in their *Women's Soccer Insider* (March 13, 2003) and *College Soccer Reporter* (November 12, 2009). Interviews were held with personnel within the University of New Mexico Athletic Department, Melissa Barbieri, and Laura Pappano. Other sources included:

"And Another Thing." *Four Four Two* (October 2007): 88–90.

Christenson, Marcus, and Paul Kelso. "Soccer Chief's Plan to Boost Women's Game? Hotpants." *The Guardian*, January 16, 2004.

Crary, David. "Soccer Punch, Hair Tug Ignite Sexism Debate." Associated Press, November 22, 2009.

Gintonio, Jim. "May-Treanor Nears Mark." *Arizona Republic*, May 10, 2007, C4.

Griffin, Pat. "Homophobia in Women's Sports: The Fear That Divides Us." In *Women in Sport: Issues and Controversies*, edited by Greta L. Cohen, 193–203. Newbury Park CA: Sage, 1993.

Hall, Matthew. "Sex, Spies, and Skill: Women's Soccer Has It All." *Sydney Sun Herald*, October 23, 2007.

Hughes, Rob. "Pulling Attention with a Yank of a Pony Tail." *New York Times*, November 10, 2009.

Lansley, Peter. "Blatter Given Clear Brief over Hotpants." TheTimesOnline, January 17, 2004.

Longman, Jere. "Those Soccer Plays, in Context." *New York Times*, November 17, 2009.

"Nude Footballers Kick Up a Fuss." BBC *News*, November 30, 1999.

Pappano, Laura. "Ponytail Pull Was Bad (but Good for Women's Sports)." TheHuffingtonpost.com, November 19, 2009.

Rudd, Alyson. "Johansson's View of the Future Is an Indecent Proposal." TheTimesOnline, June 18, 2005.

Speck, Ivan. "Chelsea Ladies Play It Fair as They Try to Hit the Top." *The Daily Mail*, February 5, 2008.

Wahl, Grant. "Revamped, Re-Focused for Goal." SportsIllustrated.com, August 5, 2008.

9. Ancestral Roots

U.S. Soccer's website had information on the U.S.–Greece opener at the 2004 Olympic Games. FIFA's website and country-specific websites were useful. On the Gaelic Games of Ireland, the Ladies Gaelic Football Association of Ireland has an informative website (http://ladiesgaelic.ie/). Interviews were conducted with Eleni Benson, Shek Borkowski, Kim Brandao, Elena Danilova, Michael Forde, Monica Jorge, Tanya Kalivas, Noel King, Aivi Luik, Anton Maksimov, Anna Picarelli, Paul Swift, Alex Valerio, Tim Ward, Tiffany Weimer, Kacey White, and Maria Joao Xavier. Other sources included:

"American-Born Greeks Ready to Face Their Idols." FIFA.com, August 11, 2004.

French, Scott. "Athens Finally Gets Its Turn." *Soccer America*, August 16, 2004.

Grainey, Timothy. "In Lusophone Ancestral Home, North Americans on a Mission as 'New Portuguese.'" Theglobalgame.com, November 2008.

———. "Ukraine: Where the Cossacks Held Sway, Women's Football Adds International Spice." Theglobalgame.com, July 10, 2009.

"Greek Coach's Epic Journey Reaches the Last Page." FIFA.com, August 10, 2004.

Levesque, John. "Renton Girl Embarks on Big Fat Greek Olympic Adventure." *Seattle Post-Intelligencer*, July 3, 2004.

Robbins, Liz. "Olympics; As Athletes Settle in, a Village Begins to Feel Like Home." *New York Times*, August 8, 2004.

"Teenage American Girl Makes History in Portugal." United Soccer Leagues' Press Release, November 11, 2004.

"22-Member Squad Will Make First Olympics Appearance at Home." Associated Press, July 21, 2004.

White, Joseph. "Early Olympic Curtain Raiser: U.S. Women Face Greece." Associated Press, August 10, 2004.

"Young Ottawa Standout Off to Portugal: Former SYL Standout Valerio Has Chance with National Team." OttawaFury.com, April 11, 2008.

"Zvezda Complete Russian Title Hat-Trick." www.femalesoccer.net, October 19, 2009.

10. National Leagues around the World

I used www.womensworldfootball.com (defunct) and Damallsvenskan-Newsblog (defunct) for information on the Swedish league, and www.femalesoccer.net on Russian football as well as the Russian Federation website. For the Australia w-league, their joint website with the men's A-League, www.a-league.com.au, was invaluable. Interviews were conducted with Shek Borkowski, Lisa DeVanna, Juliana Edwards, Jeff Hopkins, Daniel Lato, Jill Loyden, Aivi Luik, Anton Maksimov, Megan Manthey, Bonita Mersaides, Tom Sermanni, Brittany Timko, Lydia Vandenbergh, and Sarah Walsh. Other sources included:

Kennedy, Paul. "FIFA's Women's World Cup 2007—Top 10 Stories." *Soccer America*, November 2007.

Westfield W-League 2010/11 Media Guide.

11. Overcoming a Fifty-Year Ban in England

The English FA website was invaluable, particularly press releases from July 22, 2005, and September 3, 2008. *Soccer America* provided useful articles by Bryan Alvarez (November 2006) and Paul Kennedy, (February 10, 2003), and a general article (May 15, 2000). Interviews were conducted with Rachel Brown, Tonny Dijkuizen, and Emma Hayes. Other sources included:

"Battle of Sexes Charity Match Called Off by FA." Chelseafc/america.com, August 7, 2008.

Dhaliwal, Jaskirt. "Women's Football Popularity on the Rise." BBC.co.uk, October 20, 2005.

Jose, Colin. "The Dick, Kerr Ladies Soccer Tour, 1922." U.S. Soccer History Archives.

Kessel, Anna. "The Invincible." *The Observer*, May 4, 2008.

Leighton, Tony. "Fulham Disowned in Final Fall from Grace." *The Guardian*, May 22, 2006.

Newshaw, Gail J. *In a League of Their Own.* London: Scarlet, 1977.

Oatley, Jacqui. "England Women Angry at £40 Wage." BBC.co.uk, November 15, 2007.

Thornhill, Luke. "A New Dawn and a Fresh Opportunity." *The National*, March 20, 2009.

Turner, Georgina. "That's No Way to Treat the Ladies." *The Guardian*, August 4, 2005.

Williams, Jean. *A Beautiful Game: International Perspectives on Women's Football*. London: Berg, 2007.

"Women's Round-up March 2010." FIFA.com, March 24, 2010.

12. Canada's Youthful Road to Success

For research on soccer in Canada, the Canadian Soccer Association's media guides from 2002 to 2007 as well as their website were very helpful. *World Football Pages of Canada,* both the website and periodicals, was a good historical reference on the women's game in Canada from 2000 to 2007. *Soccer America* provided helpful articles, particularly those by Bryan Alvarez (November 2006), Scott French (June 21, 1999, May 8, 2000, September 23, 2002, March 5, 2003, March 29, 2004, and January 2007), and general articles (June 21, July 12, July 19, and September 20, 1999). Interviews were conducted with Bob Bolitho, Ian Bridge, Erin McLeod, Even Pellerud, Christine Sinclair, Melissa Tancredi, Brittany Timko, Amy Vermeulen, and John Walker. Other sources included:

Blair, Jeff. "Overtime Loss Ends Canada's Run." *Toronto Globe and Mail*, August 15, 2008.

FIFA *Official Program 2002 Canada Women's U-19 World Cup.*

"FIFA Women's World Cup: Last Minute Goal Crushes Canada." *Free Kick Magazine* (November 2007): 6.

Gauthier, Sebastian. "A Bright Future for the Whitecaps—Part of a Look Back at the 2008 W-League Season." *Soccer m@g* (October–November 2008).

Griffiths, Chris Vaughn. "Squeeze the Charmaine." *World Football Pages,* November 28, 2006.

Hennies, Ranier. "From Low-Key Gathering to Major Event." FIFA *Magazine* (August 2003): 7–9.

Jamieson, Jim. "Women Vow to Learn from Bitter World Cup Upset." *Vancouver Province,* May 7, 2008.

Keller, James. "Pellerud to Retire from Canadian Program in December." *The Canadian Press*, June 2, 2008.

Mallett, Peter. "Canadian Soccer Still Lacking Direction." *Toronto Globe and Mail*, May 7, 2007.

Morris, Jim. "Pellerud: I Have Almost Stopped to Hope." *Canadian Press*, October 5, 2007.

Pellerud, Even, with Sam Kucey. *Even Pellerud on Coaching and Leadership in Women's Soccer*. Auburn MI: Reedswain, 2005.

Spector, Mark. "Canada Women's Soccer Have Accomplished Something in Beijing." *National Post*, August 12, 2008.

"Tough Task Ahead for Canadian Soccer Women." *Toronto Star*, August 12, 2008.

"USA Triumph in Glorious Premiere." FIFA *Magazine* (August 2003): 23–27.

"Visit by CSA President Gives Women's Coach Hope for Changes in Organization." *The Canadian Press*, November 8, 2007.

Conclusion

FIFA's website provided statistics on the growth of female soccer. For this chapter, I conducted an interview with Mary Harvey.